RAYMOND BLANC

Photography by Jean Cazals   Illustrations by Paul Wearing

BLOOMSBURY

LONDON • NEW DELHI • NEW YORK • SYDNEY

Introduction

Think for a moment of the great times you have enjoyed at the table, and more often than not they will have involved sharing. The bread is passed around from one person to another. You pour the wine for your guests, and they are kind enough to pour some more for you. The food is shared, of course, and conversation is shared. Who knows, perhaps some healthy bickering too. Those magical meals turn strangers into the dearest of friends.

This little book is also about sharing. I suppose you could say it is my way of sharing my knowledge, through wonderful recipes and hundreds of little kitchen secrets that can improve life, save time and maybe spare embarrassment.

Perhaps I am well equipped for such a task. Over the years, both in and out of the kitchen, sharing has played a crucial role. During 35 years in this exciting profession, I have been privileged to acquire knowledge and, more importantly, pass it on to hundreds of young British people. Many of them are now the nation's most acclaimed chefs, while others have gone abroad to make their names and win their stars.

It was in my childhood that I first began to learn about food. My mother, who lives in France, shared her knowledge with me, and her cooking has inspired many of the dishes that are served in my restaurants. I was her kitchen helper, sent to the garden to pick tomatoes or lift some carrots, and to peel and chop in preparation for the meal.

My parents instilled in me a belief in the importance of using food that is seasonal, though it's true to say that we had no choice; there wasn't a supermarket selling packaged produce shipped from far-away countries. No, our food came with each season and couldn't have been more local – we ate what came from the garden, and what didn't go on to the plate immediately was pickled and jarred to eat out of season.

I really believe that we are now entering an era in which we are slowly re-connecting with our own food culture, our sense of place and traditions. Food will cease to be treated as a mere convenience or commodity. We want to know where our food comes from, how it is grown and what is in it. Food sits at the very heart of society, not on the edge of it, and it connects with every single aspect of our lives.

Cooking is actually simple. First, you need good quality and seasonal fresh ingredients. If they are local, they are seasonal; they will have a better taste, colour, texture and nutrients. In addition, local produce is abundant and therefore less expensive. So local must make sense, and by being critical and aware we have a wonderful opportunity here to re-invent our crafts, our villages and our food production.

That is your first step towards good cooking, and I hope that my culinary secrets will help you on your journey.

Among the many secrets that I will share with you in this book, the first I should tell you is that I am a self-taught chef, by which I mean that I never worked under a professional chef, not even for one minute. This has been both a blessing and a curse.

A blessing because my work was not shaped by another person's culinary philosophy. I had the freedom to investigate, to be curious, to roam and question many strict culinary rules, to bring lightness to my food and discover new techniques.

But a curse because cooking can be complex (particularly at the top end) and at times, I admit, I've missed having a mentor. I've had to learn through my many failures – small problems and occasional disasters – always trying to understand the reasons for my failure. By unravelling many of the mysteries of cooking, I gained invaluable knowledge and confidence.

When I first came to England in the early 1970s and worked as a chef at the Rose Revived in Oxfordshire, good produce was hard to come by. You knew the fish man was coming from the nasty fish smell that travelled down the road ahead of him. At my first restaurant, Les Quat' Saisons (in the Summertown part of Oxford) I struggled to buy good bread. So I set up a bakery called Maison Blanc, which also served pâtisserie like delicious chocolate éclairs. Long days of cooking and long nights of baking – I thought that was tough. But my quest for perfection continued. In 1984, when my then wife Jenny and I opened Le Manoir aux Quat' Saisons, here in the village of Great Milton, a great adventure was only just beginning...

It has been an exhausting but immensely pleasurable journey. As with any cook, my curiosity is driven by 'Why... why... why...?' I have found many answers that have helped me at Le Manoir, in my search for the best possible varieties of fruit and vegetables to grow in the gardens. And it would be comforting for me to know that my curiosity might be of benefit to you, the reader, gourmet, connoisseur... and cook.

If you were to ask me what I consider to be my finest achievement, I could answer the question without hesitation: teaching. And I have written this little book for the student, the gourmand, the *bon viveur*, the cook at home, the naive cook – as well as the experienced one. Yes, *Kitchen Secrets* is as much for the inexperienced cook as it is for the well-practised one. It is for anyone who is seeking knowledge. My aim is to tell you why, and empower you with confidence.

I so much enjoy teaching that 20 years ago I set up the Raymond Blanc Cookery School at Le Manoir. Here we actively welcome both children and adults and re-connect them with the secrets of the soil and the miracle of a simple brown seed that will transform into a flourishing vegetable, fruit or herb. We offer many courses, among them one about nutrition with Professor Jaya Henry of Oxford Brookes University. It has been a triumph of learning, of fun and of glorious food. The food is established around the simple philosophy of Maman Blanc. There's no haute cuisine!

There is a fantastic ambience, and I am reminded of the time when Kylie Minogue came for a lesson. I played one of her albums and danced along. She was concerned that I had a knee injury. 'No, that's how I always dance,' I told her. But my skills are in the kitchen, not on the dance floor, and I am happy to say that she is now a most proficient cook.

There is no elitism at the school. The classes are made up of all sorts of people with different abilities and experiences but they all come here to learn about food and the secrets of cooking. Why is my soufflé not rising? Why does my sauce separate? Should I use extra virgin olive oil or butter in this dish?

They want to find out how to save time, what to add when, and how much of it to add. Essentially, they want to master the technique of making delicious food for their family and friends. They ask, 'What sort of apple should you use for tarte tatin?' And, 'What are the best types of tomato for tomato sauce?' They want to discover the techniques of roasting the perfect joint of meat or frying a piece of fish. And they are desperate to hear secrets about cakes, pastries and chocolate.

And there you have my reason for this cookbook. It is, I hope, a sort of passport to culinary pleasure. As you read, you will come across morsels of wisdom, tips and suggestions. Such advice, of course, would be pointless unless you had wonderful recipes, too. You will find scores of them within these pages. Some are simple, some more difficult and there are some recipes for the cook who has a few hours to spare and relishes a culinary challenge. There is a star system to let you know the ease and difficulty of each recipe.

You will find 'secrets' in the introduction to each chapter, and more 'secrets' with the recipes. I know we all like to keep a few things to ourselves, but surely the real joy of a secret is in the sharing of it.

Voilà. C'est tout. Bon appétit.

Notes

Each recipe has been given a star rating to indicate its degree of complexity:

*   simple to prepare

* *   medium complexity

* * *   requires a degree of skill and will take time to prepare

All spoon measures are level unless otherwise stated:
1 tsp = 5ml spoon
1 tbsp = 15ml spoon

Always use the best-quality sea salt with the least refining, never salt with horrible anti-caking additives. Pepper should always be freshly ground from a mill.

All herbs are fresh unless otherwise suggested.

If you are using olive oil for a dressing, employ your best-quality extra virgin oil. However, when cooking with olive oil, you should use a good-quality refined (light) oil, which has a much higher burning point.

I use organic or free-range eggs – medium-sized unless otherwise indicated.

Vanilla syrup is the best way to maximise the flavour from expensive vanilla pods. To prepare, roughly chop 6 large vanilla pods, removing the hard nib at one end, then purée together with a warm sugar syrup, made by dissolving 100g caster sugar in 100ml water and boiling for 1 minute. Vanilla syrup keeps well in a sealed jar in the fridge. Good-quality vanilla extract is a suitable substitute.

If you are using the zest of citrus fruit, buy unwaxed or organic produce if possible.

The oven timings in the recipes are for fan-assisted ovens unless otherwise indicated. If you are using a conventional oven, you will need to increase the temperature by 10–15°C (½–1 Gas Mark).

Get to know your oven and use an oven thermometer to check its accuracy. Individual ovens can deviate by as much as 10°C from the designated setting, either way.

Eggs

As every cook knows, eggs are not just the symbol of life, they are the most magical of all ingredients. They are wonderfully versatile and hold incredible powers, which are critical for a host of dishes, from a simple omelette to an exquisite fluffy soufflé. Incidentally, you'll find both dishes in this chapter and when it comes to that omelette, remember to break up the eggs with a fork, not a whisk.

It is difficult to imagine where we would be without eggs – a classic English breakfast without one is unthinkable. Without doubt, this nutrient-packed ovoid is the cook's best friend, but if you want the egg to be your friend you need to tame and understand it.

Always use very fresh eggs, preferably organic, but at least free-range. Egg producers don't tell us when the eggs were laid, but they do give us a best-before date. You'll find this on the shell, along with a few red figures that call for a magnifying glass – it's a bit like trying to crack the Enigma code. O = organic; 1= free-range; 2 = barn egg; 3 = caged (nasty). The little picture of a red lion is important, especially if you intend to use raw eggs for a mayonnaise. The lion has nothing to do with English football, it is the guarantee that the laying hen has been vaccinated against salmonella. Then there is the question of size. I use medium eggs for all my recipes; these weigh approximately 60g.

Crack an egg onto a plate and it will reveal its freshness. The white should be firm, not loose; it should cling tightly to the yolk and be springy to the touch. Note that an orange yolk is not always the sign of a tasty egg. The colour is determined by the chicken's diet. A corn-fed chicken produces a pale yolk, which in my opinion is the tastiest hen's egg.

The egg white is the 'lifter' in dishes. It can be whisked into an extraordinary foam in which billions of air bubbles are harvested and trapped within a protein network. Egg whites whisk most successfully when they are at room temperature (make sure there is no trace of yolk in the white, or grease in the bowl). And add just a dash of lemon juice at the beginning to stop the foam graining.

Meringues, of course, make excellent use of this technique, incorporating sugar into the foam to give a glossy, thick texture. As I adore them, they feature in two of the desserts in this chapter – pavlova with summer berries and îles flottantes (façon Maman Blanc). They are best eaten on the day they are cooked.

The protein-packed egg yolk also has impressive culinary properties. It enriches and thickens many recipes, including crème anglaise. Egg yolks and sugar whip up to an airy mousse, creating sabayons and sponges. And brushed onto bread and pastry, beaten egg yolk bakes to an appetising golden glaze.

Smoked salmon omelette

*

Serves 1

Preparation: 2 mins

Cooking: 3 mins

Special equipment:
25cm non-stick
omelette pan

I was invited to take a televised 'omelette challenge' – to cook an omelette in the fastest possible time. One contestant managed to 'cook' their omelette in just 19 seconds, but mine took 3 minutes exactly. It was fluffy and fat, with a generous grating of truffle. I decided that if you do not have 3 minutes to cook the perfect omelette then life is not worth living. Enjoy this simple omelette as a nourishing breakfast or light meal. The filling remains your choice.

3 organic/free-range medium
  eggs
pinch of sea salt
pinch of freshly ground black
  pepper

15g unsalted butter, plus a little
  melted butter to serve
30g smoked salmon, roughly
  chopped
a few chives, finely snipped,
  to serve

To make the omelette In a bowl, gently beat the eggs together using a fork[1] with a pinch each of salt[2] and pepper.

In the omelette pan, heat the butter until it begins to foam[3]. Pour in the egg mixture and cook undisturbed for a few seconds, allowing the omelette to set lightly before stirring the set part in towards the centre. Repeat this motion 4 or 5 times until the omelette has formed but is still soft and creamy in the centre. This way you will achieve the perfect texture.

Scatter the pieces of salmon in the middle of the omelette and then fold the sides towards the centre. Turn the omelette out onto a warmed plate, brush with a little melted butter and sprinkle with snipped chives to serve.

Variations The fillings for omelettes are endless, though the simplest work best in my view. Try fines herbes (chopped chives, chervil and tarragon), sliced tomato and chopped basil, sautéed mushrooms, chopped ham, or grated cheese such as Gruyère or Comté.

[1] Don't use a whisk or break the eggs down too much because you want a contrast of textures, with a little unmixed white and yolk.
[2] You can add seasoning at any time, but you cannot take it away. Don't add too much salt to the egg as the salmon will contribute more.
[3] The butter will start to foam at about 130°C. It will turn hazelnut in colour at 150°–155°C – more appropriate for browning fish or meat than your omelette.

Comté cheese soufflé

**

Serves 6

Preparation:
20 mins

Cooking: 25 mins

Special equipment:
25–30cm oval or
round earthenware
dish[1], electric mixer
or whisk

Comté is my home, my region; it gives me a sense of place. Maman Blanc always cooked her soufflé in a large shallow earthenware dish, rather than individual moulds. She would place the dish on the table for all of us to help ourselves, or sometimes the soufflé would be encased in a flaky pastry tart. Of course, only Comté cheese would be used, never Gruyère or Emmenthal. Everyone assumes that soufflés behave like prima donnas, but I will show you how easy they can be. They are usually inexpensive, yet create a wonderful drama at the table.

Planning ahead The soufflé base can be prepared up to a day ahead and kept in the fridge, the surface closely covered with buttered greaseproof paper to avoid crusting. It will need to be warmed before the egg whites are incorporated (see note 6, overleaf). The sauce can also be made a day in advance and reheated at the last moment, but you will need to whisk in 2 tsp cold water to stop it splitting.

For lining the soufflé dish
20g unsalted butter,
   softened
20g dried, fine breadcrumbs

For the soufflé base
50g unsalted butter
50g plain flour
450ml whole milk, warmed
160g young Comté cheese,
   grated
1 tsp Dijon mustard
3 organic/free-range medium
   egg yolks
2 pinches of sea salt, or to taste
2 pinches of white pepper, or
   to taste

For the soufflé mix
7 organic/free-range medium
   egg whites
14 drops of lemon juice

To finish the soufflé
20g young Comté cheese,
   finely grated

For the sauce
150ml double cream
70g young Comté cheese,
   grated
4 turns of freshly ground
   white pepper
1 tbsp kirsch (optional)

To line the soufflé dish Using a pastry brush, grease the dish with a thin, even layer of softened butter[2], then coat with the breadcrumbs, shaking out the excess; put the dish to one side. Preheat the oven to 180°C/Gas 4 and place a baking tray on the middle shelf to heat up.

To prepare the soufflé base In a small saucepan over a medium heat, melt the butter. Add the flour, whisk until smooth and cook to a nutty blond roux[3]. Lower the heat, then gradually add the warm milk, little by little, whisking to keep the consistency smooth. Add the cheese and mustard and continue to cook, stirring from time to time, for 3–5 minutes. Remove from the heat and allow to cool a little. Add the egg yolks and stir until the mixture is silky and smooth. Season with salt and pepper to taste[4] and keep warm.

To whisk the egg whites In a large bowl, whisk the egg whites[5] with the lemon juice to medium peaks.

To incorporate the egg whites into the base Transfer the warm soufflé base[6] to a large bowl and briefly whisk in one third of the whipped egg whites[7] to lighten the base. Then carefully fold in the remaining egg whites with a spatula or large metal spoon, delicately cutting and lifting the mixture to ensure minimum loss of volume and lightness. Taste and adjust the seasoning if necessary. Pour the soufflé mixture into the prepared dish, to three-quarters fill it.

To cook the soufflé Slide the dish onto the hot baking tray and bake in the oven for 20 minutes[8]. Meanwhile, make your cheese sauce.

To make the sauce While the soufflé is cooking, bring the cream to the boil and add the cheese and pepper, stirring continuously. Once the cheese has melted, remove from the heat and taste for seasoning[9]. A dash of kirsch would not go amiss. Pour the sauce into a warm sauceboat.

To finish and serve Sprinkle the grated cheese over the surface of the soufflé and bake for a further 5 minutes. Serve immediately, placing the soufflé and sauce in the middle of the table so everyone can help themselves.

Variations Use another cheese in place of Comté. There are many different options: goat's cheese, Stilton, Emmenthal and Gruyère are just a few.

As an alternative, use individual soufflé dishes, 9.5cm in diameter and 5.5cm tall. These quantities will make 4 individual soufflés. Bake in a preheated oven at 200°C/Gas 6 for 10 minutes, then sprinkle the cheese on top and cook for a further 5 minutes.

[1] The choice of dish is important. Earthenware is a slow conductor of heat, which encourages a more even temperature distribution. A ceramic dish is the next best choice.

[2] Brushing the sides of the dish with butter will help the soufflé rise evenly; it is the lubricant. The breadcrumbs add a lovely contrasting texture. It is essential to grease the dish thoroughly; if any part is not buttered then it will hamper the rise of the soufflé.

[3] The base gives the texture, body and richness to a soufflé and it will hold the whisked egg whites. Here you are making a classic roux, which will bind and thicken the milk when they are combined and cooked together. Cook the flour and butter to a light nutty colour, to enhance the flavour and make the flour more

digestible. It is important to cook the base for 3–5 minutes to ensure that all the starch molecules have burst, grabbed as much moisture as possible, and are completely cooked.

4 Comté cheese, like Parmesan, contains quite a lot of salt, so the base should need little, if any, additional salt.

5 The whisked egg whites provide the lifting power, so it is important that they are fully whipped. The bowl must be very clean and dry, as grease and water impede the process. Lemon juice prevents the egg white graining and also heightens the flavour. Do not over-whip the egg whites to stiff peaks, otherwise they'll be difficult to incorporate into the base.

6 The base must be hot as the egg whites are folded in. It would be difficult to fold egg whites smoothly into a cold base and some of the lifting power and lightness would be lost as the air bubbles burst. It is better for the base to be wetter rather than drier. The hot base gives the soufflé a head start, enabling it to rise faster.

7 A third of the egg whites are briskly whisked in to lighten the base; this stage makes it easier to gently fold in the remaining egg whites, keeping the soufflé mixture light and airy. It is better to slightly under-mix, rather than overwork the two together, which would undermine the lightness of the soufflé.

8 Whilst cooking, a number of things will happen; not least the soufflé will rise impressively. Through the cooking process, the bubbles of air will expand and push up the mixture, while millions of droplets of moisture trying to escape are lifting the soufflé up. At the same time, whilst cooking, the egg yolks lend richness and set around the millions of bubbles, stabilising the soufflé and giving this wondrous texture.

9 If the sauce splits, whisk in 2 tsp cold water and it should re-emuslify.

Cherry clafoutis

Serves 4

Preparation:
30 mins, plus
2 hours macerating

Cooking:
30–35 mins

Special equipment:
20cm round ceramic
or cast-iron baking
dish (5cm deep),
cherry stoner

Clafoutis is one of the great classics of French family cuisine. This dessert often features on our menus, both at Le Manoir and at Brasserie Blanc. It is very easy to prepare and I would go as far as to say it is foolproof. Other stone fruits, such as peaches, plums and apricots, or indeed figs, work just as well.

Planning ahead The clafoutis mixture can be prepared a day in advance.

For the cherries
450g best-quality ripe cherries
   (such as Montmorency or
   Morello), stoned
50g caster sugar
2–3 tbsp kirsch, to taste
   (optional)

For preparing the dish
10g unsalted butter, melted
30g caster sugar, plus extra
   to finish (optional)

For the batter
2 organic/free-range medium
   eggs
45g caster sugar
½ tsp pure vanilla extract or
   vanilla syrup (see page 9)
20g unsalted butter
20g plain flour
50ml whole milk
75ml whipping cream
pinch of sea salt

To prepare the cherries Gently mix the cherries, sugar and kirsch, if using, in a bowl. Cover and leave to macerate for 2 hours[1]. Preheat the oven to 180°C/Gas 4.

To prepare the dish Brush the inside with the melted butter. Add the sugar and tilt the dish to coat the sides and base evenly; shake out the excess.

To make the clafoutis In a large bowl, whisk the eggs, caster sugar and vanilla together until creamy. Meanwhile, melt the butter in a small pan and cook to a beurre noisette[2]. Add the flour to the egg and sugar mixture and whisk until smooth, then slowly incorporate the milk, cream, salt and beurre noisette. Stir in the cherries with their juice and then pour into the prepared baking dish.

To cook the clafoutis Bake for 30–35 minutes until the clafoutis is lightly risen and a knife inserted into the middle comes out clean[3]. Leave to stand for about 10 minutes. Sprinkle with caster sugar if using and serve just warm.

[1] While macerating, the sugar slowly permeates the fruit and intensifies the taste.
[2] The foaming butter will turn a hazelnut colour at 150–155°C, i.e. beurre noisette. This butter will lend a wonderful roundness and nutty flavour to the clafoutis.
[3] The centre is always the last part to cook, so you must test it. Note that a dip in the middle suggests the clafoutis is undercooked.

Sabayon

* *

Makes 600ml
Preparation:
10 mins
Cooking: 7–8 mins
Special equipment:
electric mixer
(optional), cook's
thermometer

I love this classic recipe. Simple, yet clever, I regard it as one of my 'base recipes'. Master the technique and it will extend your repertoire of desserts – with minor adjustments, you will be able to create wonderful mousses, iced parfaits and fruit gratins (see pages 22-7).

Planning ahead The sabayon can be prepared a day in advance and refrigerated.

4 organic/free-range medium
  egg yolks
50g caster sugar

125ml Muscat or other sweet
  dessert wine
1 tbsp lemon juice, or to taste
150ml whipping cream

To prepare the sabayon In a large heatproof bowl, whisk the egg yolks, caster sugar, wine and lemon juice together for 1 minute[1].

Stand the bowl over a bain-marie of barely simmering water[2], making sure it is not touching the water, and whisk for 7–8 minutes until it reaches 78°C[3], resulting in a light fluffy sabayon. Remove the bowl from the heat and place over a larger bowl of crushed ice. Continue to whisk until the sabayon is cold.

In another bowl, whip the cream to soft peaks and then fold into the cold sabayon[4]. Cover and refrigerate until ready to use.

This sabayon can be poured onto any fruits, warm or cold. It can also be frozen (see variations).

Variations Instead of Muscat, use Marsala, sherry, white wine or any dessert wine. The sabayon can also be flavoured and frozen to make a wonderful iced parfait; flavour with 1 tsp vanilla syrup, 90ml lemon juice, 2 tbsp rum or 160g chestnut purée.

[1] Whisking the mixture homogenises it and increases the volume, resulting in a lighter, more aerated sabayon. Using an electric mixer will make it much easier.

[2] If you cook the sabayon over boiling water (or if the bowl is in direct contact with the water) the eggs are likely to scramble.

[3] Here the egg yolk is demonstrating its incredible capacity to hold air and expand. By whisking, you are introducing billions of air bubbles, doubling the volume of the sabayon very quickly. This second stage is necessary to partly cook the egg yolk around the bubbles of air, to make your sabayon fluffy and stable. I have found that 78°C is the perfect temperature to barely cook the sabayon.

[4] Ensure the sabayon is completely cold before incorporating the cream. Even slight warmth will cause the fats in the cream to melt and the sabayon to split. There is no tip to save it at this stage; if this happens you will have to start again.

Raspberry mousse

* *

Serves 6

Preparation:
10 mins, plus
making sabayon
and 4 hours chilling

Cooking: 15 mins

Special equipment:
blender or food
processor, 6
Champagne glasses

This recipe shows how the sabayon base can be transformed into a delectable mousse, simply by adding a purée of fresh fruit and a small amount of gelatine. In my opinion, the best raspberries are the late ones. Scottish raspberries, in particular, have a wonderful depth of flavour. The last of the summer fruits, they are worth waiting for.

Planning ahead This dessert can be made a day ahead and kept covered in the fridge overnight.

400g raspberries
2 sheets leaf gelatine (27x7cm)
300ml prepared sabayon
    (see page 21)

To assemble
300g ripest raspberries,
    crushed, plus extra whole
    raspberries to garnish

To make the raspberry mousse Purée the raspberries in a blender or food processor and pass through a sieve into a bowl; you will need 300ml purée for the mousse. Soak the gelatine leaves in a shallow dish of cold water to soften for 5 minutes or so[1].

In a small saucepan, bring a quarter of the raspberry purée[2] to the boil and take off the heat. Drain the gelatine leaves and squeeze out excess water, then add to the hot purée, stirring until dissolved. Now stir in the remaining cold raspberry purée. Add the raspberry mixture to the sabayon in a large bowl and carefully fold together.

To assemble Divide the crushed raspberries between the glasses and top with the raspberry mousse. Cover each glass with cling film and refrigerate for 4 hours to set. Top each mousse with a few raspberries to serve.

[1] Always rehydrate and soften your gelatine in cold water. It will then melt very quickly when added to the warm purée.

[2] I heat a small amount of fruit purée, just enough to melt the gelatine, adding the rest of the purée cold and raw – to keep the flavour fresh.

Summer fruit gratin

* *

Serves 4

Preparation:
5 mins, plus making
sabayon and 1 hour
chilling

Cooking: 1–2 mins

Special equipment:
cook's blowtorch

This simple, attractive dessert is created by topping seasonal soft fruits with sabayon and gratinéeing briefly. You can vary the fruits as you wish – try using sliced peaches, nectarines, cherries or pears. A combination of tropical fruit, such as mango, papaya and banana also works well with the shredded mint.

Planning ahead The sabayon can be made a day ahead and kept covered in the fridge overnight.

300ml prepared sabayon[1]
(see page 21)
400g mixed strawberries,
raspberries, blueberries,
blackberries or other fruit

40g caster sugar
juice of ¼ lemon
2 mint leaves, finely shredded
(optional)
icing sugar, to dust

To chill the sabayon Refrigerate the prepared sabayon for at least 1 hour before you assemble the dish[2].

To prepare the fruit Combine all the fruit in a bowl, add the sugar, lemon juice and shredded mint, if using, and mix gently. Cover and set aside to macerate for about 30 minutes[3].

To serve Divide the macerated fruit among 4 heatproof plates or place in a large heatproof dish and cover with the sabayon. Dust twice with icing sugar and caramelise by waving a cook's blowtorch over the surface or briefly placing under a preheated very hot grill. Serve at once.

[1] To give the sabayon more body and make it easier to gratiné, you can whisk in ½ softened gelatine leaf.

[2] The sabayon needs time to firm up a little in the fridge. This will give you a better caramelisation.

[3] This maceration is a very important stage. As the sugar, acid and herb flavours permeate the fruit, they will add at least 30 per cent more flavour to this dish.

Iced coffee parfait

Serves 10–12

Preparation:
15 mins, plus
making sabayon
and 12 hours
freezing

Cooking: 15 mins

Special equipment:
23 x 9cm terrine
(8cm deep)

For this marvellous dessert, all you need to do is flavour your sabayon base and freeze it in a terrine, or in individual moulds, such as ramekins, if you prefer.

Planning ahead The iced parfait can be prepared and frozen up to a week in advance. The garnish can be made a day in advance.

450ml prepared sabayon
   (see page 21)
75ml strong espresso coffee
   (ristretto) or 20ml coffee
   essence, cooled

For the garnish
50g shelled pistachio nuts
30g flaked or chopped almonds

30g icing sugar
2 tsp kirsch or Cognac

For the caramel sauce
70ml water
150g caster sugar
½ tsp arrowroot, diluted in
   a little water

To make the iced coffee parfait In a large bowl, gently fold the sabayon and coffee together[1]. Fill the terrine with the sabayon, smooth the top and freeze overnight.

To prepare the garnish Preheat the oven to 180°C/Gas 4. Mix the nuts with the icing sugar and kirsch or Cognac. Scatter on a baking tray and bake for about 7 minutes until lightly golden and crunchy. Allow to cool.

To make the caramel sauce Put 20ml of the water in a small saucepan and add the sugar. Leave for a few minutes, then dissolve over a medium heat and cook to a dark golden brown caramel[2]. Add the remaining 50ml water to stop the cooking[3]. Mix in the diluted arrowroot to thicken the sauce. Leave to cool.

To serve Dip the terrine into hot water for 4–5 seconds to loosen the parfait, then run a warmed knife around it and turn out onto a board. Cut into slices with the warm knife. Drizzle the caramel sauce onto individual plates and place a slice of parfait in the middle. Scatter the caramelised nuts around the parfait and serve.

~~~~~~~~~~~~~~~~~~~~

[1] As you fold in the coffee, make sure you don't knock out all the air you have incorporated into the sabayon.
[2] When making caramel, I always add the sugar to a small amount of water. The sugar slowly absorbs the water, helping to prevent crystallisation and ensuring even cooking. Taking the caramel to a dark golden brown is important; it will reduce the sweetness and give a more pronounced caramel flavour. If the caramel is too light or blond it will be far too sweet and will devalue the dish.
[3] Hold the pan at arm's length when adding water to hot caramel, as it will splutter.

Pavlova with summer berries

*

Makes 4 large
individual pavlovas

Preparation:
15 mins

Cooking: 2 hours

Special equipment:
electric mixer,
blender

Named after a beautiful ballet dancer, this dessert has inspired chefs around the world and it is one of my favourites. I like my meringues to be huge and shaped naturally, with a pale golden hue and bubbles of caramel oozing out, pearling into crystal formations. They are so simple to make. And, as the meringue is fat-free (never mind the calories from the sugar), you can serve it with a good dollop of ice cream and crème fraîche.

Planning ahead The meringue and coulis can be prepared up to half a day in advance. Be aware that if you cook the meringue further in advance, humidity will cause the soft inside to turn sticky and chewy.

For the meringue
3 free-range/organic medium
   egg whites
6 drops of lemon juice
100g caster sugar
75g icing sugar, sifted, plus
   extra to dust

For the fruit
150g strawberries, rinsed,
   hulled and halved
150g raspberries, washed

50g blackberries, washed
50g blueberries, washed
50g redcurrants or
   blackcurrants, washed
20g caster sugar, or to taste
squeeze of lemon juice

For the coulis
250g raspberries
30g caster sugar

To serve (optional)
vanilla ice cream

To make the meringues Preheat the oven to 120°C/Gas 1. Using an electric mixer on maximum speed, whisk the egg whites with the lemon juice for 1 minute[1], until you have soft peaks. Now gradually whisk in the caster sugar. Whisk at full speed for a further 3 minutes; the peaks will now be shiny, smooth and stiff[2]. Remove the bowl from the machine and using a spatula, fold in the icing sugar little by little; this should take about 2 minutes[3].

To shape the meringues With the spatula or a large spoon[4], drop 6 large dollops of meringue onto a baking tray lined with non-stick baking paper.

To cook the meringues Dust with icing sugar[5] and cook them in the oven for 2 hours[6]. Meanwhile, prepare the fruits and coulis.

To prepare the fruits In a large bowl, gently mix the berries together with the sugar[7] and lemon juice. Cover and leave to macerate for 30 minutes[8].

For the coulis Purée the raspberries and caster sugar together in a blender and then pass through a fine sieve to remove the seeds.

To finish the meringues Once the meringues are cooked to a light blond colour, hard on the outside and soft on the inside, remove from the oven and allow to cool for 30 minutes. You can now serve them as they are. Or, if you like, using a sharp, serrated knife, cut a lid, 5cm in diameter, from the top, then carefully scoop out and discard the soft meringue inside with a spoon.

To serve Place a meringue on each plate and spoon the macerated fruits and their juices on top or around. Trickle the raspberry coulis over the fruit. For me, a large scoop of the best vanilla ice cream on the side is a must.

Variations Use any combination of summer berries and other fruit, such as peaches, plums or cooked apricots or cherries.

Scatter toasted frosted nuts, such as almonds, hazelnuts or pistachios, over the meringue to add a great texture.

For a classic Mont Blanc, fill the meringue with a sweet chestnut purée and vanilla ice cream.

1 When whipping egg whites, it is essential to avoid adding any egg yolk, fat or water as these hinder the formation of the foam. By adding a tiny amount of lemon juice to the egg white before whisking you create a stable foam that will not separate or grain. The lemon juice can be replaced by a little cream of tartar. There is no need to add salt; it simply slows the coagulation of the egg whites.

2 Whisking egg whites traps tiny air bubbles, increasing the volume dramatically. But avoid over-whisking as this will make the egg whites turn grainy, lose volume and separate into a dry froth and a runny liquid. The caster sugar must never be added too quickly as this will reduce the volume of the meringue.

3 It is possible to incorporate the icing sugar using the mixer on the lowest speed, but there is a danger of over-mixing, resulting in a less firm meringue. So, I take the bowl from the machine and sift and fold in the icing sugar little by little.

4 I prefer the rustic, natural shape that you get from simply scooping and dropping the meringue onto the tray in a dollop. But you can, of course, pipe the meringue neatly, or shape it into large smooth quenelles, by passing between two large warm spoons. These are four very generous meringues; you can create smaller ones if you like; they will take almost the same time to cook.

5 A little dusting of icing sugar will lend an appealing colour to the meringue.

6 Should you wish to have white meringues, cook at 100°C/Gas ¼ for 3 hours; personally I prefer the pale gold-crusted exterior this recipe gives.

7 The amount of sugar required will depend on the ripeness and variety of the fruit; always taste first. As the summer progresses, the fruits will increase in natural sweetness. Blackcurrants are sharp and will add a lovely tartness.

8 Macerating the fruits will intensify the flavour and start to break down the cell walls, releasing their juices and softening the fruit.

Iles flottantes 'façon Maman Blanc'

**

Serves 4
Preparation:
40 mins plus cooling
Cooking: 20 mins
Special equipment:
electric mixer
(optional)

This is a dessert from my childhood. I have vivid memories of never-ending lunches with adults talking about politics and other serious subjects, while we sat and longed for *îles flottantes* to be served. It was worth the wait. This is probably the most celebrated dessert in France; you will find it in homes, small brasseries and Michelin-starred restaurants alike.

Planning ahead The meringues and custard can be made up to a day in advance.

For the vanilla milk
1.3 litres organic whole milk
1 tsp vanilla syrup (see page 9)
    or the best vanilla extract

For the meringues
6 organic/free-range medium
    egg whites
12 drops of lemon juice
100g caster sugar

For the crème anglaise
1 litre vanilla milk (saved from
    poaching the meringues)
85g caster sugar
10 organic/free-range medium
    egg yolks

For the caramel
50ml water
175g caster sugar

For the vanilla milk Pour the milk into a roasting tray or large frying pan, add the vanilla syrup and heat gently to a bare simmer to infuse.

To make the meringues Meanwhile, using an electric mixer on medium speed or a balloon whisk, whisk the egg whites with the lemon juice[1] to soft peaks, then slowly add the sugar, whisking constantly. Continue to whisk until the meringue holds firm peaks.

To poach the meringues Using a large spoon dipped in hot water, scoop large dollops of meringue and place in the vanilla milk. (Alternatively you can shape smooth quenelles of meringue between two spoons dipped in hot water). Poach the meringues in the shimmering milk[2] for 5 minutes on each side. Remove with a slotted spoon and place on a tray lined with non-stick baking paper to drain. Strain and reserve the poaching milk to make the custard.

To make the crème anglaise In a medium pan, bring the vanilla milk to a gentle simmer over a medium heat with 2 tsp of the sugar added[3]. Meanwhile, in a bowl, whisk the egg yolks and remaining sugar together until well mixed. Pour the hot milk onto the eggs, whisking constantly, and then pour back into the same saucepan[4]. Place over a medium-low heat and stir continuously with a wooden spoon until the custard begins to thicken and coats the back of your spoon[5]. Immediately strain into a large bowl set over ice to stop the cooking. Leave the custard to cool, stirring occasionally.

To assemble Pour the custard into individual wide serving bowls and arrange the poached meringues on top. Leave in the fridge while you make the caramel.

To make the caramel Put the water into a small saucepan, add the sugar and leave for a few minutes to allow the water to be absorbed, then dissolve over a low heat[6]. Increase the heat to medium and cook the sugar syrup to a rich caramel[7]. Immediately remove from the heat and dip the base of the pan in cold water for 8–10 seconds to arrest the cooking.

To serve Trickle the caramel decoratively over the meringues and serve at once.

Variations Flavour the custard with grated lemon zest, or grated orange zest and a splash of Grand Marnier, or melted chocolate.

[1] Whisking egg whites increases their volume by trapping tiny air bubbles inside the protein network. However, if you over-whisk the egg whites, they will become thick and grainy, lose volume and separate into a dry froth and a runny liquid.

[2] When poaching meringues ensure your vanilla milk is at a shimmer, i.e. just under a simmer. If the liquid is too hot, the meringues will soufflé dramatically and then deflate just as fast. Poach them gently and they will hold their shape and keep their fluffy texture.

[3] I always add a little sugar, 10g or so per litre, to the milk before heating; this prevents the milk proteins from sticking and burning on the bottom of the pan.

[4] When you are making a custard, always pour the hot milk/cream mixture onto the cold beaten eggs before returning to the pan to cook through. If you reverse this process you are in danger of scrambling the eggs before the sauce has had a chance to thicken.

[5] If your custard starts to scramble a little at the bottom of the pan as you cook it, immediately pour into a food processor (be careful not to over-fill) and blend until smooth again. Pour into a bowl over crushed ice to cool quickly.

[6] To prevent sugar crystallising when you make caramel, first put a little water in the bottom of the pan, add the sugar on top and let this absorb the water.

[7] Because the caramel is made in a dark pan, it can look darker than it actually is. Take a spoonful or pour a little onto a white plate. If you undercook your caramel it will be pale, too sweet and lacking in character. You need to cook it almost to a smoking point, then it will be dark brown, with a wonderful, characteristic bitter-sweet caramel flavour.

Apricot cassolette

Serves 4
Preparation:
50 mins
Cooking: 15 mins
Special equipment:
25cm round
casserole dish,
food processor,
blender, non-stick
silicone mats,
cook's blowtorch,
15cm, 9cm, 5cm
and 12cm pastry
cutters/rings, 9cm
bowl (4cm deep),
12cm diameter
metal ladle or
similar ½ sphere

This dish of poached apricots and meringue encased in fine nougatine is one of Le Manoir's best-loved classics. The delicate, almost see-through nougatine is what makes it exquisite. We adapt the dish to showcase other stone fruits in season, such as plums and greengages. It is an opportunity for the amateur cook to treasure a special craft moment. Alternatively, you can use the nougatine to create much easier desserts, such as stewed apricots topped with a nougatine disc, or a millefeuille of nougatine layered with your favourite fruit and cream.

Planning ahead Each of the components can be prepared a day in advance, ready for assembly.

For the frosted almond flakes
40g flaked almonds
1 tsp kirsch
10g icing sugar

For the nougatine
200g flaked almonds
440g caster sugar
220g liquid glucose

For the poached meringues
1 litre organic whole milk
1 tsp vanilla syrup (see page 9)
    or the best vanilla extract
6 organic/free-range medium
    egg whites
12 drops of lemon juice
100g caster sugar

For coating the meringues
crème anglaise (see below),
    made with 300ml saved
    poaching milk, 3 egg yolks
    and 25g caster sugar
60g whipping cream
a splash of kirsch

For the apricot compote/coulis
700g apricots, halved and
    stoned
40g caster sugar, or to taste
25ml water
1 tbsp lemon juice

To finish (optional)
a few pistachio nuts, crushed

For the frosted almond flakes Preheat the oven to 160°C/Gas 3. Mix the almonds, kirsch and icing sugar together. Scatter on a baking tray and toast in the oven for 4–6 minutes until the nuts are lightly coloured and glazed. Set aside to cool.

To make the nougatine Scatter the almonds on a baking tray and warm in the oven for 3–5 minutes until pale blond[1]. Put the sugar and liquid glucose into a medium saucepan, dissolve over a medium heat and cook to a light golden caramel. Add the almonds, mix well and pour onto a silicone liner or tray lined with non-stick baking paper. Leave to cool for about 20 minutes until set hard.

For the poached meringues Pour the milk and vanilla syrup into the casserole and bring to a simmer over a low heat. Using an electric mixer on medium speed,

Trimming the edge of the nougatine sheet.

Cutting the nougatine discs for the cassolette bowls and lids.

Fixing the handles to the nougatine cassolette bowls.

whisk the egg whites with the lemon juice to soft peaks, then slowly whisk in the sugar. Continue to whisk to almost firm peaks. Using two large spoons dipped in hot water, scoop half the meringue into 4 quenelles[2]. Poach in the shimmering milk[3] for 2 minutes on each side. Remove with a slotted spoon and leave to drain on a tray lined with non-stick baking paper. Repeat to make another 4 quenelles. Cool and refrigerate. Strain and reserve the poaching milk for the custard.

For the crème anglaise to coat the meringues Use the above-listed quantities and make the custard as for îles flottantes (see page 31). Fold in the cream and kirsch.

For the apricot compote and coulis Gently mix the apricots with the sugar, water and lemon juice in a large bowl and leave to macerate for 30 minutes. Put the macerated apricots with their juice into a saucepan and bring to a gentle simmer over a medium-low heat. Cover and cook for about 15 minutes until the apricots are soft but still holding their shape. Taste and add a little more sugar if required.

To make the coulis Purée 160g of the fruit and juices in a blender until smooth. Pass through a sieve into a bowl. Set the apricot compote and coulis aside to cool.

To make the nougatine sheet Using a rolling pin, break the set nougatine into smaller pieces. Then, in four batches, blitz in a food processor to a fine powder, using the pulse button. Line a baking tray with a silicone liner. Using a large sieve, sprinkle half of the powdered nougatine evenly onto the silicone mat, to create a 2mm layer[4]. Push the nougatine away from the edge of the mat using a knife to create a 1cm margin. Cook in the preheated oven[5] for 4 minutes until the powdered nougatine melts to form a perfect thin sheet. (You'll need to cut the shapes from this nougatine before baking and shaping a second sheet[6].)

To make the nougatine shapes On removing from the oven, let the nougatine rest for ½ minute or so until it has just cooled enough to handle. Cut out two 15cm discs for the cassolette bowls, two 9cm discs for the lids and two 5cm discs – halve these to make the handles and trim to crescent shapes. In each case, press the cutter onto the nougatine and with a small knife cut around the shape. Lift all the shapes onto a clean tray with a spatula. Reserve. Repeat with the second tray of powdered nougatine.

To mould the nougatine shapes Reheat them, two at a time, in the oven for about ½ minute to re-introduce some suppleness to the nougatine. To shape each cassolette, upturn the 9cm bowl, lift the 15cm nougatine disc over it and wrap the disc tightly around the bowl with your hands. Press the 12cm cutter over the moulded nougatine and use a small knife to cut around it. Leave to cool until firm, then lift the nougatine bowl from the mould and reserve. Soften the inner edge of one crescent-shaped handle by waving a cook's blowtorch over it and then stick to one side of the nougatine cassolette. Repeat for the other handle.

To shape the lid Upturn the 12cm ladle (or half-sphere), lift the warmed 9cm disc of nougatine and mould it tightly around the ladle with your hands (shaping a handle too, if you wish). Leave to cool, it will solidify; lift the shaped nougatine from the ladle. Repeat to shape and assemble the other 3 cassolettes and lids.

To serve Spoon some apricot coulis into the middle of each plate and position a nougatine cassolette on top. Fill with apricot compote, top with two meringues and spoon crème anglaise over them. Sprinkle the toasted nuts and pistachios, if using, on top and position the nougatine lid, at an angle. Serve at once.

---

[1] Warming the almonds enhances the flavour and appearance, but avoid browning them as they will continue to colour in the hot caramel.

[2] To shape a quenelle, dip two large spoons in hot water, then take up a scoop of meringue on one spoon and pass it back and forth between the spoons, turning to create a neat oval.

[3] When poaching meringues ensure your poaching liquor is just under a simmer; if it is too hot then the meringues will soufflé very fast and deflate afterwards.

[4] The thickness and evenness of the nougatine powder is important. If too thick, it will be difficult to shape; if too thin it will cool quickly, becoming too brittle to use.

[5] Have your cutters and moulds ready before baking your nougatine sheets.

[6] You will need to bake, cut and shape the nougatine in two batches, to ensure it will be pliable enough to cut. If you do break your shapes, allow to cool, grind back into a powder, re-bake and mould again.

Bread & Yeast

One of the most exhausting periods of my life came shortly after opening Maison Blanc. We would bake bread through the night and at dawn I'd climb into the van and head for London – to deliver my loaves to the capital's finest restaurants. Dodging traffic wardens was the easy part.

But there are few things in life as rewarding as baking your own bread at home. Forget the cheap, long-lasting, chemically enhanced stuff on the supermarket shelves. Become your own master baker and give your home the warm, comforting scent of a cheerful boulangerie. Your family and friends will love it.

Bread is made from four basic ingredients – flour, yeast, salt and water – yet thousands of different loaves can be produced from this simple combination, by adjusting the method and adding a flavouring or two. However, it is important to realise that baking is a science and there are essential rules to follow. It helps to understand how the ingredients behave.

Yeast is used to make three of our favourite things – beer, wine and bread. It's a fungus – a living organism – that requires moisture and warmth. It feeds on the sugar present in flour, transforming it into billions of pockets of carbon dioxide, and these pockets expand during the proving process. Yeast sleeps at 4°C and can be kept frozen. It is best used at 20°C and it dies at 45–50°C. After so many years as a cook, I am still fascinated by the miraculous powers of yeast and its role in baking.

Flour is the main ingredient in bread and the source of carbohydrate; it also contains up to 14 per cent protein. It is the gluten protein within flour that gives bread its structure and enables it to rise. Strong flour, which is high in gluten, is the type to use for your bread. Salt enhances the taste of bread and strengthens the gluten network, but mixing it directly with yeast will disable it and must be avoided.

Water helps the protein bind together to create the wonderful elastic network. It must be used at the right temperature; if too hot it will kill the yeast. Unless otherwise indicated, start the dough with cold tap water.

Proving is a vital stage in bread-making as it enables the dough to develop flavour and texture. I prove my doughs at standard room temperature (about 20°C). Above 25°C a dough begins to ferment, adversely affecting the taste. The proving dough must be kept covered to prevent it forming a skin and drying out.

When the dough is proven you should see signs of blistering on the surface. It is fragile at this stage but proving it on silicone paper makes it easier to transfer to the oven.

Generating steam in the oven will give your bread a wonderful crust. Pour some hot water into a baking tray in the oven before sliding in the bread and it will create the steam you need.

Pain de campagne

* *

Makes 4 crusty
loaves (each 500g)

Preparation:
30 mins, plus
overnight
fermenting and
2½ hours proving

Cooking:
20–25 mins

Special equipment:
electric mixer
with dough hook
attachment, peel
(optional), baking
stone (optional),
Stanley knife or
razor blade

Of course you can buy your bread from your local bakery, or you can make it at home using a bread maker, which gives satisfactory results and a little pride. But this simplified traditional bread recipe is the real thing. The natural, slow proving gives character and depth of flavour, in contrast to breads that we find in our supermarkets, which rely on flour improvers and rising agents to speed up the process. Hopefully it will introduce you to an exciting and lifelong love affair with yeast and home-made breads, breeding confidence and knowledge, and delighting your friends and family... And another little secret: it is the best stress reliever, especially if you decide to knead the dough by hand.

Planning ahead Prepare the dough starter 12 hours in advance. The bread can be cooked a few hours before serving; it can also be sliced and frozen. But French bread, with its wonderful crust, is at its best warm from the oven.

For the dough starter/leaven	*For the campagne dough*
100g strong plain white organic bread flour[1]	950g strong plain white organic bread flour[1]
100g dark rye flour	130g dark rye flour
5g fresh yeast, crumbled[2]	15g salt[4]
135ml cold water[3]	22g fresh yeast, crumbled
	680ml cold water[3]

For the dough starter/leaven[5] A day ahead, mix all the ingredients together in a medium bowl. Cover the bowl with cling film and leave to ferment overnight, i.e. about 12 hours at room temperature.

To make the bread dough The following day, put all the ingredients into the bowl of the mixer fitted with the dough hook and add the dough starter. Beat together on the lowest speed for 5 minutes and then on medium speed for approximately 5–7 minutes to knead the dough[6]. Alternatively, you can knead the dough by hand on a lightly floured surface, stretching and kneading it for 10 minutes or so. Test the elasticity of the dough by making sure that you can stretch a small piece between your fingers without it breaking (illustrated overleaf).

For the first proving Shape the dough into a ball, cover loosely with a clean cloth or cling film and leave at room temperature for 1 hour; it will increase in bulk[7].

For the second proving Divide the dough equally into four (500g portions) and shape each into a loaf of your desired shape on a lightly floured board. Place each one on a peel or flat tray lined with a silicone liner or non-stick baking paper. Cover loosely with a plastic sheet or a clean cloth to prevent it from

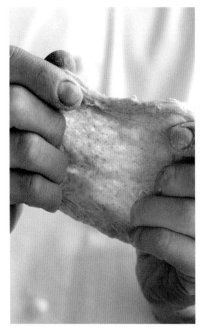

Stretching a piece of dough to test the elasticity after kneading.

Proving doubles the volume of the dough and develops the flavour.

Scoring the loaves at an angle to create an attractive finish.

drying out and leave the loaves to prove at room temperature for about 1½ hours until doubled in volume[8].

To prepare for baking While the loaves are proving, preheat the oven (without the fan) to its highest setting, 250°C/Gas 10. Slide a baking stone[9] or sturdy baking tray onto the middle shelf and place a small roasting tin on the oven shelf below[10].

To bake the bread Dust the loaves with flour, then score lengthways at an angle with a Stanley knife or razor blade[11], making the cuts about 2mm deep. Slide the bread onto the preheated tray or baking stone in the oven. Pour a jug of boiling hot water into the roasting tin and quickly close the oven door[12]. Bake for 20–25 minutes. Remove the loaves from the oven[13] and cool on a wire rack.

Variations French bread is usually shaped by hand and then baked, but you can of course bake the dough in loaf tins.

Alternatively you can mould the loaves in special bread baskets lined with flour (see page 310) and then turn them out to bake them.

---

[1] The choice of flour is important; I recommend Shipton Mill flour. Depending on the time it has been stored, the variety and its nutritional composition, the flour

will absorb more or less water when making the dough. Bread requires a 'strong flour' with a high protein (gluten) content. It provides better elasticity to the dough and gives the loaf a better texture. I also add rye flour to this recipe for flavour.

2 If fresh yeast is unavailable, then dried yeast can be used but you should use half the quantity.

3 The water must be cold, directly from the tap, since you are going to work the dough, which will warm it. If you use warm water then the fermentation process will be activated too quickly and this would undermine the taste.

4 Always weigh yeast and salt separately, as the salt will dehydrate and kill the yeast if it is in direct contact.

5 Using a starter/leaven in bread-making gives a greater complexity of flavour. As the yeast activates and slowly feeds on the natural sugars present in the flour, over time it produces a distinctively tangy or sour taste. Equally it creates a wonderful light-textured bread. If you make your bread regularly, keep back 300g of the dough to use as a starter for the next batch.

6 The initial slow mixing will amalgamate all the ingredients together, giving the flour the opportunity to fully absorb the water (and without flour flying in your face). Then the faster speed will warm the gluten in the flour, making the dough elastic and creating the right environment for fermentation to happen.

7 Ensure that the proving takes place in a draft-free room to prevent a crust from forming on the dough. The room temperature is hugely relevant to the proving; if it were too high then the fermentation process would be activated too quickly, undermining the taste. Standard room temperature is 20°C, which is about right.

8 Once the bread has proven, it will show some signs of blistering on the surface. At this stage the loaves will be fragile to handle; placing them on silicone mats or non-stick baking paper makes it easier to transfer them to the oven.

9 A baking stone will give you a superior crust and will diffuse the heat better.

10 I preheat a small roasting tin, about 20cm wide, in the oven to half-fill with hot water as we put the bread in. This will generate steam, which will help the development of the loaf and create a wonderful crust.

11 I use an old-fashioned razor blade here, but a Stanley knife is a safer tool and I would recommend keeping one of these especially for scoring dough. The sharpness of the blade will avoid any drag on the dough. Ensure the cut is at an angle and not too deep to create an attractive finish. If the cut is vertical it will open up the bread. Practice makes perfect and you can design your own patterns after a few attempts, if you so wish.

12 The high temperature inside your oven is critical. It will decrease significantly when you open the door to place the bread in. If the bread appears to be colouring too quickly, lower the setting slightly.

13 Be very careful when opening the oven door as there will be a lot of hot steam generated. Leave the door ajar for 5 seconds before taking the bread out of the oven to avoid burning yourself.

Seeded cereal bread *Illustrated overleaf*

** **

Makes 3 loaves
(each 600g)

Preparation:
25 mins, plus
2–2½ hours proving

Cooking: 25 mins

Special equipment:
electric mixer with
dough hook
attachment, three
26 x 9cm loaf tins
(8cm deep), peel
(optional), baking
stone (optional)

This bread is very straightforward to make as it doesn't require a starter dough. Enhanced by the textures, flavours and nutrients of a variety of seeds and grains, including malted wheat flakes, barley flakes, sunflower seeds, millet and oats, it has a lovely texture and a wonderful depth of flavour. I buy my seed mix from Shipton Mill, my local mill, which I have used for the past 30 years; it is also available online.

Planning ahead These loaves freeze successfully.

200g seed blend (malted
    wheat, barley, oats, millet and
    sunflower seeds), such as
    Shipton Mill 5
900g strong plain white
    organic bread flour[1]

100g buckwheat flour[2]
24g sea salt
30g fresh yeast[3], crumbled
670ml cold water[4]

To mix and knead the dough Put all the ingredients into the bowl of the mixer, fitted with the dough hook. Mix on low speed for 5 minutes, then on medium speed for 6-7 minutes[5] to knead the dough. Alternatively, you can knead the dough by hand on a lightly floured surface, stretching and kneading it for 10 minutes or so. Test the elasticity of the dough by making sure that you can stretch a small piece between your fingers without it breaking.

For the first proving Scoop out the dough and place in a lightly floured bowl. Cover loosely with a clean cloth or cling film and leave to rise at room temperature for 1 hour.

For the second proving Divide the dough into three (600g portions), shape into oblongs and place each in a lightly greased loaf tin[6]. Cover loosely with a plastic sheet (tented to avoid sticking) or a clean cloth and leave to prove at room temperature for 1-1½ hours[7] or until doubled in bulk.

To prepare for baking While the loaves are proving, preheat the oven (without the fan) to its highest setting, 250°C/Gas 10. Slide a baking stone or sturdy baking tray onto the middle shelf and place a small roasting tin on the shelf below[8].

To bake the bread Slide the loaf tins onto the hot baking stone or tray in the oven. Pour a jug of boiling hot water into the roasting tin and quickly close the oven door. Bake for 25 minutes.

On removing from the oven, upturn the tins and de-mould the bread. Leave to cool on wire racks [9].

1 For advice on bread flour, see page 42.

2 Buckwheat isn't actually a cereal flour, it is a fruit seed, related to rhubarb, which can be used as a highly nutritious, gluten-free alternative to wheat flour.

3 If fresh yeast is unavailable then dried yeast can be used, but halve the quantity.

4 Use cold water from the tap rather than warm water, which would activate the fermentation process too quickly and undermine the taste.

5 There are two mixing speeds. The slow start mixes all the ingredients together. Mixing on the faster speed subsequently warms the dough and stretches the gluten in the flour, making the dough elastic and creating the right environment for fermentation to take place.

6 Alternatively, you can shape the dough into balls or oval loaves by hand. Prove the loaves as above but on a baking peel or flat tray lined with silicone mats or non-stick baking paper. Flour the loaves lightly before baking directly on the baking stone or tray for the same time as above.

7 If the dough dries out, it will form a crust and not prove properly, so cover it with a cloth and ensure that proving takes place in a draft-free room, at around 20°C (standard room temperature). A warm room would speed up fermentation, undermining the development of the flavour. A long, slow proving is always better for taste.

8 I preheat a suitable container, about 20cm wide, in the oven to half-fill with boiling hot water as I put the bread in. This will generate steam, which will delay the formation of a crust and give the bread a longer opportunity to rise. It will also, at a later stage, give a better colour to the crust.

9 Don't leave the bread in the tin, otherwise the trapped steam will soften the crust. Should you want a crustier loaf, you can bake the bread for 20 minutes in the tin, then de-mould and bake directly on the baking stone or tray for the last 5 minutes. The heat will be intense, so to avoid burning yourself, leave the door ajar for 5 seconds before taking the bread out of the oven.

Rye bread galette *Illustrated on previous page*

*
Makes 2 large
galettes
Preparation:
10 mins, plus
1¼ hours proving
Cooking: 50 mins
Special equipment:
electric mixer with
dough hook
attachment, baking
stone (optional),
2 baking peels
(optional)

A wonderful rustic loaf. For bread-making, rye flour, which is very low in gluten, is a good alternative to heavily processed white flour. It produces a dense-textured loaf with an excellent full flavour.

Planning ahead This bread needs to be made a day in advance as it is very sticky when just baked and therefore difficult to cut. A rye loaf will keep for up to 5 days. At home I pre-slice my bread, wrap and freeze it, then take out slices as I need them.

160ml cold water
30g fresh yeast[1], crumbled
1060g organic rye flour (such
   as Shipton Mill Type 1350
   Rye), plus extra for sprinkling

32g sea salt
970ml warm water
   (at about 50ºC)

To mix and knead the dough In a small bowl, whisk together the cold water and yeast. Put the rye flour, salt and warm water[2] into the bowl of the mixer fitted with the dough hook and mix for 2 minutes on low speed. Add the yeast liquid and mix for a further 2–3 minutes on medium speed. Divide the dough into 2 equal pieces.

To prove the dough Generously sprinkle the base of two medium bowls with rye flour[3] and scoop a portion of dough into each one. Cover each loosely with a clean cloth to prevent crusting and leave to prove at room temperature for about 1¼ hours[4].

To prepare for baking While the loaves are proving, preheat the oven (without the fan) to its highest setting, 250°C/Gas 10. Slide a baking stone or sturdy baking tray onto the middle shelf to heat up.

To bake the bread Upturn the bowls to de-mould the dough carefully over two peels or trays lined with squares of non-stick baking paper. Slide the dough directly onto the preheated tray or baking stone in the oven and bake for 20 minutes, then turn the setting down to 230ºC/Gas 8 and bake for further 40 minutes[5]. Transfer to a wire rack and leave to cool overnight.

Variations For a slightly less pronounced rye taste, you can replace 100g of the rye flour with 120g strong white organic wheat flour.

   To develop more of the fermentation flavours, and slightly lighten the texture, make a bread starter: Mix 80ml of the cold water with the yeast and 100g of the flour and let it ferment at room temperature for 2–3 hours. Add this as if it were the yeast liquid in the recipe.

1 If fresh yeast is unavailable, then dried yeast can be used but you should use half the quantity.

2 As rye flour contains very little gluten, there is little to provide elasticity and it is therefore important to maximise the yeast's potential. Using warm water at around 50°C (i.e. the usual temperature of hot tap water) will give a warm dough, activating the yeast more quickly and speeding up the fermentation process. Use water from the kettle cooled to this temperature rather than directly from the hot tap (which is not necessarily suitable for drinking). This is one of the few breads to have such a high proving temperature; most other breads benefit from a slow fermentation at around 20°C (standard room temperature).

3 You need to sprinkle the bowls with flour quite heavily, to prevent the moist rye dough sticking. The rye dough is wetter than a wheat dough and will spread a little when turned out.

4 Because a rye dough has very little gluten protein, just 2–3 per cent, it will not double in volume in the way a wheat dough does. There will be a slight lift, but the texture will remain quiet dense. That is the character of rye bread…

5 Note that rye dough takes much longer to cook than breads made with wheat flour and darkens much more during baking.

DID YOU KNOW?
One possible reason for the increased incidence of gluten intolerance is the higher percentage of gluten in modern strains of wheat compared to older strains.

** **

Brioche

Serves 10

Preparation:
20 mins, plus
2½ hours proving

Cooking:
20–25 mins

Special equipment:
electric mixer with
dough hook
attachment,
26 x 9cm loaf tin
(8cm deep)

Still today, I find brioche immensely satisfying to make, and magical in many ways. The dough can triple in size, creating wonderfully light, butter-rich melting crumbs, with that irresistible yeasty fermented flavour. You must try this recipe; it is not over complicated and the reward is immense. If you have any brioche left over, use it to make pain perdu (see page 234). The dough also forms the basis for my gâteau à la crème fraîche (overleaf).

Planning ahead The brioche can be made a day in advance; it can also be frozen.

250g strong white organic bread flour (Shipton Mill No. 4)	4 free-range/organic medium eggs
3 pinches of sea salt	150g unsalted butter, at room temperature, cut into small cubes
30g caster sugar	
12g fresh yeast[1]	

To make the brioche dough Place the flour, salt, sugar[2] and yeast in the bowl of an electric mixer fitted with the dough hook, keeping the salt and yeast apart. Add the eggs and mix on the lowest speed for 5 minutes until completely absorbed[3]. Increase to the next speed setting and mix for another 5 minutes until the dough comes away from the side of the bowl. Now add the cubes of butter[4] and continue to mix for 2–3 minutes until fully incorporated.

For the first proving Remove the mixer bowl from the machine and cover the brioche dough loosely with a tea towel to prevent the surface from drying and to stop a crust forming. Leave to rise at room temperature[5] for 1 hour. Then refrigerate the dough for 1 hour[6].

For the second proving Lightly oil your loaf tin, dust with flour and shake out the excess. With a scrape card or spatula, release the dough from the bowl onto a lightly floured board and shape it into a cylinder that will fit into the tin. Place in the loaf tin, pat down lightly and leave at room temperature for 25 minutes until it has doubled in size[7].

To cook the bread Preheat the oven to 200°C/Gas 6. Bake the brioche for 20–25 minutes. Remove from the oven, slide the brioche out of the tin onto a wire rack[8] and allow to cool.

Variations There are various flavourings you could add to the dough, such as grated lemon or orange zest to taste, or 1 tsp ground ginger and 45g finely chopped fresh root ginger, blanched and refreshed in fresh boiling water 3 times to remove bitterness.

To make individual brioches, on a lightly floured surface, divide the dough into 60g pieces and shape into balls or other shapes. Brush with egg wash (beaten egg yolk) and bake for 10 minutes.

1 If fresh yeast is unavailable then dried yeast can be used, but halve the quantity.

2 The inclusion of sugar is to help the yeast ferment and produce carbon dioxide – creating wonderful bubbles and air pockets, giving a light and soft bread.

3 At this stage the proteins within the gluten are being worked, making them more elastic. This happens as the liquid, i.e. the eggs, is absorbed into the flour.

4 Adding the butter in small pieces at room temperature enables it to be incorporated quickly into the dough, producing a silky smooth texture.

5 Here, the optimum proving temperature is around 22°C, which is more or less kitchen temperature. The warmer the room is, the faster the proving time, but a slow fermentation creates a better flavour and also a greater rise.

6 You will need to chill the dough at this stage, otherwise it will be too soft to work with. Chilling will also slow down the proving.

7 The same chemistry is happening in the second proving as the first. The second proving will increase the activity of the yeast, creating wonderful sweet and sour flavours and, of course, puffing out the dough.

8 Ensure that you remove the brioche from the tin as soon as it is baked. If left in the tin, the brioche is likely to become soggy due to moisture trapped in the tin.

DID YOU KNOW?
This wonderful egg-enriched yeast dough dates back a long way in French history. Marie Antoinette's solution for the bread-starved Parisians was to: 'Let them eat brioche!'

Gâteau à la crème fraîche

* *

Serves 6–8

Preparation:
20 mins, plus
making brioche
dough and
25 minutes proving

Cooking: 25 mins

Special equipment:
25cm tart ring (3cm
high)

Rustic, rich and heavenly, this is very much a Maman Blanc dessert. The proof is in the proving... Just inhale the warmly provocative vapours of the rising dough.

Planning ahead Both the filling and brioche dough can be made a day ahead.

For the dough
400g prepared, risen and
    chilled brioche dough
    (see page 50)

For the crème fraîche filling
4 free-range/organic medium
    egg yolks
45g caster sugar

finely grated zest of ½ lemon
juice of ¼ lemon
150g crème fraîche

To finish
2 egg yolks, lightly beaten
    (for egg wash)
caster sugar, for sprinkling

To make the crème fraîche filling In a large bowl, mix all the ingredients together until evenly combined, then cover and reserve in the fridge.

To shape and prove the dough Lay a 35cm square of greaseproof paper on your peel (or tray) and sit the tart ring on top[1]. Place the dough in the middle. With lightly floured hands, flatten the brioche dough, pushing it from the middle to the outside until you have an even thickness of 3–4mm and a raised rim of about 1cm. Leave to prove at room temperature for 25 minutes[2]. Preheat the oven to 200°C/Gas 6 and place a baking stone or tray on the middle shelf.

To prepare for baking Knock back the dough base with your fingertips, to the edge of the raised rim[3]. Brush the rim with egg wash. Pour three-quarters of the crème filling into the brioche case. Carefully slide the gâteau onto the baking stone or hot baking tray and pour in the rest of the filling.

To bake the gâteau Bake for 10 minutes, then sprinkle caster sugar over the surface and bake for a further 15 minutes until golden brown and cooked[4]. Remove the ring and transfer to a wire rack to cool slightly. Serve warm.

[1] A ring mould isn't essential. You could simply shape the round with your hands and let the gâteau take its own shape, flattening the base until you have the desired thickness and creating the rim as described.

[2] This second proving will help to develop the flavour and puff up the dough.

[3] You will need to knock back the dough to create a well for the crème fraîche mixture; do not touch the risen rim.

[4] To make sure the gâteau is cooked, gently lift one edge with a spatula and check that the base is golden brown in colour.

Apple croustade

Serves 4

Preparation:
2 hours, plus
1½ days resting

Cooking: 50 mins

Special equipment:
electric mixer with
dough hook
attachment,
4 individual
8–10cm tart tins,
4 non-stick 14cm
round moulds,
mandolin (optional),
blender

This famous croustade from southwest France features a rosace of Cox's apples in their own coulis, crowned with the finest and flakiest caramelised pastry. I love it, even though it doesn't originate from my region, and interestingly, the recipe has similarities with the legendary strudel. It does require patience and delicate handling, but it's a highly rewarding dish and a wonderful treat for a special occasion. Should you decide not to attempt it, then come to Le Manoir during the autumn – it will be on the menu. I like to serve it topped with a scoop of apple sorbet or honey and ginger ice cream and a little diced stem ginger.

Planning ahead The croustade will take 2 days to make, as the dough needs to be prepared the day before, then refrigerated overnight, then stretched and allowed to dry for another 24 hours. The dough recipe makes enough for 16 croustade crowns, but it isn't practicable to make a smaller amount, so divide the dough into 4 batches and wrap each in cling film. Freeze all but one batch for future use – for up to a month. Once defrosted, the dough can easily be stretched again and shaped into croustades.

For the croustade dough
2 organic/free-range egg
    whites
2 pinches of salt
1 tsp caster sugar
2 egg yolks
260ml warm water
    (at about 50°C)[1]
500g strong plain white
    organic bread flour (ideally
    Shipton Mill)
3g fresh yeast, crumbled[2]
2 tbsp grapeseed oil

To finish the dough
15g clarified butter
30g caster sugar

For the apple rosace
30g clarified butter
½ tsp Calvados (or brandy)
10g caster sugar
½ tsp lemon juice
8 Cox's Orange Pippin apples[3]
    (1.6kg)

For the apple coulis
80g Cox's Orange Pippin
    apple, peeled and chopped
80ml water
40g caster sugar
10ml lemon juice
½ tsp vanilla syrup
    (see page 9)

To make the croustade dough In a bowl, whisk the egg whites with the salt and sugar to a foam[4]. In a separate bowl, whisk the egg yolks with 240ml of the warm water and stir this into the whites. Put the flour and yeast into the bowl of the electric mixer, with the dough hook fitted, and mix on a low speed, then slowly incorporate the egg mixture.

When the dough starts to come away from the side of the bowl, add a third of the oil[5] and continue mixing until it is completely absorbed, then add the remaining 20ml water and mix for 10 minutes, still on low speed. Add the remaining two-thirds of the oil and mix for 3–4 minutes on medium speed until it is all absorbed.

Turn the dough onto a lightly floured surface and knead by hand into a smooth ball. Divide into 4 portions, wrap each in cling film and refrigerate overnight. (The following day, freeze all but one dough batch for future use.)

The following day Take the croustade dough from the fridge and leave it, still wrapped, in a warm place[6] for 4 hours before shaping.

To shape the croustades Here you need a friend. Cover your work surface with a large, clean cloth and gradually pull and stretch the dough on the cloth with your friend, handling it extremely carefully. Using the minimum of flour and the back of your hands, continue to stretch until the dough is very thin[7].

Using a wide, soft pastry brush, apply a thin coat of clarified butter lightly over the dough[8] and sprinkle evenly with the caster sugar. Cut out four 20cm squares, allow them to dry a little and then invert each one into an individual 8–10cm tart tin[9]. Press into the base and edges of the tin and fold and shape the overhanging pastry decoratively into the tin with your fingers, to create the croustades, giving them height. Leave to dry at room temperature overnight.

To bake the croustades Preheat the oven to 220°C/Gas 7. Bake the croustades for 3 minutes or until golden brown and crisp[10].

To make the apple rosace Lower the oven to 200°C/Gas 6. Line the bases of 4 non-stick 14cm moulds with a disc of non-stick baking paper. In a small bowl, mix the clarified butter with the Calvados, sugar and lemon juice until the sugar has dissolved. Lightly brush the moulds with the Calvados butter.

Peel, core and slice the apples across into fine 2mm slices, using a mandolin if you have one. Place an apple slice in the centre of each mould and fan the remaining apple slices around it, overlapping them tightly in a rosace shape[11]. Brush the apple slices with the remaining Calvados butter. Cook in the oven for 40 minutes.

Once removed from the oven, cover each mould with cling film and leave for 10 minutes or so – the trapped heat will cook the apples through.

To make the apple coulis Put all the ingredients into a small saucepan and bring to a simmer. Cook gently for 2 minutes. Blitz in a blender for 1 minute, then pass through a sieve into a bowl and leave to cool.

To serve Turn out the rosace onto a sheet of greaseproof paper. Place one in the middle of each plate and spoon the apple coulis around it. Top with a croustade and crown with a scoop of ice cream or sorbet. Simple, yet perfect!

Variation As a quick alternative to making your own dough, use filo pastry lightly brushed with clarified butter, dusted with caster sugar and arranged as a crown in a small container. Dry overnight and then bake at 200°C/Gas 6 until golden. Not quite the same, but still delicious.

1 Use water from the kettle cooled to this temperature. It should be roughly the temperature of hot tap water (which isn't always suitable for drinking, so we don't recommend using it).

2 Here yeast is used as an agent to sour the dough, rather than lift it. If fresh yeast is unavailable, then substitute dried yeast but use half the quantity.

3 I have found Cox's Orange Pippins to be the best apples to use for this recipe, as they have just the right texture and level of acidity.

4 To enable the egg whites to mix easily into the dough, you need to break down their albumen, so whisk them to a light foam, i.e. just under soft peaks.

5 The oil is added in two stages, to ensure it is completely absorbed. The oil enriches the dough and gives it elasticity, helping the stretching later on.

6 The warmer the dough, the easier the stretching will be and the thinner you will be able to get it. The best place to leave the dough is in an airing cupboard.

7 Stretching the croustade dough is the most delicate part and you may hate me for it! But such is the price for a truly exquisite dessert. We use the back of the hands and arm to gently stretch the dough to the finest possible thickness; it should be almost transparent. Using your fingertips would damage it. Even though you may be extremely careful, you will probably still have a few tears through the pastry, but it doesn't matter as you will cut these out later on.

8 Brush extremely lightly with butter, barely touching the dough, or it will be too oily. In the same way, just lightly sprinkle the sugar over the buttered dough.

9 Ensure the sugar-coated side of the croustade dough is on the outside, as this will caramelise the most and will be the presentation side.

10 Watch closely, as it will only take 2–3 minutes to bake the croustades and they can quickly over-darken and burn.

11 The rosace will be about 2–3cm in height. On cooking it will settle into a truly delicious, melting apple experience.

Fish

Some predict that the world's fish stocks will be extinct by 2050, others say there are plenty more fish in the sea, that we should continue to catch and eat them with a clear conscience. I sit somewhat uncomfortably between these two extremes, but I am proud to say that Le Manoir is the only Michelin-starred restaurant to be accredited by the MSC.

The sale of commercial fishing is without precedent, as industrial fishing vessels are now able to locate and suck out tens of tonnes of fish at a time. Immense drift nets harvest the seas and beam trawlers scour the ocean floor for deep-dwelling fish, damaging the seabed and fish habitats in the process. Perhaps most worryingly, as much as a third of the catch is discarded – either because it is undersized or because the fishermen have already reached their permitted quota for that particular species. Few of these discarded fish are able to survive.

However, it is not all gloom and doom. Passionate individuals and organisations are actively campaigning to make us aware of the problems. The Marine Conservation Society (MCS), Marine Stewardship Council (MSC) and Sustain are working to change the way we fish, the way we buy fish and the way we cook it. Whether we are fishermen, retailers, chefs or consumers, we all share a responsibility. The future of our fish is in our hands.

As consumers, we should certainly be looking to buy sustainable species. When it comes to choosing fish, freshness is critical. Look for fish with bright bulging eyes, firm flesh and bright red, fresh-looking gills. The fish should be slippery and stiff to the touch, and have an agreeable smell. If the fishmonger is filleting the fish for you, ask for the bones and use these to make soup or stock.

The simplest cooking methods are the best. Delicate whole fish and fillets are excellent pan-fried in a little foaming butter in a good non-stick frying pan over a medium heat. Or you could use your best extra virgin olive oil, keeping the temperature moderate; above 190°C the oil loses its special characteristics. If very fresh, the fish will curl as it touches the pan. Wait 15 seconds, then gently press it using a fish slice to ensure the skin is in contact with the pan and it will stay that way. Your prize will be a lovely crisp skin.

Steaming is another excellent simple technique as it preserves the natural flavours and textures of the fish beautifully; it is also the best way to retain nutrients.

I often cook whole fish and chunky fillets in a court bouillon. The beauty here is in the exchange of flavours. As the fish gently cooks through, it releases its flavour into the cooking liquor. In return, the delicate flavours of the aromatics permeate and scent the fish flesh.

Hot-smoked salmon, beetroot salad and horseradish crème fraîche

Serves 4
Preparation:
20 mins
Cooking: about
1 hour

This is a simple dish that combines some interesting autumnal flavours and textures. Please try to buy the best salmon you can find. Organic farmed salmon costs a lot more than conventionally farmed salmon but it is definitely worth it. Today we have access to a large, exciting range of beetroot varieties, ranging from ruby red to yellow and white. The less familiar ones are mostly old varieties that are enjoying a revival. Tiny beetroot are often disappointing in flavour. My best beetroot experience was a huge root – about half a kilo. Was it French, Italian or English? I don't remember, but it was just divine.

Planning ahead The beetroot can be cooked ahead and the salad prepared up to a few hours in advance.

120g hot-smoked salmon
(preferably bradon rost)

For the beetroot salad
480g mixed small beetroot
(about 4), such as Candy,
Bull's Blood and Golden,
washed and trimmed
½ shallot, peeled and finely
chopped
2 tsp aged balsamic vinegar
(at least 8 years old)
2 tbsp extra virgin olive oil[1]
1 tbsp water
2 pinches of sea salt
2 pinches of freshly ground
black pepper

For the dressing
100g crème fraîche
1 tsp finely grated fresh
horseradish
2 pinches of sea salt
pinch of cayenne pepper
squeeze of lemon juice

For the garnish
a few dill sprigs

To make the beetroot salad Put the beetroot into a large saucepan, add enough cold water to cover and bring to the boil. Reduce the heat and simmer for about 1 hour until tender[2]. (Alternatively you could steam the beetroot.) Drain and leave to cool slightly, then peel[3]. Cut the beetroot into even-sized wedges and toss in a bowl with the remaining salad ingredients. Taste and adjust the seasoning if necessary[4].

To make the dressing In a bowl, mix all the ingredients together until evenly combined. Taste and adjust the seasoning if necessary.

To serve Divide the beetroot salad among individual bowls. Break the salmon into generous flakes and scatter on top. Spoon the horseradish crème fraîche over and garnish with dill.

~~~~~~

1   Use your best extra virgin olive oil in salad dressings.
2   In order to gain the maximum flavour from the beetroot, you must cook it through to ensure the starches are fully converted into sugars. Depending on size, your beetroot may take anywhere between 40 minutes and 1½ hours. To test, insert a small knife through to the centre; it should meet with little resistance and the texture should be soft and melting.
3   I would recommend wearing rubber gloves when preparing the beetroot, to prevent your hands from staining red.
4   The salmon is relatively high in salt, as salt is involved in the curing process prior to smoking, so very little needs to be added to the salad.

DID YOU KNOW?
Bradon rost is a Scottish type of hot-smoked salmon. Unlike more familiar cold-smoked salmon, heat is involved for part of the smoking process, which effectively cooks the salmon. Bradon rost has a big smoke flavour.

Fillet of mackerel, shaved fennel salad and soy lime glaze

Serves 4

Preparation: 20 mins, plus 2 hours soaking fennel seeds

Cooking: 5 mins

Special equipment: mandolin

Mackerel is one of the most plentiful species of fish in our seas; it is also inexpensive and delicious. It can be prepared in many ways – as sushi, pickled, smoked, barbecued, grilled, baked, pan-fried or steamed – but to appreciate this fish at its best it must be very fresh. This little dish has the virtue of being very simple, and it is packed with flavours.

Planning ahead To lend even more flavour to the fish, pickle it for 20 minutes before you grill it (see variations, overleaf). In this case, you will need to prepare the pickling liquor a day in advance.

4 mackerel fillets (skin on)

For the glaze
1 tbsp water
2 tbsp soy sauce (Kikkoman brand)
1 tbsp palm sugar or dark muscovado sugar
1 tsp finely chopped fresh root ginger
½ tsp lime juice

For the fennel salad
150g fennel bulb, trimmed
15g rocket leaves
juice of ¼ lime
4 tsp extra virgin olive oil
pinch of sea salt
pinch of freshly ground white pepper
1 tsp fennel seeds, soaked in warm water for 2 hours and toasted in a dry pan[1]

To prepare the fennel For the salad, remove the core from the fennel, then cut into wafer-thin slices, using a mandolin[2]. Immerse in a bowl of iced water and set aside for 20 minutes[3].

To prepare the glaze In a small saucepan, combine the water, soy sauce, sugar, ginger and lime juice. Bring to the boil and let bubble for 10 seconds only[4], then remove from the heat.

To prepare the mackerel Check the mackerel for pin bones[5] and lightly score the skin at 2cm intervals[6]. Preheat your grill to high. Place the mackerel fillets skin side up on a baking tray. Place under the hot grill for 4–5 minutes depending on the thickness of the fillets, until the fish is just cooked.

To make the fennel salad While the mackerel is under the grill, drain the fennel, pat dry in a tea towel and place in a large bowl with the rocket leaves, lime juice, extra virgin olive oil and seasoning[7]. Toss lightly together to combine and sprinkle with the toasted fennel seeds.

To serve Divide the salad among individual plates and lay the grilled mackerel fillets on top. Spoon the glaze over and around the fish. Serve immediately.

Variations Other oily fish, such as tuna or salmon, could be used in place of the mackerel. And the salad leaves can, of course, be varied – try adding baby spinach or watercress, for example. Some caramelised almonds or peanuts would make an interesting addition, too. You could also replace the fennel seeds with anise seeds.

For an interesting flavour variation, you might like to try lightly pickling the mackerel fillets for 20 minutes before grilling. To prepare the pickling liquor, pour 250ml each white wine vinegar and water into a large saucepan and add 2 pinches of crushed pink peppercorns, a pinch of crushed toasted coriander seeds, a good pinch of sea salt, 40g caster sugar and 35g thinly sliced shallot or red onion. Bring to the boil, then remove from the heat and add 3–4 lemon slices and 10g coriander stalks. Leave to infuse at room temperature overnight. The next day, strain the pickling liquor and add the mackerel fillets. Leave in the fridge for 20 minutes, then remove the mackerel, pat dry and grill as above.

1 Soaking the fennel seeds in water will re-hydrate them, making them a little plump and easier to eat. By toasting in a dry pan you add a little crunch to them, and a toasted fragrant flavour. A lovely little addition of texture to the salad.

2 The finer the fennel slices the better, and a mandolin is the best tool to use here. Mind your fingers, though; I have nearly lost a few myself over the years! Always use a guard.

3 The iced water will crisp and curl up the fennel giving it a great texture. It will also remove some of the sugars, which can otherwise be too pronounced. Make sure the fennel is well drained before using.

4 The glaze is meant to be light and fresh in flavour, so make sure you cook it very briefly: 10 seconds is plenty; any longer and it will be over-reduced and salty; it is also liable to caramelise.

5 Run your fingers over the fillets to feel for any tiny 'pin' bones that might have escaped the filleting process and remove these with kitchen tweezers.

6 To score the skin, with a sharp knife, make shallow incisions, 2–3mm deep. Scoring makes it easier for the marinade to permeate the fish. It will also prevent the mackerel fillets from curling up in the pan during cooking and allows the heat to penetrate faster and more evenly.

7 As there is soy sauce in the glaze, you hardly need any salt in the dressing for the salad.

Cornish fish soup

*

Serves 4

Preparation:
20 mins, plus
making rouille
and 30 minutes
marinating

Cooking: 45 mins

Special equipment:
blender or food
processor

When you think of fish soup, inevitably the heady flavours of Provence spring to mind. On the Atlantic, we do not have the same varieties that are caught in the Mediterranean, but you can still make a lovely fish soup with some Cornish red and grey mullet and gurnard, using the technique from the south of France.

Planning ahead Order the fish from your fishmonger well in advance and ask him to scale and gut it for you, and to chop the bones into small pieces[1]. The soup, garnish and rouille can be prepared a day in advance.

2 red mullet, cleaned and filleted, bones reserved and chopped

2 gurnard, cleaned and filleted, bones reserved and chopped

1 grey mullet, cleaned and filleted, bones reserved and chopped

1 sachet (0.25g) saffron strands[2], soaked in 1 tbsp hot water and 2 tbsp extra virgin olive oil for 15 minutes

For the soup
50ml olive oil
1 small onion, peeled and cut into 1cm dice
1 medium carrot, peeled and cut into 1cm dice
25g fennel trimmings, washed and chopped

4 garlic cloves (unpeeled), lightly crushed

100g vine-ripened tomatoes, cut into 1cm dice

2 sachets (0.5g) saffron powder[3]

7.5g tomato purée

100ml white wine

1 bouquet garni (1 bay leaf, 4 thyme sprigs and 2 parsley stalks, tied together)

750ml water

1½ tsp Pernod

salt and freshly ground pepper

2 pinches of cayenne pepper

For the garnish
20 thin croûtes (see page 136), rubbed with a cut garlic clove

To serve
rouille (see page 68)

To marinate the fish Check the fish for any pin bones and remove any you come across with kitchen tweezers. Cut the flesh into bite-sized pieces and place in a large bowl. Add the infused saffron mixture and leave to marinate in the fridge for at least 30 minutes.

To make the soup In a large saucepan over a medium heat, warm the olive oil and gently sweat the onion, carrot, fennel, garlic and tomatoes with the saffron powder for 4–5 minutes, without colouring. Stir in the reserved chopped fish bones and tomato purée and sweat a further 2 minutes.

Meanwhile, boil the wine in a small pan for 2 minutes. Add to the soup base with the bouquet garni. Pour in the water to cover, add the Pernod and bring to the boil. Skim and then simmer for 30 minutes. Allow to cool slightly.

Remove the bouquet garni, then blitz the soup in a blender or food processor, in batches if necessary, for 3 seconds only – to pulverise the fish bones and other flavourings. Now force the soup through a fine sieve into a clean saucepan, pressing with the back of a ladle to extract as much liquid as possible.

To finish and serve Bring the soup to the boil and then skim off any oil from the surface. Taste and heighten the seasoning with salt, pepper and cayenne. Add the marinated pieces of fish and simmer gently for 6–8 minutes. Pour into a large tureen and serve at once, with garlic croûtes and rouille on the side.

Variations Add a few crushed, chopped lemongrass stalks for a fresh lemony scent, or a little finely chopped fresh root ginger and chilli.

You might like to enrich the soup with a swirl of your best extra virgin olive oil and a little sprinkling of cayenne.

Rouille

Serves 4

Preparation: 5 mins

Smooth and delicious, this classic sauce is very simple to make. It is an emulsified sauce and uses the same techniques as a traditional mayonnaise.

2 organic/free-range medium
  egg yolks
2 pinches of sea salt
2 pinches of freshly ground
  white pepper
2 garlic cloves, peeled and
  crushed

1 sachet (0.25g) saffron strands,
  soaked in a little warm water
  for 15 minutes
125ml grapeseed oil
125ml extra virgin olive oil
2 tsp lemon juice

To make the rouille Have all the ingredients at room temperature before you start[4]. In a large mixing bowl, whisk together the egg yolks, salt, pepper, garlic and saffron-infused water. Start adding the grapeseed oil, then the olive oil, in a steady trickle, whisking energetically until the oil is absorbed and the mixture turns pale orange and thickens, usually after about 150ml oil has been added[5]. Thin down or loosen the consistency with the lemon juice, then whisk in the remaining olive oil[6]. Taste and correct the seasoning if necessary. Store the rouille in a covered container in the fridge and use within 2–3 days.

Variation Omit the saffron from this sauce and you will have a simple aïoli (garlic mayonnaise).

1 If you want to make a 'low budget' soup, it is possible to use only the fish bones and the soup will still be quite delicious.

2 Good saffron stamens can be difficult to source and they are expensive. To get the best out of them, soak in hot water to rehydrate and draw out their wonderful colour, flavour and aroma.

3 Saffron powder is less expensive than saffron strands and readily passes on its flavour and colour. You can find some good saffron powder.

4 For the rouille, all the ingredients must be at room temperature, especially the oil. If too cold, it will be difficult to incorporate and emulsify.

5 Here the egg yolk it is acting as an emulsifier. When you whisk the egg yolks slowly, they absorb all the droplets of oil, forming an emulsion which thickens and gives you a rich, stable and delicious sauce. The most difficult stage is at the start. If you add the oil too quickly, the sauce is very likely to curdle, as the emulsifiers in the egg yolk will not be able to absorb it.

6 If the rouille separates, add 1 tsp hot water and whisk until smooth. Or, if this doesn't work, take a clean bowl, add 1 egg yolk and slowly whisk in the split rouille, little by little, to incorporate and emulsify.

DID YOU KNOW?
The oleic acid in extra virgin olive oil gives it a relatively high acidity, which can interfere with emulsifying, resulting in a thin sauce. Also, the flavour of extra virgin olive oil can dominate, so I like to use half a mild-tasting oil, such as grapeseed, adding it to begin with and finishing with extra virgin olive oil to taste.

Chargrilled Dover sole, spiced butter

*

Serves 4

Preparation:
15 mins, plus
30 minutes chilling

Cooking: 10 mins

Special equipment:
griddle pan or
barbecue

What can be better than a beautifully grilled, very fresh Dover sole that you know has been responsibly caught off the nearest coastline? Top with a chilli and smoked paprika butter and serve with some seasonal vegetables and you will have a superb meal. Of course, sole is expensive, but you could use sustainable plaice, lemon sole or megrim instead. And if you don't fancy the chilli, flavour the butter with crushed garlic, chopped parsley or chopped anchovies instead.

Planning ahead Ask your fishmonger to remove the dark skin from the fish for you. The butter can be made a few days in advance and refrigerated or frozen.

4 Dover soles (350–450g each),
   heads and dark skin
   removed, trimmed
plain flour, for dusting
sea salt and freshly ground
   black pepper

For the spiced butter
100g unsalted butter, at room
   temperature
5g medium-strength red chilli,
   deseeded and finely chopped
½ tsp smoked paprika
2 tsp lemon juice

To make the spiced butter Mix together the butter, chilli, paprika and lemon juice. Taste and adjust the spice if necessary. Scoop the butter onto a sheet of cling film and wrap in the film, forming the butter into a sausage shape. Twist the ends of the cling film to secure. Place in the fridge for 30 minutes to firm up (or freeze).

To prepare the fish An hour before cooking, take your fish from the fridge and firmly pat dry with a cloth or kitchen paper[1]. Preheat the oven to 180°C/Gas 4 and your griddle pan to full heat[2]. Lightly dust the fish with flour and pat off the excess[3]. Season lightly with sea salt and black pepper.

To cook the fish Lay the fish on the grill or barbecue and cook, without moving, for 1 minute on each side[4]. Lift into a lightly buttered baking tray and finish cooking in the oven for 8–10 minutes. Serve topped with the spiced butter.

[1] It is important to remove as much surface moisture as possible to prevent the fish sticking to the grill during cooking, so give it a firm rub with a dry cloth.
[2] If you don't have a griddle pan, brush the fish with olive oil or melted butter, season and do the initial cooking under a preheated grill or directly in the oven.
[3] A dusting of flour will help to stop the fish from sticking and give it a golden crust.
[4] By marking the fish over a high heat you will get a smoky chargrilled flavour; you can then finish cooking the fish gently in the oven. If you cooked the fish completely on the grill it would become dry and tough, and the skin would burn.

Pollock fillet grenobloise, pomme purée

*

Serves 4
Preparation:
10 mins
Cooking: 10 mins,
plus 30 mins for
pomme purée
Special equipment:
ovenproof frying
pan

We have fished our cod to near extinction and whilst stocks are hopefully replenishing, it is lovely to have a fish like pollock. Although not as sumptuous as cod, it has a great texture and big flavour and is underrated, in my view. After all, it is a member of the cod family. Cooked in homes all over France, this recipe is part of the classic French repertoire. The method of pan-frying lends itself to other round fish, including salmon, cod, hake and mullet.

Planning ahead The croûtons can be prepared well in advance and reheated in the oven.

4 pollock fillets (skin on), each
   180g and 3cm thick
4 pinches of sea salt
2 pinches of freshly ground
   white pepper
40g unsalted butter

For the pomme purée
1kg Desirée, Belle de Fontenay
   or Estima potatoes[1]
170–200ml whole milk,
   warmed
70g unsalted butter, melted
2 pinches of sea salt
2 pinches of freshly, finely
   ground white pepper

For the sauce
50ml water
½ lemon, peeled and segments
   cut free from the membrane,
   juice reserved
2 tbsp capers, washed and
   drained
30g shallot, peeled and finely
   chopped
10g flat-leaf parsley, finely
   chopped

To finish
30g small croûtons[2]

To cook the potatoes for the pomme purée Peel and quarter the potatoes, cutting them into even-sized pieces. Place in a large saucepan, add enough cold water to cover and bring to the boil over a high heat. Reduce the heat so that the water is gently simmering and cook for 25–30 minutes[3] until the potatoes are soft.

To finish the purée Tip the cooked potatoes into a colander to drain and leave for 2–3 minutes to allow excess steam to escape. Pass the potato through a mouli or fine potato masher and return to the saucepan. Using a wooden spoon, gradually mix in 170ml warm milk and then stir in the melted butter and seasoning. Taste and correct the seasoning if necessary. If the purée is too firm, thin it down with a little more milk. You know you have the perfect purée when it is fluffy, forms firm peaks and melts in your mouth. Keep warm over a pan of simmering water.

To cook the fish Preheat the oven to 200°C/Gas 6. Pat the pollock fillets dry and season the flesh side with salt and pepper. In a large ovenproof frying pan over

a medium heat, melt the butter and heat until foaming, then add the fish fillets flesh side down and colour for 5–6 minutes[4]. With the aid of a fish slice, carefully turn the fillets onto the skin side and cook for a further 1 minute.

Now place the pan in the hot oven for 4–5 minutes. Take out the pan and place back on a high heat for 1 minute. Carefully transfer the fish fillets from the frying pan to a warm serving dish.

To make the sauce Add the water to the hot pan and stir so that the caramelised juices dissolve and emulsify into the liquid as it boils[5]. Add the lemon segments and juice to the frying pan with the capers, shallot and parsley. Bring back to the boil, taste and correct the seasoning if necessary.

To serve Spoon the pomme purée onto warmed plates and place the fish on top. Pour the sauce on and around the fish[6], scatter over the hot croûtons and serve.

Variations You can replace the water with brown chicken stock to give more depth of flavour to the sauce.

Flavour the potato purée with crushed garlic, freshly grated nutmeg, olive oil, freshly grated horseradish, mustard or any chopped herbs you like.

[1] Choosing the right potatoes is important: too waxy or too starchy and they won't purée very well; too watery and they will be tasteless. Get to know your potatoes and which varieties are best for different cooking purposes. You also need to appreciate that storage alters potato characteristics, so be prepared to change to a different variety every few months.

[2] To make the croûtons, cut crustless white bread into 1cm cubes, toss in melted unsalted butter or olive oil and scatter on a baking tray. Toast in a preheated oven at 200°C/Gas 6 for 5–6 minutes.

[3] Do not boil the potatoes rapidly or they may overcook and absorb excessive water, making a watery purée.

[4] The success of this dish lies in the understanding of the simple technique of pan-frying and regulating the temperature to achieve the right degree of heat. The butter will start to foam at about 130°C. At about 150–155°C it will go hazelnut colour. This is the perfect stage to caramelise the fish without drying it. If the butter becomes too hot, it will burn and the fish will dry out. However, if the butter isn't hot enough, the fish won't brown and it will stew in its own juices. At this stage, if the temperature is right, the smells are invading your kitchen. And while the fish proteins are browning, the juices are seeping out and collecting at the bottom of the pan – begging for a splash of water to create a heavenly jus.

[5] Simply adding water to the pan the fish has been cooked in can create a most exciting jus, as it dilutes the caramelised juices at the bottom of the pan.

[6] Often people discard the skin, but to me this is the best part, and the most nutritious as it is where the essential omega fatty acids are concentrated.

Braised fillet of turbot, scallops, herbs and garden vegetables

***

Serves 4
Preparation:
30 mins, plus
1 hour freezing
Cooking: 15 mins
Special equipment:
mandolin (optional)

This dish encapsulates modernity, freshness and purity of flavours. It has been a classic at Le Manoir for many years. As with all of my dishes, it embraces the seasons and uses the very best ingredients. The recipe is straightforward enough to prepare in your own home, unless you decide to make it for a crowd, then you will be in trouble. The fish is delicately steamed on a bed of shallot and mushrooms, allowing its natural juices to leak out and create a wonderful jus.

Planning ahead Prepare the cucumber ribbons a few hours in advance. Brush the turbot fillets with the flavoured softened butter and refrigerate an hour or two ahead. Have the other ingredients weighed out in advance.

For the cucumber ribbons
½ cucumber
sea salt

For cooking the fish and scallops
4 turbot fillets (150g each)
4 tbsp softened unsalted butter
4 squeezes of lemon juice
4 pinches of sea salt
2 pinches of freshly ground
   black pepper
20g knob of unsalted butter
50g banana shallot, peeled and
   sliced
120g girolles, chanterelles or
   white button mushrooms,
   cleaned and sliced
100ml dry white wine, such as
   Chardonnay

80ml water
4 hand-dived large scallops
   (about 120g), cleaned and
   halved

To finish the sauce
1 tbsp whipping cream
20g cold unsalted butter, diced
100g baby spinach, washed
1 tsp lemon juice, or to taste
½ tbsp chopped chives
½ tbsp chopped chervil
20g diced, skinned plum
   tomato flesh (optional)

For the garnish
baby cress or other salad leaves
a little extra chopped chives
   and chervil

To prepare the cucumber ribbons Peel the cucumber, then cut 12 long thin ribbons, using a mandolin or swivel vegetable peeler, turning as you go, until you are left with the seeds, which can be discarded. Season lightly with salt and freeze on a tray for 1 hour[1]. Rinse under cold water to defrost and remove the salt.

To prepare the fish Lay the turbot fillets on a board. Mix the softened butter with the lemon juice and seasoning and brush over the turbot fillets. Refrigerate until ready to cook[2].

To cook the fish and scallops Preheat the oven to 190°C/Gas 5. In an ovenproof sauté pan over a medium heat, melt the knob of butter and sweat the shallot for 2 minutes. Add the mushrooms and sweat for a further minute. Meanwhile, bring the wine to the boil in another pan and boil for 10 seconds[3]. Add the boiled wine, water and some seasoning to the sauté pan and bring to the boil.

Sit the turbot fillets on top of the mushrooms and cover with a lid. Cook in the oven for 5 minutes. Place the scallops on top of the turbot fillets and cook for another minute. Transfer the fish and scallops to a small baking tray and set aside to rest for 3 minutes[4], then put back in the oven for 1 minute to keep warm while you finish the sauce and cook the vegetables.

To finish the sauce While the fish is resting, add the cream to the pan, bring to the boil and whisk in the butter [5]. Add the spinach, cook for 10 seconds, then add the cucumber and take off the heat[6]. Check the seasoning and add a little lemon juice to lift the sauce. Finish with the chopped herbs and diced tomato, if using.

To serve Place the vegetables in the middle of each warmed large serving bowl. Top with the turbot fillet and scallop, spooning the sauce over and around. Garnish with the salad leaves and an extra sprinkling of chopped herbs.

Variations You can substitute brill, plaice, lemon sole or Dover sole for the turbot, adjusting the cooking times accordingly. A few cockles, clams and/or mussels would also be nice. The fish can be portioned and cooked on the bone if you wish; this would lend more flavour to the sauce.

Vary the vegetables according to the season. Excellent additions are lightly blanched asparagus, freshly podded peas or broad beans, or baby courgettes with flowers.

[1] Lightly seasoning the cucumber with salt cures it, then freezing the cucumber ribbons breaks down the cell walls, releasing the chlorophyll to give you a brilliant colour. Usually cucumber loses texture, flavour and colour in cooking, but here it will be lively, clean and fresh tasting.

[2] The butter will season the fish first, then as the fish is chilled, the butter will solidify and prevent the salt from curing the fish.

[3] Boiling the wine drives off the alcohol, leaving the fruity qualities, enough acidity and a good depth of flavour.

[4] The residual heat will finish cooking the fish perfectly during this brief resting. Some of the juices will escape during this time; pour these into the sauce to enrich it. Once rested, the fish will need to be flashed in the oven before serving.

[5] It is important to use cold butter, adding it in little pieces and whisking to create an emulsion. Butter at room temperature would melt too quickly and not emulsify.

[6] The heat from the boiled sauce is enough to just cook the delicate cucumber.

Confit of salmon, apple and lemon verbena

Serves 4

Preparation:
40 mins, plus
3–4 hours
marinating

Cooking: 25 mins

Special equipment:
blender, cooking
thermometer,
sous-vide (optional)

I created this delicate dish with subtle hints of flavours over a decade ago and it's still a classic at Le Manoir. To achieve it I cured salmon fillets lightly, then applied a very low heat – just enough to lose the rawness, but ensuring the salmon would keep its wonderful colour. The texture was melting and the flavour delicate.

Here I use the advantages of the sous-vide technique. As the food is cooked in a pouch under vacuum at a low temperature, the flavours, colours and textures are superior; you also minimise the loss of nutrients. However, as most domestic kitchens do not have a sous-vide machine, I have also given you the method I used before I acquired one; it works perfectly.

Planning ahead You can cure the salmon, marinate the apples and make the apple purée a day in advance.

For the cured salmon
480g organic or sustainable
    wild salmon fillet, skinned
1 tsp chopped dill
1 tsp chopped lemon verbena
grated zest of ¼ lemon
10g sea salt
1 tsp caster sugar
2 pinches of freshly ground
    white pepper

For the apple purée
2 large Braeburn apples
2 tbsp water
squeeze of lemon juice

*For the apple and lemon
verbena jelly*
250g apple juice, ideally freshly
    juiced Discovery apples
20g lemon verbena, chopped
1g agar agar

For marinating the apples
10g lemon verbena, roughly
    chopped
100ml extra virgin olive oil
    (40ml if using sous-vide
    technique)
2 Cox's Orange Pippin apples

For cooking the salmon
400ml extra virgin olive oil
    (200ml if using sous-vide
    technique)
1 lemon verbena sprig

For the garnish
a few drops of verbena oil from
    the marinated apples (above)
micro sorrel or other tiny salad
    leaves
1 tbsp crème fraîche (optional)
1 tsp osetra caviar (optional)

To cure the salmon Place the salmon fillet in a shallow dish. Mix together the ingredients for curing and distribute evenly over the fish. Cover and leave to marinate in the fridge for 1 hour[1].

Wash off the marinade and pat the salmon dry. Cut into 4 portions, place on a plate, cover and refrigerate.

To make the apple purée Peel, core and dice the apples. Put into a medium saucepan with the water and lemon juice, cover with a tight-fitting lid and cook over a high heat for 8 minutes. Transfer to a bowl and cool down quickly over ice. Purée in a blender until smooth, then transfer to a bowl and set aside.

To make the apple and lemon verbena jelly In a medium saucepan, bring the apple juice to just under a simmer (about 80°C). Take off the heat, add the lemon verbena and set aside to infuse for 8 minutes. Now whisk in the agar agar[2] and bring gently to the boil, whisking all the time until the liquid is clear. Pass through a fine muslin-lined sieve into ice-cube trays or other small containers and allow to set at room temperature.

To marinate the apples in verbena oil In a small saucepan over a medium heat, bring the chopped verbena and olive oil to about 60°C; remove from the heat and set aside to infuse. Once cooled, blitz in a blender for 3–5 seconds, then pass through a fine sieve into a bowl and reserve. Halve the apples, cut into 5mm slices and lay in a shallow tray. Pour the lemon verbena oil over the apple slices and leave to marinate for 2–3 hours.

Alternatively, place the apple slices in a medium sous-vide pouch, add the verbena oil and vacuum pack[3]. Marinate as above.

To cook the salmon Line a small, shallow sauté pan with a piece of greaseproof paper, pour in the olive oil and heat to 42°C. Add the salmon portions[4] with the lemon verbena and 'confit' for 25 minutes, maintaining the temperature. Lift out the salmon, drain and place on kitchen paper to remove excess oil.

Alternatively, if using a sous-vide, preheat the water bath to 42°C [5]. Slide your salmon portions into a medium sous-vide pouch, adding the olive oil and sprig of verbena. Vacuum pack and cook in the water bath for 25 minutes. Remove the salmon fillets from the bag and drain as above.

To serve Place a portion of warm salmon[6] in the middle of each plate. Surround with tiny spoonfuls of the apple purée, nuggets of jelly, marinated apple slices, drops of verbena oil and micro leaves. Spoon the crème fraîche on top of the salmon and finish with the caviar, if using.

Variation As a simple alternative, serve the cured salmon with a cucumber salad lightly dressed with a dill and mustard or horseradish dressing.

[1] Here we are giving the salmon a light cure to firm up and season the flesh. It will not preserve the fish, as there is not enough salt – or time – to do so.

[2] Agar agar is a setting agent derived from red algae, in powder form. Unlike gelatine it is suitable for vegetarians. When you add agar agar to a hot liquid, it will turn cloudy. You need to whisk over a gentle heat until the liquid is clear, which indicates the agar agar has fully dissolved; this will take about 1 minute.

3 Using a sous-vide and vacuum pack enables you to halve the oil and dispense with heat. It aids the breakdown of the cells within the apple, pushing the flavour of the verbena oil into the apple and slightly bruising the flesh, which gives another texture.

4 Ensure you place the fish on top of the greaseproof paper as this will protect the flesh from the direct heat at the bottom of the pan. It is difficult to maintain the temperature when cooking the salmon this way, but as long as the temperature does not exceed 42°C the result will be fine.

5 Using a sous-vide machine and vacuum pack makes low temperature cooking much easier to control and results in superior flavours, textures and colours. At 42°C the fish protein is denatured and the collagen and fats dividing the flakes will melt; this allows the flakes to separate easily and lends flavour.

6 The fish must be barely warm – not hot, as this would spoil the dish.

DID YOU KNOW?
Our Atlantic wild salmon is now on the MCS Fish to Avoid list, but you can buy very good quality farmed organic salmon or MSC-certified Pacific salmon from Alaska.

Shellfish

After a career of cooking and eating lobster, I travelled last year to Fife – Scotland's only kingdom – to fish for them. The fishing boat was called West Haven II. When I asked Stuart the skipper what happened to West Haven I, he didn't answer, which made me slightly nervous as we set sail. Our catch included lobsters with small claws. Stuart explained that these crustaceans fight frequently and rip off each other's claws, but not to worry because the claws re-grow. I didn't know that.

No doubt you are aware that live lobsters are blue, turning bright red when they are cooked. They are also blue-blooded, like the inhabitants of my adopted nation and the Frenchman's cherished snail – the high level of copper in the blood makes it look blue.

Buy a live lobster that looks lively. A dying or dead one releases enzymes which give the flesh a nasty, cotton wool texture. To promote breeding and sustainability, female lobsters carrying eggs under their tail should not be caught and eaten; it is illegal to do so in some areas. As for frozen shellfish, freezing does not affect the quality of crustaceans – lobster and prawns freeze particularly well.

A lobster has a complex series of brains and nerve centres, so it is not easy to kill one without inflicting pain. When I was trying to establish the most humane method of despatch, a friend came to my rescue. He devised his version of an electric chair, called a Crustastun. It is RSPCA-approved and delivers an electric charge to the lobster, killing it instantly and possibly helping to keep the flesh firm. I realise you might not have a Crustastun to hand so I have given an alternative method (see page 96).

Mussels are another of my favourite shellfish. The best ones are grown on ropes or poles away from the sea floor, with fresh seawater flowing through them, which provides food and cleans the mussels at the same time. Fresh mussels are heavy with seawater and have tightly closed, shiny shells. Like all shellfish, they should have a pleasant smell of the sea rather than a 'fishy' taint.

The sure sign of a great mussel is in the eating. During cooking the shells open, releasing a small amount of trapped seawater, which perfectly seasons the dish and creates a wonderful juice.

Scallops are another beautiful bivalve, with sweet-tasting flesh. Large 'king' scallops are the best. There are two methods of catching them – dredging and scuba diving. I only use hand-dived scallops, mostly from Scotland. Dredging the seabed damages scallops, leaves them full of sand, and destroys the habitat of other sea creatures. Like mussels and most other shellfish, scallops need fast cooking to avoid the flesh toughening.

Moules marinière

Serves 4

Preparation:
20 mins

Cooking: 5 mins

Special equipment:
large sauté pan with
tight-fitting lid

This Normandy classic is easy to reproduce in your kitchen. It is now possible to buy excellent fresh mussels – cleaned and ready for the pot.

Planning ahead This dish can be prepared 4–6 hours in advance.

1.8kg very fresh good-quality
   mussels[1]
100ml dry white wine
20g unsalted butter
1 small white onion, peeled and
   very finely chopped

4 bay leaves
8 thyme sprigs
2 tbsp whipping cream
3 tbsp roughly chopped
   flat-leaf parsley

To prepare the mussels Wash the mussels thoroughly in a bowl under cold running water, removing any barnacles and beards that are still present. Discard any mussels that float, including those that are closed[2]. Drain the mussels in a colander. Meanwhile, boil the wine in a small pan for 30 seconds[3].

To cook the mussels In a large saucepan over a high heat, melt the butter. Add the onion, bay leaves and thyme, stir and then add the wine after 10 seconds. Bring to the boil, add the mussels and cover with the tight-fitting lid. Cook for 2–3 minutes until the mussels open. Stir in the cream and chopped parsley[4].

To serve the mussels Tip into a large dish or divide among warmed soup plates Provide your guests with finger bowls and serve with lots of good French bread to mop up the wonderful juices.

Variations For an Indian flavour, add a generous pinch of Madras curry powder to the onion and finish the dish with lemon juice and freshly chopped coriander.
   For a Thai flavour, add some chopped fresh chilli, garlic, lemongrass and a kaffir lime leaf; replace the cream with creamed coconut or coconut milk.

[1] The secret, as ever, is in the freshness of the mussels. A fresh mussel is shiny, closed and heavy with seawater, with no 'fishy' smell.

[2] Mussels should be tightly closed – any that are not should be discarded as they will be dead. Don't scrub the shells with a knife as you clean them, as their colour will leach into the juices during cooking, giving an unappetising grey hue.

[3] It is essential to boil the wine before you use it, to remove most of the harsh alcohol taste, leaving the fruity, acidic qualities of the wine to balance the dish.

[4] No seasoning is required in this dish as when the mussels open, they release a small amount of trapped salt water, which is enough to season the dish perfectly.

Seared scallops, cauliflower purée and curry oil

Serves 4

Preparation:
40 mins, plus
1 hour infusing

Cooking: 20 mins

Special equipment:
blender

A dish very much inspired by simple Indian spicing. I use a high-quality Madras curry powder sourced from my local Indian supermarket and I suggest you do the same. If you do not have time to make the cauliflower bhaji accompaniment, this is a lovely, elegant dish in its own right.

Planning ahead The curry oil can be made up to a week ahead. The cauliflower purée can be made up to half a day in advance.

For the scallops
6 hand-dived large scallops
    (about 180g), cleaned[1]
pinch of sea salt
1 tbsp olive oil
squeeze of lime juice
1 tbsp curry oil (from below)

For the curry oil
1 tsp Madras curry powder
100ml extra virgin olive oil,
    warmed
1 lemongrass stalk, bruised and
    finely chopped[2]
2 kaffir lime leaves, finely sliced
grated zest and juice of ½ lime
pinch of sea salt

For the cauliflower purée
65g unsalted butter
½ large cauliflower (250g),
    cut into small florets
2 pinches of sea salt
250ml whole milk
1 tsp lemon juice

For the seared cauliflower slices
2 tbsp olive oil
16 fine cauliflower slices (200g)
pinch of sea salt (optional)

To serve
20g mixed baby salad leaves
2 tsp curry oil (from above)
a few finely chopped chives
cauliflower bhajis (optional,
    see page 88)

To prepare the curry oil In a small frying pan over a medium heat, toast the curry powder for 5 minutes[3] then add to the warm olive oil with the lemongrass, lime leaves and lime zest. Stir and set aside to infuse in a warm place for 1 hour.
   Strain the oil through a fine sieve[4] into a bowl and add the salt and lime juice. Cover and set aside until needed.

To make the cauliflower purée In a large saucepan, melt 25g butter over a medium heat and gently sweat the cauliflower for 3 minutes, seasoning with the salt[5]. Add the milk, bring to the boil, then lower the heat and simmer for 10 minutes until tender. Using a slotted spoon, transfer the cauliflower to a blender and purée with just enough of the cooking liquor to make a smooth purée. In another

pan, heat the remaining 40g butter to the beurre noisette stage[6]. Stir into the cauliflower purée with the lemon juice, then check the seasoning; keep warm.

To sear the cauliflower slices Heat the olive oil in a medium frying pan over a medium heat, then add the cauliflower slices and sear for 1 minute on one side until golden brown; they should be half raw with a wonderful crunch. Transfer to a warm plate, season with a pinch of salt, if needed, and keep warm.

To cook the scallops Season the scallops with the salt. Heat the olive oil in a medium, heavy-based frying pan over a medium heat. Add the scallops, flat side down, and sear for 1½ minutes until golden brown[7], then turn the scallops over and continue to cook for 30 seconds. Remove the pan from the heat and deglaze with a squeeze of lime juice and 1 tbsp of the curry oil.

   Transfer the scallops and the juices to a warm plate, season with another pinch of salt, if needed, and keep warm.

To serve Put two spoonfuls of cauliflower purée on each plate and arrange the scallops in the middle. Lay the caramelised cauliflower around the outside of the plate and drizzle the deglazed pan juices over. Garnish with baby salad leaves, curry oil and chopped chives and accompany with the bhajis, if serving.

Cauliflower bhajis

Serves 4

Preparation:
20 mins, plus
30 mins marinating

Cooking: 5 mins

An excellent accompaniment to the seared scallops, you might also like to try serving this side dish with your favourite Indian curry.

¼ red chilli, deseeded and
   finely chopped
1 tbsp finely chopped coriander
   leaves
1 tsp curry oil (see page 86)
40g gram flour

pinch of ground turmeric
30ml cold water
2 pinches of sea salt
50g cauliflower, cut into
   12 small florets
grapeseed oil, for deep-frying

To prepare In a large bowl, mix the chilli, coriander and curry oil with the flour, tumeric, water and a pinch of salt. Marinate the cauliflower florets for 30 minutes.

To cook the bhajis Heat the oil for deep-frying in a deep-fryer or other suitable deep, heavy pan to 170°C. You will need to cook the bhajis in 2 or 3 batches. Dip the marinated florets into the spiced batter to coat lightly and then drop them individually into the hot oil[8]. Deep-fry for 1½–2 minutes until golden brown. Remove with a slotted spoon and drain on kitchen paper.

   Season with a pinch of salt and keep warm while you cook the rest. Serve the bhajis as soon as possible.

1. We only source hand-dived scallops, as dredging the seabed for these prized shellfish leaves them full of sand and is liable to damage them. It also destroys their habitat and that of other marine life.
2. Bruising the lemongrass with the back of a large knife draws out the natural oils, intensifying its aromatic flavour and making the curry oil more flavoursome.
3. By toasting the curry powder you will bring out the natural oils present, making it more fragrant.
4. At Le Manoir, we use very fine sieves and damp muslin cloths to strain out all solids from infused oils and sauces. You can easily do the same at home. Alternatively, the curry oil can be left to stand for an hour to allow the solids to sink to the bottom. You can then spoon off the clear oil from the top.
5. By gently sweating vegetables you convert the natural starches into sugars, sweetening them and maximising their flavour.
6. The butter will start to foam at approximately 130°C, turning a hazelnut colour at 150–155°C; i.e. the required beurre noisette stage.
7. Searing the scallops slowly will release their natural sugars, promoting a golden brown crust. Be sure to regulate the temperature of the pan; too high and the scallops will over-caramelise and burn; too low and they will release their juices but not caramelise at all.
8. Hot oil is dangerous. Make sure the pan handle is to the side (not the front) of the hob and drop the cauliflower florets in from a low height – just above the oil – to avoid splashing.

Salad of grilled squid and Provençal vegetables

Serves 4

Preparation:
20 mins, plus
30 minutes
marinating

Cooking: 5 mins

Special equipment:
griddle pan,
mandolin

A juicy, colourful summer salad of flavours from Provence. Combining protein-rich squid, fabulous vegetables and the best extra virgin olive oil, it is simple, satisfying and nutritious.

Planning ahead The Provençal vegetables may be prepared and marinated a day in advance. Oven-dried tomatoes can be prepared up to a week ahead.

For the grilled squid
3 medium squid (each 300g),
    cleaned, tentacles reserved
2 tbsp olive oil
squeeze of lemon juice
1 red chilli (ideally Rio Grande),
    deseeded and finely chopped
10g grated palm sugar (or dark
    muscovado)[1]
2 pinches of sea salt

For the Provençal vegetables
1 courgette (150g), trimmed
1 fennel bulb (300g), trimmed
200g oven-dried or sun-dried
    tomatoes[2]
1 tbsp extra virgin olive oil
pinch of sea salt
pinch of freshly ground black
    pepper

For the rocket salad
4 handfuls of rocket leaves
    (100g), washed
1 tbsp balsamic vinegar (at least
    8 years old)
2 tbsp extra virgin olive oil
pinch of freshly ground black
    pepper

To garnish
a little extra virgin olive oil
Parmesan shavings

To prepare the squid Cut open the squid pouches along the body line and score on the inside[3], then cut each one into 3 pieces. Place in a bowl with the tentacles, olive oil, lemon juice, chopped chilli, sugar and salt. Toss to mix and leave to marinate for 30 minutes[4].

To prepare the Provençal vegetables Heat your griddle pan. Using a mandolin, cut both the courgette and fennel lengthways into long, wafer-thin (2mm) slices. Cook the courgette and fennel slices in the hot griddle pan, in batches as necessary, for 1 minute on one side and then remove from the heat and place in a shallow dish. Add the oven-/sun-dried tomatoes, drizzle with the olive oil and season with salt and pepper; set aside.

For the rocket salad Place the rocket leaves in a bowl. For the dressing, whisk together the balsamic vinegar, olive oil and pepper.

To grill the squid Preheat the griddle until very hot[5] then add the squid and cook for 15–30 seconds on each side. Immediately remove from the griddle to a warm plate. Taste and adjust the seasoning if necessary.

To serve Pile the rocket salad in the middle of each plate and dress lightly. Surround with the grilled squid and Provençal vegetables. Drizzle with extra virgin olive oil and top with some Parmesan shavings.

Variations Scatter over some freshly chopped parsley, chervil or chives to serve.
  Grill a wider variety of vegetables, perhaps including sliced peppers, red onions and aubergines. English asparagus spears – blanched for 2 minutes before grilling – make a lovely addition when in season.

[1] Palm sugar lends a bit of sweetness and helps with the browning of the squid. Muscovado or brown sugar can be substituted.

[2] Preparing your own oven-dried tomatoes will be much more satisfying and delicious. Cut each of 4 medium tomatoes into 8 wedges, lay on a baking tray and brush with olive oil. Place in a low oven at 100°C/Gas ¼ for 1½ hours to dry and intensify the flavour. Leave to cool then pack in a jar, add olive oil to cover and keep in the fridge for up to a week until ready to use.

[3] Scoring the inside of the squid will assist in even cooking and encourage the squid to roll up attractively during cooking.

[4] Marinating will boost the delicate flavour of the squid.

[5] The griddle pan must be very hot indeed to ensure quick, short cooking and a golden caramelisation of the squid. If it is not hot enough you run the risk of boiling the squid in its own juices. If the squid is cooked for too long, it will become tough and rubbery. This high heat technique produces a lot of smoke, however, so make sure the kitchen is well ventilated and your extractor is on full.

Lobster plancha with red pepper and cardamom jus

Serves 2

Preparation:
50 mins, plus
1 hour infusing

Cooking: 10 mins

Special equipment:
blender or juicer

A wonderful special occasion dish, created by Gary Jones, my executive head chef at Le Manoir. Our native lobsters are best and plentiful during the summer and autumn, so do make the most of them. Here the sweet lobster meat is mildly spiced with cardamom and ginger, and cooked simply *à la plancha* (see page 311).

Planning ahead The curry oil can be made a week in advance.

For the lobster
1 live Cornish or Scottish
   lobster (800g), cleaned, tail,
   claws and head separated[1]
½ tsp finely grated fresh root
   ginger
pinch of freshly ground
   cardamom
2 tsp curry oil (see below)
4 pinches of sea salt

For the curry oil
1 tsp Madras curry powder
100ml extra virgin olive oil,
   warmed
1 lemongrass stalk, bruised and
   finely chopped[2]
2 kaffir lime leaves, chopped
10 curry leaves, chopped
grated zest and juice of ½ lime
pinch of sea salt

For the red pepper reduction
500g red peppers (about 3),
   deseeded, pith removed,
   flesh chopped
100g lobster shell, chopped
   (reserved from the lobster)
1 tbsp olive oil
4 tbsp dry white wine
½ tsp finely grated fresh root
   ginger
2 cardamom pods, lightly
   crushed
pinch of cayenne pepper

For the potatoes
100g Jersey potatoes (about 3)
1 tbsp curry oil (from above)
2 pinches of sea salt

For the garnish
2 tbsp Greek-style natural
   yoghurt
1 tsp osetra caviar (optional)
1 tbsp curry oil (from above)
20g baby salad leaves
crispy deep-fried potato skins,
   (optional)

To parboil the lobster Have ready a large bowl of crushed ice. Bring a large pan of water to the boil. Blanch the lobster tail for 10 seconds, then remove with a slotted spoon and immerse in the crushed ice for 10 minutes; drain and place in the fridge[3].

Add the lobster claws to the boiling water, turn the heat to a very low simmer and cook for 5 minutes. Remove and place in the crushed ice for 10 minutes. Drain and reserve in the fridge.

To make the curry oil Toast the curry powder in a small frying pan over a low heat for 5 minutes[4]. Add to the warm olive oil along with the chopped lemongrass, lime leaves, curry leaves and lime zest. Stir to combine and set aside to infuse in a warm place for 1 hour. Strain the oil through a fine sieve (preferably lined with muslin) into a bowl and add the salt and lime juice. Cover and leave at room temperature until needed.

To shell the lobster Carefully remove the meat from the tail and reserve. Chop the shell into 2cm pieces, using a pair of kitchen scissors: save for the sauce.

To extract the meat from the claws, using a pair of scissors, cut the tendons holding the small pincer to the claw, twist side to side to loosen and then remove and discard the pincer shell (if this is not done then you risk ripping off the flesh from the small pincer). Using a meat hammer, break the claws and gently extract the meat, trying to keep it intact as much as possible; discard the claw shells (as they will be too hard to break up to use in the sauce).

In a large bowl, mix the lobster flesh with the ginger, cardamom, curry oil and sea salt to coat[5]. Cover and refrigerate until ready to serve.

To make the red pepper reduction Juice the red pepper flesh[6] and pass through a fine sieve into a bowl. In a medium frying pan over a high heat, quickly sauté the chopped lobster shell in the olive oil for 2–3 minutes. Deglaze the pan with the white wine and then add the red pepper juice along with the ginger, cardamom pods and cayenne pepper. Turn off the heat and leave to infuse for 5 minutes, then strain into a clean pan and bubble to reduce for about 10 minutes[7]. Pass through a fine sieve, making sure you press all the liquor from the lobster shells. The reduction should lightly coat the back of a spoon once cooled to room temperature; you should have approximately 50ml. Taste and add a little more cayenne if desired. Set aside until needed.

To prepare the new potatoes Cook the potatoes in simmering, salted water for 15–20 minutes until tender. Drain well, cut in half and toss them with the curry oil and salt. Taste and adjust the seasoning. Put to one side until needed.

To finish cooking the lobster Preheat the oven to 180°C/Gas 4. On a lightly oiled plancha over a high heat, sear the pieces of lobster meat for 1 minute to colour a little, then place the tails on an oiled baking tray in the oven for 3 minutes to finish cooking. Remove to a warm bowl, then taste the lobster and adjust the seasoning if necessary.

To serve Place three potato halves down the middle of each plate and top with the yoghurt and caviar, if using. Lightly glaze the lobster pieces with half the red pepper reduction. Place the tail and lobster claw on the plate and drizzle the remaining red pepper reduction and curry oil over the dish. Arrange the salad leaves and deep-fried potato skins, if serving, on the plate and serve at once.

1 At Le Manoir we use an electric stunner called a 'Crustastun' (see page 310) to kill shellfish humanely. The electric stun renders them immediately anaesthetised. As you are unlikely to have one of these at your disposal, the best way to kill them is by putting the point of a large knife through the cross on the back of their head and splitting the head in two. Then turn the lobster around and split the tail in two. The lobster, like most other crustaceans, has nerves along their tail. By piercing the head you do not kill the lobster – the animal is still alive. You have to split the lobster down the full length of its body to fully kill it humanely. This ensures that you have severed all the nerve centres of the animal before you cook it. At this stage you should remove the dark intestinal tube that runs down the length of the shell. Also remove and discard the dead-man's fingers from the head.

2 By bruising the lemongrass with the back of a large knife, you draw out the natural oils, intensifying its aromatic flavour, thus making the curry oil more flavoursome.

3 Blanching the lobsters in boiling water for 10 seconds and refreshing them in crushed ice will not cook the lobster flesh, but it will allow the flesh to separate from the shell, making it easy to remove from the shell.

4 By toasting the curry powder you will bring out the natural oils present, making a more fragrant curry oil.

5 Adding the spices and curry oil at this stage will allow time for them to permeate the flesh of the lobster.

6 The red pepper flesh can either be put through a juicer, or puréed in a blender.

7 Use a wide pan over a high heat to reduce the liquor as quickly as possible in order to retain maximum flavour and freshness.

Lamb

When I opened Les Quat' Saisons, my first restaurant, in Summertown, Oxford, I had just 3 months of cooking experience. Today the aspiring restaurateur would have a decade of experience and a 5-year business plan, but back then I took things day by day.

It was an awesome struggle, and the search for quality produce was the greatest challenge. However, lamb was always good. I got spring lamb for about 8 months of the year, starting with lamb from the Pyrenees in France, then from the South of England, and in the autumn months it came from Shetland.

I bought the whole carcass and every bit of the animal was used. This enabled me to apply different cooking techniques, boosting the restaurant's profits at the same time. You will find that today's good chefs will similarly buy a whole lamb carcass. So, as a salute to this reconnection with gastronomy, this chapter is a celebration of the succulent beast.

Before you turn to the recipes, there are a few essential tips to relay here. Firstly, invest in the best temperature probe that you can find; this will give you more control over the accuracy of your cooking.

Secondly, never cook a joint directly from the refrigerator. When a piece of meat is chilled, it is at approximately 4°C. In order to cook your meat faster and more evenly, take it out of the refrigerator first to allow the core temperature to reach room temperature. The time this takes depends on the size of the joint, but one weighing 2kg might take as long as 3–4 hours.

After roasting, you will need to cover the meat loosely with foil and leave it in a warm place – to 'rest'. The reason for this is that whilst cooking, the juices are pushed towards the centre of the joint. Resting is essential as it allows the muscles of the meat to relax and the juices to redistribute through the joint, making it tender. Always allow half an hour's resting time before carving.

It is crucial to remember that while the meat is resting, its internal temperature continues to rise, and so the meat continues to cook. In fact, I've discovered from my tests that during a 30-minute 'rest' the meat can gain 5–10°C – that's the difference between pink and a horrible grey.

Always allow for this. Use the probe and take the meat from the oven when it is at least a few degrees *below* your desired temperature. To measure this, insert the probe into the middle of the joint (make sure it is not touching a bone). For rare lamb, remove the joint from the oven when the probe reads 50°C (it will reach 60°C after 30 minutes' resting), for medium-rare 53°C (61°C after resting), for medium 58°C (66°C after resting), and for well done 65°C (72°C after resting).

Slow-roasted shoulder of lamb, braised summer vegetables

Serves 4–6

Preparation:
30 minutes, plus
1 hour marinating

Cooking: 4½ hours

This dish epitomises good home cooking. Shoulder is one of the cheaper cuts of lamb, yet here it is transformed into a wholesome meal – the long, slow cooking rendering the meat tender, juicy and incredibly tasty. Maman Blanc never used stock – just water, herbs and the occasional splash of wine to create delectable cooking juices.

A shoulder of lamb will vary in weight according to the time of year. In May and June, it will be about 1.5kg, while in August it could be 2kg, and in November around 3kg, so you'll need to adjust the cooking time accordingly; a 2kg shoulder will take 4½ hours; one weighing 3kg will need 5½ hours.

Planning ahead The lamb can be scored and marinated several hours ahead.

1.5kg new season's shoulder of
   lamb, plus 700g lamb bones
   and trimmings
4 pinches of sea salt
4 pinches of freshly ground
   black pepper
2 rosemary sprigs, leaves
   picked, finely chopped
3 sage leaves, finely chopped
2 tbsp olive oil
2 tbsp rapeseed oil
1 garlic bulb, halved
   horizontally
100ml white wine, such as dry
   Chardonnay
400–500ml hot water
1 bay leaf
3 thyme sprigs

*For the braised summer
vegetables*
3 Swiss chard stalks (250g)
2 medium onions (250g)
250g carrots, peeled
250g yellow beetroot, peeled
2 Gem lettuces
2 tbsp olive oil
sea salt and freshly ground
   black pepper
50ml water
10g flat-leaf parsley, roughly
   chopped

To prepare the lamb Lightly score the skin of the lamb. Rub all over with the salt, pepper, chopped herbs and olive oil. Set aside to marinate at room temperature for 1 hour[1].

Preheat the oven to 230°C/Gas 8. Heat the rapeseed oil in a large heavy-duty roasting pan over a medium heat. Add the lamb bones and meat trimmings and colour, turning from time to time, for 7–10 minutes until lightly golden[2]. Add the garlic and brown for 3 minutes, then take the roasting pan off the heat.

To roast the lamb Sit the seasoned lamb shoulder on top of the bones[3] and roast in the oven for 20 minutes. Meanwhile, in a small pan, bring the wine to the boil and let bubble for 30 seconds, then add 400ml water, the bay leaf and thyme.

Take the lamb out of the oven and baste the joint with the pan juices, removing any excess fat. Add the wine mixture to the roasting pan, stirring to scrape up the sediment on the base of the pan[4].

Turn the oven to 150°C/Gas 2. Cover the meat loosely with a piece of foil and return to the oven. Roast for a further 4 hours, basting every 30 minutes with the pan juices. If, at the end of cooking, the pan juices are reduced right down, stir in about 100ml water to extend the jus.

To braise the vegetables Start to prepare the vegetables about half an hour before the lamb will be cooked. Slice down either side of the Swiss chard stalks to separate them from the leaves. Halve the stalks lengthways and cut across into 3cm lengths; set the leaves aside for later. Cut each onion into 6 wedges, keeping the base intact. Halve the carrots lengthways and cut into 3cm pieces. Cut the beetroot into similar sized pieces. Cut each lettuce into 6 wedges, keeping the stalk intact.

In a large saucepan over a medium heat, sweat the onions, chard stalks, carrots, beetroot and lettuces in the olive oil with a little seasoning for 5 minutes. Add the water, cover and cook over the lowest possible heat for 35 minutes[5].

Finally add the Swiss chard leaves, replace the lid and cook over a high heat for a further 3 minutes. Transfer to a warmed serving dish.

To serve Remove the lamb from the oven. Strain the juices into a small saucepan and remove the excess fat from the surface. Set the lamb aside to rest. Reheat the juices until bubbling, then taste and adjust the seasoning. Pour into a warmed sauceboat.

Place the lamb and braised vegetables on the table so your guests can help themselves. The lamb will be tender enough to be portioned with a spoon, though you can carve it with a knife if you prefer. A turnip and potato gratin (see page 222) would be an excellent accompaniment here.

Variations Flavour the seasoning rub for the lamb with spices rather than herbs – cumin and coriander seeds will give it an Indian flavour.

Vary the root vegetables – turnip, parsnip, butternut squash and celeriac would all be suitable.

---

[1] The salt and herb rub will permeate the lamb with a subtle flavour. The meat needs to be out of the fridge for at least a couple of hours before cooking to ensure it reaches room temperature before going into the oven.

[2] Do not colour the bones too much, or the resulting jus will taste bitter and astringent. And remember there is 4 hours of slow cooking ahead.

3 The bones serve two purposes. Firstly, they provide a platform for the lamb joint, allowing the heat to circulate all around it, facilitating even cooking. If the joint sits directly on the base of the pan, the meat in direct contact is liable to dry out. Secondly, the caramelised bones provide the basis for a wonderful pan jus.

4 Adding water to the pan will lift the caramelised meat juices from the bottom of the pan and the bones, creating a flavourful jus at the end. It will also keep the shoulder of lamb moist during cooking.

5 By slow-cooking the vegetables you allow the sugars to develop slowly, ensuring a wonderful depth of flavour and a soft melting texture.

DID YOU KNOW?

Skimming removes most of the fat, but there will still be some dispersed through the juices. I like to retain this, as it carries a huge amount of flavour from the roasting process.

Lamb's liver with persillade *Illustrated overleaf*

Serves 4
Preparation:
15 mins
Cooking: 6–7 mins

*

Not only is this dish truly delicious, it is also highly nutritious. Of course, the lamb's liver must be very fresh – pale pink in colour and firm to the touch, with no trace of stickiness or smell. And it must be cut no more than 1cm thick, otherwise the texture will be quite wrong. A short cooking time is essential.

400g lamb's liver[1], cut into
   8 slices, 1cm thick
2 pinches of sea salt
pinch of freshly ground
   black pepper
40g unsalted butter

For the persillade[2]
large handful of flat-leaf parsley
   (50g), finely chopped
½ medium shallot, peeled and
   finely chopped
1 garlic clove, peeled and
   finely chopped

For the sautéed potatoes
4 medium potatoes
   (Maris Piper or King
   Edward)
2 tbsp rapeseed oil
2 pinches of sea salt
2 pinches of freshly ground
   black pepper
20g unsalted butter

For the pan juices
120ml water
juice of ¼ lemon

To prepare the persillade Mix the chopped parsley, shallot and garlic together in a small bowl; set aside.

For the sautéed potatoes Peel the potatoes, cut into small dice and rinse under cold water; drain. Blanch the diced potatoes[3] in boiling water for 30 seconds, then tip into a colander to drain so the steam can escape.
   Heat the rapeseed oil in a large frying pan over a high heat. Add the diced potatoes, season with salt and pepper and sauté for 4–5 minutes until golden brown. Lower the heat and add the butter and two-thirds of the persillade. Taste and adjust the seasoning if necessary. Set aside; keep warm.

To cook the lamb's liver At the last moment, season the liver slices evenly on both sides with the salt and pepper. In a large frying pan over a medium heat, melt the butter and heat until it is blond in colour and begins to foam[4]. Immediately add the liver slices and cook for 30 seconds on each side for medium rare, or 1 minute each side for medium[5].

To finish and serve Using a pair of tongs, transfer the liver slices to a warmed serving dish. Quickly add the water, lemon juice and remaining persillade to the pan, scraping up the sediment on the bottom[6].
   Pour the pan juices and persillade over the liver and serve at once, with the sautéed potatoes.

Variations Replace some of the parsley in the persillade with another chopped fresh herb, such as chervil, thyme, sage or marjoram.

Use calf's rather than lamb's liver.

~~~~~~

1   A whole lamb's liver will serve 4–6. If you buy a whole liver, I recommend you soak it overnight in 500ml each water and whole milk with ½ tsp salt added. This will extract a lot of the blood, lending a creamier colour and a more subtle, superior taste.

2   In France, persillade is added liberally to many dishes. Traditionally it comprises parsley, shallots and garlic, but you can include other fresh herbs if you like (see variations). It is always added towards the end of cooking.

3   The potatoes can be sautéed from raw, but all too often they will brown before they are cooked through. Blanching avoids this problem and gives the potato a better texture.

4   The butter will start to foam at about 130°C. At about 150–155°C it will go hazelnut colour. This is the perfect stage to caramelise the liver without drying it. Be careful not to colour the butter too much initially, as it will continue to cook with the liver.

5   To fully appreciate the texture and flavour of the lamb's liver, it must be cooked medium rare or medium. If you cook it until well done the texture will be ruined.

6   Adding water to the pan will dissolve the caramelised juices in the bottom of the pan and form an emulsion with the butter, creating a delectable jus to pour over the liver.

Provençal best end of spring lamb, ratatouille *Illustrated on previous page*

Serves 4

Preparation:
30 mins

Cooking: 35 mins

Special equipment:
food processor,
ovenproof frying
pan

This stunning dish is effortless to prepare, yet guaranteed to impress. French-trimmed racks of lamb are available from good butchers and supermarkets. The garlicky herb flavours of the Provençal crust permeate the meat beautifully and a classic ratatouille is the perfect complement.

Planning ahead The Provençal breadcrumbs can be prepared a few days in advance and kept in a sealed container in the fridge. The ratatouille can be made a day in advance. Several hours ahead, the lamb racks may be roasted (initial stage) and coated with the herb crust ready to finish in the oven.

2 French-trimmed racks of
   spring lamb, each with 6–8
   ribs, plus 200g lamb bones
   and trimmings, chopped
2 pinches of sea salt
2 pinches of freshly ground
   black pepper
2 tbsp olive oil
1 tbsp Dijon mustard

For the Provençal breadcrumbs
80g white or brown bread,
   dried[1]
2 garlic cloves, peeled and
   crushed
2 pinches of sea salt
2 pinches of freshly ground
   black pepper
handful of flat-leaf parsley
2 thyme sprigs, leaves picked
   and finely chopped
1 small rosemary sprig, leaves
   picked and finely chopped
60ml extra virgin olive oil

For the ratatouille
2 tbsp olive oil
2 medium onions, peeled and
   cut into 2cm pieces
4 garlic cloves, peeled and
   crushed
1 large red pepper, cored,
   deseeded and cut into
   2cm pieces
2 medium courgettes,
   quartered lengthways and
   cut into 2cm pieces
1 medium aubergine, cut
   into 2cm pieces
4 large marmande tomatoes,
   roughly chopped
2 thyme sprigs
pinch of sea salt
pinch of freshly ground
   black pepper

To make the Provençal breadcrumbs Put the bread, garlic, salt and pepper into a food processor and pulse until you achieve a sandy texture. Add the parsley and chopped herbs, and pulse until you have a crumbly texture. Drizzle in the olive oil, mix briefly, then taste and correct the seasoning.

To cook the lamb Preheat the oven to 190°C/Gas 5. Season the lamb racks with the salt and pepper. Heat half the olive oil in a large ovenproof frying pan and brown the lamb bones over a high heat for 7–8 minutes. Set aside.

In another large frying pan, heat the remaining olive oil over a medium heat. Add the racks of lamb, fat side down, and lightly colour for 3–4 minutes, then turn onto the meat side and colour for 1 minute only. Place the racks on top of the browned bones[2] and roast in the oven for 15 minutes. Transfer the lamb to a warm plate and leave to rest[3].

To prepare the ratatouille Heat the olive oil in a large saucepan over a medium heat and sweat the onions for 5–7 minutes. Add all the remaining ingredients and stir to combinc. Bring to the boil, put the lid on and simmer over a medium heat for 20 minutes. Taste and adjust the seasoning before serving.

To coat the lamb Scatter the Provençal breadcrumbs on a tray. Brush the lamb all over with the mustard and press the fat side into the Provençal breadcrumbs to coat thoroughly. Place on a baking tray and set aside until needed.

To finish and serve Put the lamb into the preheated oven at 190°C/Gas 5 and cook for 15 minutes. Divide the ratatouille among warmed shallow serving bowls. Cut each lamb rack in two and place on the ratatouille. Serve at once.

Variations Instead of ratatouille, serve the lamb racks with a seasonal vegetable or two, such as green beans, courgettes or grilled aubergines.

The provençal breadcrumbs have many other uses – in particular, they make a delicious coating for fish, beef, veal and pork.

[1] To dry the bread, toast it in the oven at 80°C for 2 hours. Fresh breadcrumbs are likely to give you a wetter crumb, making it difficult to achieve a good crust on the lamb.

[2] The lamb bones and trimmings will act as a platform for the lamb racks, enabling the heat to circulate around the meat, resulting in more even cooking.

[3] Should you wish to make a simple jus to accompany the meat, add 300ml water to the roasting pan of browned bones and simmer for 10 minutes.

Assiette of lamb

Serves 4

Preparation:
30 mins, plus lamb
shoulder and rack

Cooking: 40 mins,
plus 2 hours for
oven-dried tomatoes

Special equipment:
blender

The variety of tastes and textures that come from one beast is extraordinary and this dish is a real celebration of the lamb. It brings together the different elements from the three previous recipes on one sumptuous 'plate'. Any seasonal vegetables can be introduced here. As we move closer to the winter months, lamb will be more strongly flavoured and perfectly complemented by the more hardy root vegetables.

Planning ahead The oven-dried tomatoes and olive tapenade can be prepared several days ahead. The onion and garlic purée can be made a day in advance.

4 pieces (200g) slow-roasted
    shoulder of lamb
    (see page 100)
1 roasted Provençal best end of
    spring lamb (see page 108)
4 uncooked slices lamb's liver
    (100g), 1cm thick
    (see page 104)
sea salt and freshly ground
    black pepper
25g unsalted butter

For the oven-dried tomatoes[1]
4 medium plum tomatoes, cut
    into quarters
about 100ml olive oil (to store)

For the black olive tapenade
100g black olives (ideally
    kalamata), pitted
60ml extra virgin olive oil
30ml water (at room
    temperature)

For the onion and garlic purée
3 tbsp olive oil
700g onions, peeled and finely
    chopped
6 garlic cloves, peeled and
    finely sliced[2]
4 thyme sprigs, leaves picked
pinch of sea salt
4 turns of freshly ground white
    pepper
50ml extra virgin olive oil

For the braised shallots
4 banana shallots, peeled, root
    left on
1 thyme sprig
2 pinches of sea salt
2 black peppercorns
2 tbsp olive oil
400ml water

To serve
steamed spinach

To prepare the oven-dried tomatoes Preheat the oven to 100°C/Gas ¼. Place the tomato quarters, cut side up, on a baking tray and dry in the low oven for 2 hours. Leave to cool, then store in a small jar covered in olive oil.

To make the black olive tapenade Place all the ingredients in a blender and purée until smooth, stopping to scrape down the sides once or twice to ensure an even, fine purée. Transfer to a jar and refrigerate until needed.

To make the onion and garlic purée Heat the olive oil in a heavy-based saucepan over a very low heat and add the onions, garlic and thyme with the seasoning. Cover and cook for about 30 minutes, stirring occasionally; do not allow to colour[3]. Allow to cool, then blitz in a blender to a smooth velvety purée. Enrich with the extra virgin olive oil, then taste and adjust the seasoning if required.

To prepare the braised shallots Put the shallots into a small saucepan with the thyme, salt, peppercorns, 1 tbsp olive oil and the water. Bring to the boil over a medium heat, cover with a lid and cook at a gentle simmer for 40 minutes[4] until soft but still holding their shape. Leave to cool.

Once cooled, cut each shallot in half and pat dry with a clean cloth. Heat the remaining 1 tbsp olive oil in a medium frying pan and add the shallots, flat side down. Caramelise over a high heat for 1–2 minutes until golden brown. Place the shallots on a tray and reserve until needed.

To serve Preheat the oven to 190°C/Gas 5. Reheat the shoulder and lamb cutlets and caramelised shallots in the oven for 4 minutes. Meanwhile, cook the lamb's liver (following the method on page 104) and put to one side while you dress the plate. Spoon the onion purée onto the centre of each warmed plate and top with the spinach and oven-dried tomatoes. Arrange the shoulder, cutlet and liver on top, scatter over the braised shallots and spoon over the jus. Serve at once, with the tapenade in a bowl on the side.

Variations Garnish with any seasonal vegetable, such as grilled aubergines, green beans or braised carrots.

Replace the liver with lamb's kidneys or sweetbreads.

---

[1] Oven-dried tomatoes are easy to prepare and so much better than the alternative sun-dried tomatoes on supermarket shelves. San Marzano or Roma plum tomatoes are ideal as they have relatively few seeds, little acidity and dry successfully. Halved cherry tomatoes will also do very well. These oven-dried tomatoes can be kept in a jar covered with olive oil for up to a week.

[2] If you are able to find new season's garlic, so much the better, but you will need 12 cloves as the flavour is much more delicate. If garlic is left to sprout and develop a central green shoot within the clove, this can be bitter, so remove it.

[3] Gently cooking the onion and garlic will convert their natural starches into sugars, giving you a wonderful purée, which will complement many other dishes, including pork, poultry and game.

[4] Undercooked shallots are unappetising and indigestible. It takes 40 minutes' cooking to render them completely soft and sweetened.

Navarin of lamb

Serves 4–6
Preparation:
20 mins
Cooking: 2½ hours

This dish is a perfect example of slow cooking, where a cheaper cut of meat, cooked gently over a long period of time becomes meltingly tender and wonderfully full flavoured. Here I am using slices of neck on the bone, as the bone imparts a rich flavour during cooking. It is a very straightforward dish to prepare. With minimum effort at the start, you will be rewarded with a nourishing meal that the whole family will enjoy.

Planning ahead The navarin can be cooked up to 2 days in advance and gently reheated to serve.

1.2kg new season's neck or
  shoulder of lamb on the
  bone[1], trimmed and cut into
  4–5cm pieces
2 tbsp rapeseed oil
100ml white wine
  (such as dry Chardonnay)
1 tsp sea salt
6 black peppercorns
bouquet garni (2 bay leaves,
  4 thyme sprigs, 5 parsley
  sprigs, 1 rosemary sprig,
  tied together)

4 plum tomatoes, roughly
  chopped
1 litre cold water
2 onions, peeled
1 large carrot, peeled
1 celery stick
2 turnips, peeled
8 garlic cloves, peeled

To brown the lamb Check that the lamb is trimmed of excess fat. Preheat the oven to 110°C/Gas ½. Heat the rapeseed oil in a large flameproof casserole and colour the pieces of lamb over a medium heat for 5–10 minutes until lightly browned[2]. Meanwhile, in a small pan, bring the wine to the boil and let bubble for 30 seconds[3].

To cook the navarin Season the lamb with the salt, then add the peppercorns[4], wine, bouquet garni and chopped tomatoes and cook, stirring, for 1 minute. Pour on the cold water to cover the lamb and bring just to the boil, then skim off any scum that rises to the surface[5]. Put the lid on, place the casserole in the oven and cook for 1½ hours[6].

To prepare the vegetables While the lamb is in the oven, cut each onion into 6 wedges, keeping the base intact. Cut the carrot in half lengthways and slice into 6cm lengths. Cut the celery into similar lengths. Cut each turnip into at least 6 wedges.

To cook the vegetables Take out the casserole after 1½ hours, add the vegetables and garlic and bring back to the boil on the hob. Replace the lid and return to the oven for 1 hour until the vegetables are cooked and the lamb is very tender. Taste and correct the seasoning. Serve straight from the casserole.

Variation Lamb shoulder steaks on the bone, lamb shanks or lamb's tongues would also work well in this recipe.

1   For this recipe, you need a cut that can withstand long, slow cooking. Here we have used slices of neck on the bone, as the bone imparts a full, rich flavour during cooking. It also helps reduce shrinkage in the meat. Get your butcher to cut the lamb for you, asking for 1.2kg of trimmed neck on the bone.

2   I have browned the meat first to enhance the flavour, but you could omit this stage for a lighter taste.

3   I boil the wine first to remove most of the alcohol and tannins, while retaining its freshness and character.

4   The peppercorns are added whole at the start, as they will slowly release their aromatic flavour through the long cooking.

5   Cold water is added to the pan, so when the heat rises, it encourages impurities to move up to the surface, allowing them to be skimmed off easily. This results in a delicate, clear stock.

6   When you are cooking in a low oven, it is important to bring the cooking liquor to the boil before the dish goes in the oven, otherwise it will take a long time to come up to temperature. With your oven set at 110°C, the meat will reach a temperature of around 85°C. This is sufficient to break down the collagen and fibrous tissues, making the lamb perfectly tender. The stock must not boil; if it did it would become cloudy, the meat would shrink and toughen, and the vegetables would disintegrate.

Charcuterie & Terrines

Looking back on my childhood in Franche-Comté, the rural part of France close to both the rugged Jura mountains and Burgundy, I remember vividly the spectacular feast days. Pig was the main staple of the region, and to honour the beast we even celebrated *la fête du cochon*, or 'Saint-Cochon' as we called the pig.

In France there is a tacit arrangement between man and pig and it is this: the pig roams free, chomping on apples, cereals and boiled potatoes, all at man's expense. Then it's payback time, and the pig must provide for the table. It's a fair arrangement, I think.

The slaughtering of the pig was a village highlight, taking place not in an abattoir but in a butcher's shop backyard. As curious kids, we never missed it. After the slaughter came the feast, and villagers gathered to celebrate.

The venerable animal was eaten from tail to snout – every morsel used in one way or another. Obviously, there were the favourite cuts of pork, such as leg, shoulder and chops. But the pig also brought us black pudding, andouillettes, a few metres of sausages, pâtés and four fine trotters.

Then, of course, there was the meat to be cured, air-dried and often smoked, thus preserving it for future months. This is part of the great art of charcuterie (which translates from old French as 'cooked flesh'), an art that is pretty much nothing without the pig.

Today, in many villages in the Haut-Doubs, this ceremony still takes place. A celebration of traditions and region, it is a strong part of our identity.

Charcuterie is also becoming an interesting part of Britain's food culture. On a recent visit to Trealy Farm, in Monmouthshire, I learnt how the young Trealy farmers had travelled through France, Germany, Spain and Italy on a mission to master the art of charcuterie... They succeeded.

Curing at home is very rewarding and the results will keep for a few weeks in the fridge, but you must use a trusted recipe and follow strict hygiene practices. Always cure smaller pieces of meat, as this reduces the health risk.

A humid environment encourages the growth of bacteria and moulds, so make sure there is plenty of dry air circulating around the meat. Often air-drying will discolour the surface of the meat and dry it out. To overcome this, paint a thin layer of melted pork fat mixed with cracked pepper onto the surface.

There are three main ways to cure meat: in a mix of sea salt, herbs and spices; in a brine solution made of salt and sugar, sometimes with vinegar and spices added; and smoking. Smoking gives a special flavour to meats and fish, of course, but it also preserves them, as wood smoke contains chemicals that slow down and inhibit the growth of microbes.

Ham hock terrine, soused vegetables

*

Serves 12

Preparation:
50 minutes, plus
overnight setting

Cooking: 3–4 hours

Special equipment:
large stockpot,
23 x 9cm terrine
(8cm deep)

I simply love this rustic terrine. The flavour is superb and it looks so attractive as you slice it – revealing a mosaic of vegetables, herbs and ham. It is also inexpensive to make and can be prepared well ahead. The pig's trotter isn't essential but it will add flavour and natural gelatine to your terrine.

Planning ahead The soused vegetables can be made a week in advance and the terrine up to 2 days ahead.

For the terrine
1 large ham hock, about 1.5kg
   (or 2 smaller ones)
1 pig's trotter, cut in half
   lengthways (optional)
2 litres cold water
1 bouquet garni (2 bay leaves,
   5g parsley, 2g thyme, tied
   together)
8 black peppercorns
1 large carrot (100g), quartered
   lengthways
2 celery sticks (100g), halved
1 medium white onion (100g),
   peeled and cut into 6 wedges
1½ sheets leaf gelatine (27x7cm)
40ml white wine vinegar
35g flat-leaf parsley

For the soused vegetables
400ml water
80ml white wine vinegar
90g clear honey
1 thyme sprig
1 bay leaf
6 pinches of sea salt
2 pinches of freshly ground
   white pepper
160g baby onions, peeled,
   root left on
100g carrot, peeled and cut into
   3cm long sticks
70g cauliflower, cut into
   small florets
1 tarragon sprig
60g small gherkins, rinsed
10g dill sprigs, chopped

To cook the meat for the terrine Put the ham hock(s) and pig's trotter into a large stockpot or saucepan, cover with the cold water and bring to the boil, skimming to remove the impurities[1]. Let bubble gently for 1 minute. Turn down the heat to a gentle simmer, add the bouquet garni and peppercorns and put the lid on, leaving a slight gap[2]. Cook for 3–4 hours, adding all the vegetables 45 minutes before the end of the cooking time. The cooking time will depend on the size of the hock(s); the meat should be tender enough to pull the small bone out easily.

Once cooked, lift out the meat onto a board and leave until cool enough to handle. Strain the liquor through a sieve set over a large pan, reserving the vegetables. Soak the gelatine leaves in a shallow dish of cold water to soften for 5 minutes or so. Bring the strained liquor to a simmer and take off the heat. Drain the gelatine and stir into the hot liquor with the wine vinegar. Reserve 400ml for the terrine (any excess can be used as a broth with noodles).

To prepare the terrine Peel off the rind and fat from the ham hocks. Cut off and discard the fat from the rind; cut the rind into 1cm pieces[3]. Flake the meat from the hock into a bowl, reserving 3 large pieces. Add the rind to the flaked meat. No additional seasoning should be needed as the hock's cure provides enough.

Set aside a quarter of the meat and rind mixture; mix the drained vegetables into the rest. Blanch the parsley in boiling water for 15 seconds, drain, pat dry and chop roughly, then mix into the meat and vegetable mixture.

To build the terrine Line the terrine with two layers of cling film for extra support, leaving a 10cm overhang all around (to wrap the terrine once formed).

Pack the meat and vegetable mixture into the terrine, placing the 3 reserved pieces of ham hock in the centre, then top with the reserved meat and rind mix[4]. Pour in enough of the warm cooking liquor to come to the level of the mixture, then press down lightly so a thin layer of liquor covers the meat and vegetables.

Gently fold the overhanging cling film over to cover the top and place in the fridge overnight to set[5].

To prepare the soused vegetables Put the water, wine vinegar, honey, thyme, bay leaf and seasoning into a large saucepan and bring to the boil. Add the onions and carrot and simmer gently for 20 minutes, then add the cauliflower and tarragon and simmer for a further 10 minutes. Take off the heat, add the gherkins and pour into a bowl set over ice to cool quickly. Once cooled, add the chopped dill and store in airtight jars until needed.

To firm up the terrine When set, carefully remove the terrine from the mould and wrap tightly in an extra two layers of cling film[6]. Refrigerate until ready to serve.

To serve Remove the cling film from the terrine, place on a board and cut into slices. Put the soused vegetables in a pot and serve on the side, along with a basket of freshly toasted pain de campagne or warm French bread.

---

[1] Bringing the cold water to the boil coagulates the blood and lifts the impurities to the surface, so they can be skimmed away easily – resulting in a clearer stock.

[2] The liquor must be simmering not boiling, otherwise the meat will become tough and the broth will be very cloudy. When covering with a lid it is important to leave a gap; if the lid is on tight, the heat will accumulate and the broth will boil.

[3] There is a common misconception that the rind and cartilage are fatty parts of the animal, but they are mostly protein and will give your terrine added texture.

[4] A third of the chopped meat and rind is reserved for the top, which will become the base of the terrine once it is turned out. This mixture, which excludes vegetables, will provide firm support for the terrine.

[5] The gelatine needs at least 12 hours to set to its maximum capacity.

[6] This helps to set the shape and stop the terrine from falling apart as you slice it.

Chicken liver parfait

Serves 10–12

Preparation:
20 mins, plus
1–2 days chilling

Cooking:
45 mins–1 hour

Special equipment:
blender, 23 x 9cm
terrine (8cm deep),
temperature probe

Rich, silky, melting and totally delicious, this pâté remains one of the most popular dishes at Brasserie Blanc. If you like, you can accompany it with chutney or pickled vegetables to cut the richness. The parfait is also perfect spread on small croûtons and served as a canapé, with a glass of red wine.

Prepare ahead The parfait is improved if it is made a couple of days in advance, to allow time for the flavours to mature.

400g free-range/organic
chicken livers, cleaned and
sinews removed[1]
100ml dry Madeira
100ml ruby port
60g shallots, peeled and
finely chopped
4 thyme sprigs, leaves picked
and finely chopped
1 garlic clove, peeled and
crushed
50ml Cognac

5 free-range/organic
medium eggs
400g unsalted butter, melted
and kept warm
10 pinches of sea salt
2 pinches of freshly ground
black pepper

To finish the parfait
75g butter, softened
75g lard, softened

To make the parfait Preheat the oven to 130°C/Gas 1. Rinse and drain the chicken livers well. Put the Madeira, port, shallots, thyme, garlic and Cognac into a small saucepan and bring to the boil over a high heat. Let bubble to reduce by a third[2], then remove from the heat and set aside.

In a blender, purée the raw livers with the reduced alcohol and flavourings. Now add the eggs, one at a time, blending for 3–4 minutes until the mixture is silky smooth. Gradually incorporate the warm melted butter[3]. Season with the salt and pepper.

To mould the parfait Line the base of the terrine with greaseproof paper. Pass the contents of the blender through a fine sieve into the terrine mould, forcing them through the sieve with the back of a ladle. Cover the surface closely with a piece of greaseproof paper[4] and lay a piece of foil loosely over the top of the mould.

To cook the parfait Stand the terrine in a roasting tray and pour enough boiling water into the tray to come two-thirds of the way up the side of the terrine[5]. Cook in the oven for 45 minutes to 1 hour, until the terrine reaches 67–70°C in the middle[6]. Remove the terrine from the water bath and leave to cool for 30 minutes, then refrigerate for at least 30 minutes to chill.

To smooth the parfait Discard the greaseproof paper on top and dip the terrine mould briefly into hot water. Slide the blade of a hot knife around the edge of the terrine, to liberate the parfait, then lift out onto a board. Using a warm palette knife, smooth the sides and the top of the parfait[7]. Refrigerate for at least 30 minutes to firm up (or place in the freezer for 15 minutes).

To finish the parfait Mix the softened butter and lard together until evenly blended. Using a palette knife, spread some on top of the parfait to create a smooth, even layer. Flip the parfait over onto a tray lined with greaseproof paper and coat the rest of the parfait with the softened lard/butter mix in the same way[8]. Refrigerate for at least a day; 2 days would be preferable.

To serve Using a knife dipped in hot water, cut the pâté into thick slices and serve with chutneys, pickles and warm sourdough bread.

Variation I adore the silkiness and richness of this pâté, but if you prefer it a little less rich then you can reduce the amount of butter and replace with more chicken livers.

[1] I recommend pre-soaking the livers in 500ml each water and whole milk, with 10g salt added, for an hour. Soaking will draw out most of the blood and bitterness, giving them a more delicate flavour. Drain them thoroughly before you use them.

[2] By boiling the wine you are evaporating some of the alcohol, removing the harsh bitterness and leaving the fruity qualities of the wine. The heat will also draw out more flavour from the herbs.

[3] If the butter is not warm enough, it will start to solidify when you add it to the cold, raw chicken livers and the mixture will split. It needs to be at about 40°C and incorporated gradually; if added too quickly, the mixture is liable to split.

[4] The paper must be cut to fit exactly. It will protect the parfait from the direct heat of the oven, preventing it from discolouring and developing a crust.

[5] Using a bain-marie moderates the heat of the oven, ensuring the parfait cooks slowly and evenly. If it were to cook too quickly, or at too high a temperature, it would be overcooked on the outside but raw in the middle.

[6] Begin testing the parfait after 45 minutes, by inserting a temperature probe into the middle. Once the temperature is 67–70°C it is ready. Do not overcook the parfait or it will split and lose its fine, smooth texture.

[7] When cooled, there will be a slight depression (and discolouration) on the top of the parfait. With the blade of a knife dipped in hot water, level and smooth the top. Smooth the sides at the same time.

[8] The butter and lard coating will stop the parfait from oxidising and discolouring. You might like to add a touch of spice to the butter coating – roughly crushed black peppercorns, ground cinnamon or dried grated orange zest, perhaps.

Duck ham

Serves 4

Preparation:
30 mins

Curing: 24 hours
salting, plus 12 days
hanging

Special equipment:
muslin cloth

While it might be hard to cure and dry a whole pig leg at home, a duck ham is a more realistic and achievable aim. This little recipe is simple and I have prepared it many times. It will also reconnect you with the forgotten art of home-curing, bringing to your table a delicious treat.

Planning ahead The duck ham must be prepared and hung in the fridge 12 days in advance of serving.

For preparing the duck ham
2 magret duck breasts,
    250–300g each (or
    4 smaller ones)
100g coarse sea salt
2 tsp black peppercorns,
    crushed
4 thyme sprigs, leaves picked
pinch of juniper berries,
    crushed

For the salad
150g mixed salad leaves
    (batavia, frisée, chicory etc,)
4 tsp extra virgin rapeseed oil
2 tsp walnut oil
2 tsp white wine vinegar
pinch of sea salt
pinch of freshly ground
    black pepper

For the garnish
crispy duck skin (reserved from
    preparing the duck)
2 tbsp walnuts, toasted and
    crushed (optional)
2 tbsp flaked almonds, toasted
    (optional)

To prepare the duck breasts Place the duck breasts, flesh side down, on a board. Using a very sharp knife, slice off the skin, leaving a 3mm layer of fat[1]. Roll the skin up, wrap in cling film and freeze for later.

To cure the duck breasts Place in a small container[2] and sprinkle with the salt, pepper, thyme and juniper. Turn to coat all over. Cover with cling film and place in the bottom of the fridge to cure for 24 hours, turning halfway through[3].

To dry the duck breasts Remove the duck breasts from the fridge and brush off the salt and spices, then rinse under cold running water, drain and pat dry. Wrap each duck breast separately in muslin, tie with string and hang in your fridge for 12 days[4]. Thereafter the duck can be kept in a sealed container in the fridge for up to a month.

To finish and serve Preheat the grill to high. Unwrap the frozen duck skin and cut into fine slivers, then grill until crispy and golden. Season lightly and set aside.

Unwrap the duck hams. If any parts of the flesh surface appear to be slightly over-dry, trim these pieces.

Wash the salad leaves and pat dry. In a small bowl, whisk together the oils, wine vinegar and seasoning to make a dressing.

Toss the salad leaves in the dressing and pile in the centre of each plate. Garnish with the crispy grilled duck skin and toasted nuts, if using. Cut the duck hams into very thin slices and arrange around the edge of the salad to serve.

1   It is essential to leave a layer of fat on to protect the meat and lend flavour.

2   The container must be small so that the two breasts are packed together with a layer of salt below, above and in between.

3   Salting is the first stage of the curing process. It is important to use sea salt, which has natural curing agents in addition to sodium chloride, rather than rock salt, which does not. This recipe uses 18–20 per cent salt in proportion to the weight of meat, which is the right amount for curing small cuts. During this stage, the concentration of salt on the surface of the meat will draw out water by osmosis, killing the majority of bacteria by drying them out. The salt will also denature the protein, making the texture and flavour hugely appetising.

4   Hanging (or air-drying) is the second stage of the curing process. It both dries the duck ham and further matures the meat in a controlled environment (the fridge must be at 4°C or below to minimise bacterial growth). Hanging the duck breasts in muslin allows air to circulate around the meat. Before wrapping, you can paint a little duck fat spiced with cracked pepper on the inside of the duck breast to prevent the surface drying. The optimum time is 12 days; beyond this the duck will dry out too much and become leathery.

DID YOU KNOW?
To fully appreciate the duck hams, they must be sliced very thinly. If cut too thickly, the meat will be very firm, almost chewy.

Pot au feu

Serves 8
Preparation:
30 mins, plus
soaking ham hock
Cooking: 2¼ hours
Special equipment:
large stockpot

The quintessence of French family cuisine, this must be the most celebrated dish in France. It honours the tables of the rich and poor alike. Despite its lack of sophistication, it has survived the passage of time. Pot au feu is a triumph of simplicity and the inspiration for many other dishes, such as poule au pot, potée au choux, navarin, daubes, carbonnades and not forgetting the beautiful chicken soup. You can feast on it for several days.

Planning ahead You can prepare this dish a day or two in advance and keep it in the fridge, ready to reheat and serve as required.

1 ham hock, about 1kg, soaked in cold water in the fridge for 6 hours or overnight
500g flank of beef, outer fat removed
300g smoked streaky bacon, rind on
3 litres cold water
2 pinches of sea salt
1 bouquet garni (6 bay leaves, 10g parsley, 4g thyme, tied together)
20 black peppercorns
3 garlic cloves (unpeeled)
1 Morteau sausage, about 350g[1]
1 marrow bone, about 400g (optional)

For the vegetables
1 Savoy cabbage, cut into 6 wedges, core retained
6 medium carrots (480g), peeled and quartered
2 celery stalks (120g), cut into thirds
2 large turnips (300g), peeled and halved
2 onions (300g), peeled and quartered, root left on

For the garnish
chopped flat-leaf parsley

To cook the meat and vegetables Place all the meat, except the Morteau sausage and marrow bone, in a large casserole. Pour on the cold water to cover, add the salt and slowly bring to the boil. Let bubble gently for 1 minute while skimming to remove the impurities[2].

Turn down to a gentle simmer, add the bouquet garni, peppercorns and garlic and cover with a lid, leaving a small gap[3]. Cook very gently, with one bubble just breaking the surface, for 1½ hours. Skim off most of the fat[4], then add the Morteau sausage and marrow bone.

Blanch the cabbage wedges in boiling water for 3 minutes, then add to the pan with the rest of the vegetables. Cook very gently for a further 30 minutes or until the meat just starts to come away from the bone and the vegetables are soft but still holding their shape. Taste the liquor and correct the seasoning.

To serve You could simply serve the pot au feu straight from the casserole and let guests help themselves, but serving will be easier if you portion the meat in the kitchen. Divide the meat between warm soup plates, surround with the vegetables and pour on some of the cooking liquor. Sprinkle with chopped parsley and accompany with Dijon mustard, gherkins and a French baguette.

Variations Other cuts of meat, such as feather blade steak, shin of beef, lamb shank or pig's cheeks could be added to the dish at the start of cooking. Other root vegetables could be used, such as parsnips, swede, potatoes, celeriac etc.

[1] This smoked French sausage from Morteau in Franche-Comté is probably the best quality sausage you can ever eat. It is strongly flavoured and densely textured. In fact, the flavour is so pronounced you could use the sausage alone in this pot au feu, doubling the quantity and leaving out the other meats, as I often do. Morteau sausage can be easily purchased online.

[2] This clarification process coagulates the blood and impurities, which can then be skimmed away, producing a much clearer stock.

[3] The pot au feu must be simmered not boiled, otherwise the meat will become tough and the broth will turn very cloudy. When covering with a lid, it is important to leave a gap – if the lid is on tight, the heat will accumulate and the broth will boil.

[4] A little fat will improve and enhance the flavour of the broth, so I recommend that you do not skim all of it away. However, if you are determined to remove all the fat, the best way to do so is to allow the pot au feu to cool completely; the fat will then solidify on the surface of the liquor, making it easier to remove.

Mushrooms & Game

Many people who indulge in good food eagerly await the twelfth day of August; the start of the grouse season. It is also about then that chanterelles, girolles, black trumpets and ceps are springing up on the mossy forest floor.

I remember vividly this season in France, when both mushrooms and game are abundant within the forests, and gum-booted little Frenchmen stalk the woods armed with guns. They are dangerous, so if ever you go, please wear red clothing and sing loudly to ensure you're not mistaken for grouse or rabbits.

Mother Nature has been kind by giving us game and mushrooms at the same time of year. They are the perfect marriage on the plate and it makes sense for them to share this chapter.

I've been mushroom-foraging all my life, and as a child I was taught which ones were edible, though my parents also told me, 'All mushrooms are edible... once.'

A few years ago, I met Richard Edwards, an extraordinary man, who is immensely knowledgeable about all things mushroom. I was touched by his enthusiasm and immediately connected it to a shady mini valley at Le Manoir. It is 123 metres long and has a little brook running through it, and I had been wondering for a long time what to do with it. With Richard's help we landscaped it with hundreds of logs and injected each of them with many strains of mushrooms and mycelium. We also created a propagating and growing room, which sits under a bridge spanning across the little mushroom *vallée* – the only one of its kind in Great Britain.

As for the controversial subject of washing mushrooms: do you or don't you? My advice is to first scrape away any forest debris and cut off the end of the bases. Large mushrooms (mostly ceps) don't need to be washed at all, just brushed. The others should be washed very quickly – 5–10 seconds - in a bowl of cold water and drained immediately.

If you have an abundance of mushrooms, why not dry some? Slice them finely and lay on a baking tray, then put into a preheated oven at 100°C for 3 hours. Rehydrate in plenty of water before cooking. Their flavour will be enhanced ten-fold, so use sparingly. You can also powder dried mushrooms to add magic to risottos, pasta and other dishes. Dried mushrooms are an essential store-cupboard ingredient.

As for game... I recall being told, 'Look out for the pheasants in the bathroom.' The birds would hang there until the head had separated from the body. Hanging must be done in a cold place to prevent spoiling. It improves a meat's 'gamey' flavour and makes it tender, but a lot of game doesn't need lengthy hanging. Grouse, for instance, doesn't need hanging at all. Remember, game often has a low fat content. Don't overcook it or it will be dry and tough.

Chicken with morels and sherry wine sauce

*

Serves 4

Preparation:
10 mins, plus
2 hours soaking
mushrooms

Cooking: 20 mins

This is a great classic of French cuisine and it originates from my own region. It is quick and easy to prepare and I urge you to cook it for your friends. To me, morels are the finest mushrooms in the world and you can now find them dried in good supermarkets. I even prefer the dried ones to the fresh ones as their flavour is so much more pronounced. The traditional Jura wine is the best, if you happen to have some, otherwise a dry sherry works very well.

Planning ahead The dried morels need to be soaked for at least a couple of hours. You can prepare the chicken half an hour in advance and warm it through in the morel sauce to serve.

30g dried morels[1], soaked in
   250ml water for at least
   2 hours
4 organic/free-range chicken
   breasts (180g each), skinned
sea salt and freshly ground
   black pepper
15g unsalted butter
250g firm button mushrooms,
   washed quickly, patted dry
   and quartered
120ml dry sherry or Jura wine
400ml double cream

For the leeks
2 medium leeks, trimmed, cut
   into 2cm pieces and washed
200ml boiling water
pinch of sea salt
15g unsalted butter

To prepare the morels Drain the morels, reserving the soaking liquor, and squeeze to extract as much of the liquor as possible. Rinse the morels, drain and squeeze dry. Cut larger morels into smaller pieces; set aside. Pass the reserved liquor through a muslin-lined sieve to remove any sand or grit and save 100ml.

To cook the chicken Season the breasts with salt and pepper. In a large frying pan, melt the butter over a medium heat until it is foaming[2]. Add the chicken breasts and colour lightly for 3 minutes on each side. Remove from the pan and reserve.

In the fat remaining in the frying pan, soften the soaked morels and button mushrooms together, for 1–2 minutes. Meanwhile, boil the sherry or wine in a small pan for 30 seconds. Add the sherry or wine[3] to the mushrooms with the reserved morel liquor and a pinch of salt. Pour in the cream and bring to the boil.

Place the chicken breasts back in the pan, making sure the cream sauce covers them. Lower the heat to a gentle simmer and cook for 10 minutes, depending on the size of the chicken breasts, until they are just cooked through[4].

To cook the leeks While the chicken is cooking, put the leeks into a saucepan, pour on the boiling water and add the salt and butter. Cover and cook at a full boil for 5–10 minutes until tender.

To finish the dish Using a slotted spoon, lift out the chicken breasts and place in a warm dish; keep warm. Boil the sauce rapidly to reduce until it is thick enough to coat the back of a spoon. Taste and adjust the seasoning. Place the chicken breasts back in the sauce to reheat for 2 minutes.

To serve With a slotted spoon, lift the leeks from their liquor and arrange on warmed plates. Sit the chicken breasts on top and pour the morel sauce over and around. By this time your kitchen will be filled with heavenly smells. Accompany with a chilled bottle of Jura wine for a perfect moment. *Bon appétit.*

Variations Use dried ceps in place of the morels. Or you can use fresh wild mushrooms, adding them with the button mushrooms.

Replace the chicken with guinea fowl or pork chops, adjusting the cooking time accordingly.

[1] Dried morels are highly prized by the gourmet. These mushrooms grow in many parts of Europe during the spring. Conical-shaped, with a distinctive honeycomb structure, they hold sand and grit, so need to be washed a few times in fresh water to ensure they are thoroughly cleaned.

[2] The butter will start to foam at about 130°C. At 150–155°C it will turn a hazelnut colour. This is the perfect stage to caramelise the chicken without drying it.

[3] I boil the sherry or wine before adding it to the dish to remove most of the alcohol, retaining the flavour and character.

[4] It is essential to avoid overcooking the chicken, or it will become dry. The timing here should ensure that your chicken is tender and succulent.

Brown chicken stock

Makes 1.2 litres
Preparation:
15 mins
Cooking: 1½ hours

I use this stock as the base for several of my sauces to be served with game. It lends a delicate flavour, which will not overpower the flavour of the dish the sauce is served with. You can make a lovely stock from veal or lamb in the same way.

Planning ahead Once this stock is made, it can be stored in small containers in the freezer to be used as and when required.

100ml neutral-flavoured oil
(sunflower, groundnut or
rapeseed)
2kg chicken wings, chopped
into 3 pieces
1 Spanish onion (250g), cut
into 5mm dice
150g flat mushrooms, cleaned
and thinly sliced

4–6 garlic cloves, skin on,
crushed
2 litres cold water
1 bay leaf
1 thyme sprig
2 parsley stalks
8–10 black peppercorns
1 tsp arrowroot or cornflour
diluted in 2 tbsp water

To brown the chicken wings Divide the oil between two large roasting trays and place over a high heat until almost smoking. Add the chicken wings and colour for 15 minutes, turning occasionally with a wooden spoon[1]. Add the onion, mushrooms and garlic and continue to colour for 5 minutes until the bones and vegetables are golden brown. Drain off excess fat if necessary.

To make the stock Transfer the chicken wings, vegetables and garlic to a large saucepan and pour on the cold water to cover. Add the herbs and peppercorns and bring to the boil. Let bubble for 2 minutes, skimming off the impurities as they rise to the surface[2]. Turn the heat down to a gentle simmer so that the bubbles just break at the surface, and cook for 1 hour.

Whisk the diluted arrowroot[3] into the stock and bring to the boil, stirring, to bind the stock very lightly. Strain the stock through a fine sieve[4]. Cool, then refrigerate[5] or freeze until needed.

---

[1] The browning of the bones will determine the taste and quality of the stock. If you do not colour the bones enough, the stock will be lacking in colour and flavour. But, if you colour them too much, the resulting stock may have a bitter edge.

[2] Removing the impurities makes for a clearer stock.

[3] The arrowroot will give a little body to the stock.

[4] No salt is added to the stock as it may need to be reduced before using, which would make it too salty. Adjust the seasoning of a sauce once the stock is added.

[5] As the stock is chilled, any fat will solidify on the surface and is easily removed.

Fricassée of wild mushrooms

Serves 4
Preparation:
20 mins
Cooking: 2 mins

I am lucky to have an ancient wood forest close to my Oxfordshire home. The forest floor is thick with mosses and lichens, and wild mushrooms are abundant. This dish should be redolent with heady forest flavours, but feel free to include some cultivated mushrooms. Provide good French bread to mop up the juices.

400g mixed wild mushrooms[1]
   (chanterelles, girolles etc.)
5g black trumpet mushrooms[1]
   (optional)
½ shallot, peeled and chopped
40g unsalted butter
100ml dry white wine
1 garlic clove, peeled and
   crushed
4 pinches of sea salt

4 pinches of freshly ground
   black pepper
juice of ¼ lemon
handful of flat-leaf parsley
   leaves, coarsely chopped
120g vine-ripened tomatoes,
   deseeded and diced

For the croûtes
½ small baguette
1 garlic clove, peeled and halved

To prepare the mushrooms Pick off any forest debris and cut off the base of the stalks. Wash the mushrooms very briefly[2] in plenty of water and lift them onto a clean tea towel to drain. Pat dry and cut off the base of the stalks.

To prepare the croûtes Cut the baguette into fine slices, no more than 3mm thick, and toast under the grill (or in the oven at 180°C/Gas 4) until lightly golden brown. Rub the slices on both sides with the garlic.

To cook the mushrooms In a large frying pan over a medium heat, soften the shallot in 1 tsp butter for 30 seconds without colouring. Meanwhile, boil the wine in a small pan for 30 seconds.

Increase the heat under the frying pan to high and add the garlic and wild mushrooms, except black trumpets[3]. Add the salt, pepper and wine. Cover and cook at a full boil for a minute. Add the lemon juice and remaining butter.

Lastly, add the black trumpets, if using, chopped parsley and diced tomatoes; cook for a further 10–30 seconds. Taste and correct the seasoning. Serve in warmed soup plates, with the croûtes on the side.

[1] If you are foraging, get a mushroom expert to check what you have gathered, unless you are 100 per cent confident of identifying them.

[2] Ensure that the washing process is no more than 5–10 seconds. Mushrooms are sponges and readily absorb water, adversely affecting both taste and texture.

[3] If you add the black trumpets too early they will release too much juice and discolour the sauce.

Cep ravioli, sage and toasted nut butter

** **

Serves 2 as a main dish, 4 as a starter

Preparation: 1 hour, plus 1¼–1½ hours resting

Cooking: 4 mins

Special equipment: food processor, pasta machine, 8cm round cutter

I have fond memories of this recipe. I was in Tuscany, at Villa San Michele, working in the cookery school. On a glorious autumn day, we visited the market with the guest students to appreciate the abundance of local and fresh fruits. Some beautiful freshly picked fat ceps caught my eye and this little dish was created the same day.

Planning ahead The pasta can be prepared a day in advance and kept tightly wrapped in cling film in the fridge. The ravioli can be assembled a few hours in advance and reserved on a plate dusted with semolina to prevent sticking, ready for cooking.

For the pasta
200g pasta flour (type 00)[1]
1 tbsp water
5g sea salt
2 organic/free-range medium eggs
1 tbsp extra virgin olive oil

For the filling
15g unsalted butter
½ medium shallot, peeled and finely chopped
300g ceps[2], trimmed, cleaned and cut into 3mm dice
sea salt and freshly ground black pepper
juice of ¼ lemon, or to taste

For the sauce
10g hazelnuts
10g pine nuts
40g unsalted butter
2–3 ceps, trimmed, cleaned and sliced
4 sage leaves, finely chopped
50ml water or brown chicken stock (see page 135)

To serve
fried sage leaves, (optional)
freshly grated Parmesan

To make the pasta dough Put all of the ingredients in a food processor and process for about 1 minute until the dough is just coming together.

Turn the dough onto a lightly floured surface and knead for 5 minutes until perfectly smooth. Shape into a ball, then flatten roughly to the width of your pasta machine. Wrap in cling film and leave to rest[3] in the fridge for 1 hour.

To prepare the filling Melt the butter in a medium sauté pan over a low heat, add the shallot and cook gently for 2 minutes or until softened and translucent. Add the diced ceps and cook over a high heat, stirring continuously, for 2 minutes. Remove from the heat and season with salt, pepper and a dash of lemon juice to taste. Cool down on a tray in the fridge.

To roll out the pasta Fix your pasta machine to the side of a table. Flatten the dough with a rolling pin to the width of the machine. Cut it in half and roll one piece through the machine, on the thickest setting[4]. Seal the two ends together to make a conveyor belt and continue to roll the pasta, gradually narrowing the setting until you reach the thinnest setting for ravioli on your machine[5]. Repeat with the other piece, then lay, interleaved with cling film, on a tray in the fridge[6].

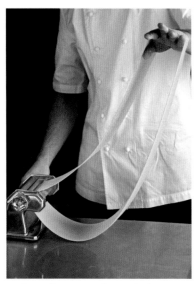

Rolling the pasta through the machine to the correct thickness.

Enclosing the mounds of filling between the sheets of pasta.

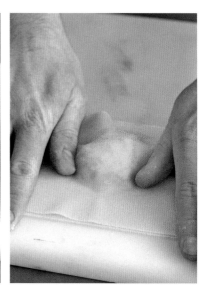

Pressing the pasta around the filling to expel air.

Neatening the shape with cling film and the inverted cutter.

Cutting out the individual ravioli.

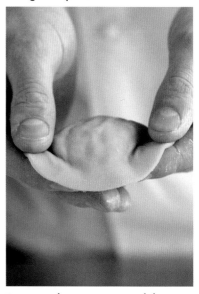

Pressing the pasta around the filling to ensure a tight seal.

To fill the pasta Lay one pasta sheet on a clean surface. Lightly put teaspoonfuls of the filling in mounds at 6cm intervals along the middle of the sheet. Ensure that a gap of 3cm is maintained between each mound. Take the second sheet and drape it loosely over, pressing around the mounds of filling with the back of your thumbs to seal and expel any air bubbles.

To shape the ravioli Now cover the filled pasta with a sheet of cling film. Using the inverted 8cm cutter, press down over the cling film around the filling mounds to neaten the shape. Turn the cutter the right way up and cut out the ravioli. Reserve on a cling film-lined tray to prevent the pasta from sticking.

To make the sauce Preheat the oven to 170°C/Gas 3. Scatter the hazelnuts and pine nuts on a baking tray, keeping them separate, and toast in the oven for 10 minutes. Cool slightly, then lightly crush the hazelnuts.

To cook the pasta Bring a large pan of water to the boil and cook the ravioli for 4 minutes exactly. Meanwhile, for the sauce, heat the butter to the noisette stage[7] and quickly sauté the sliced ceps for a couple of minutes until softened. Add the chopped sage, toasted pine nuts and hazelnuts, and water or brown chicken stock (if you have some to hand) to create an emulsion.

To serve Drain the ravioli, add to the sauce and toss carefully, then arrange in warmed bowls. Top with the fried sage leaves, if using, and serve with freshly grated Parmesan.

Variations The fillings for ravioli are endless. Diced fish, roasted pumpkin, diced courgettes with basil and tomato – these are just a few delicious options.

[1] For pasta you need a high gluten flour to give the dough elasticity. Durum wheat flour is by far the best, lending a wonderful texture to your pasta.

[2] If you are unable to find fresh ceps you could use flat cup or field mushrooms and enrich them with a little dried cep powder, which is available from delicatessens and good supermarkets.

[3] By kneading the pasta dough you will activate the gluten in the flour; this will cause the pasta to retract if it is not allowed to rest thereafter.

[4] When rolling out the dough, ideally use no flour, or as little as possible, as it will be absorbed. Too much flour will make the pasta glutinous once cooked.

[5] Ensure that the pasta is no thicker than 1mm. If it is any thicker it will be doughy and unpleasant.

[6] Again it is important to allow the pasta to rest in the fridge for 20 minutes after working it through the pasta machine.

[7] The butter will start to foam at about 130°C, turning hazelnut in colour at 150–155°C; i.e. the required beurre noisette stage.

**

Roast wild duck, blackberry sauce and celeriac purée *Illustrated overleaf*

Serves 2

Preparation: 30 mins

Cooking: 35 mins, plus resting

Special equipment: blender

This is a great autumnal dish. Wild duck has a fantastic gamey flavour and blackberries are a perfect match, as their acidity cuts the richness of the meat. Wild duck is best appreciated if you serve it medium rare. Overcook it and it will quickly become dry, as there is hardly any fat within the muscle. Remember to ask your butcher for extra duck bones for the sauce.

Planning ahead You can make the blackberry sauce and celeriac purée a day in advance.

2 tbsp groundnut oil
2 wild ducks, prepared and
   oven-ready[1]

For the blackberry sauce
300g wild duck bones,
   chopped into 2cm pieces[2]
2 tbsp groundnut oil
120g shallots, peeled and finely
   sliced
100g flat cup mushrooms,
   cleaned and sliced
150ml red wine (ideally
   Cabernet Sauvignon)
500ml brown chicken stock
   (see page 135) or water
¼ tsp juniper berries, crushed
15g unsalted butter
25ml whipping cream
2 pinches of sea salt

small pinch of freshly, finely
   ground black pepper
60ml blackberry purée[3]
2 tsp balsamic vinegar
½ tsp arrowroot, mixed with
   a little cold water (if needed)

For the celeriac purée
300g celeriac, peeled and cut
   into 3cm pieces
600ml whole milk
2 pinches of sea salt
small pinch of cayenne pepper
½ tsp lemon juice
20g unsalted butter

For the garnish (optional)
whole blackberries
celeriac crisps (deep-fried
   wafer-thin slices)

To make the blackberry sauce In a cooking pot over a medium heat, colour the chopped duck bones in the groundnut oil for 10 minutes[4]. Add the sliced shallots and mushrooms and cook, stirring occasionally, until golden brown. Meanwhile, boil the wine in a small pan to reduce by half.

Spoon off the excess fat, then add the reduced wine, stock or water, juniper berries, butter, cream and seasoning to the cooking pot. Bring to the boil and let bubble gently for 15 minutes[5]. Strain into a clean pan and stir in the blackberry purée. Taste, correct the seasoning and add a dash of balsamic vinegar to balance the sauce. Thicken with a little diluted arrowroot if needed[6].

To make the celeriac purée Put the chopped celeriac into a medium saucepan with the milk and bring to the boil. Lower the heat and simmer for 15–20 minutes until soft. Drain the celeriac, reserving some of the milk.

Purée the celeriac in a blender until smooth, adding a little of the milk to achieve a good consistency. Season with the salt, cayenne and lemon juice[7]. Taste and adjust the seasoning if necessary. In a small saucepan, heat the butter until it foams and reaches the noisette stage[8], then whisk into the purée. Cover and leave to one side.

To roast the ducks Preheat the oven to 180°C/Gas 4 while cooking the celeriac. Heat the groundnut oil in a large frying pan over a medium heat and colour the ducks for 8 minutes on each side, then for 2 minutes on each breast, so they are golden brown all over. Transfer the ducks to a roasting tray and roast in the oven for 12 minutes. Remove and leave to rest, breast side down and loosely covered with foil, in a warm spot for at least 10 minutes. Meanwhile, reheat the sauce and the celeriac purée if necessary.

To serve Carve the ducks as you would a roast chicken onto a flat dish. Serve accompanied by the blackberry sauce and celeriac purée and garnished with blackberries and celeriac crisps, if you like.

[1] As they are smaller and leaner, wild ducks need less cooking than farmed ones. Ask your butcher to remove the wishbone from the ducks as this will make it easier to carve the breast when you come to serve the dish.

[2] If you don't have enough duck bones, you can supplement with chopped chicken wings, which have an even ratio of meat to bone.

[3] To obtain this quantity of purée, you will need to blend about 75g blackberries in a blender or food processor, then sieve to remove the pips.

[4] Do not over-colour the bones, as this would impart a bitter taste to your sauce.

[5] I find that 15 minutes of simmering is just the right amount of time for the proper exchange of flavours between ingredients. Do not boil the sauce, as it would become cloudy and lose its freshness.

[6] If the sauce needs thickening slightly, add just a little diluted arrowroot to begin with and stir over a medium-low heat. You can always add a little bit more later if necessary.

[7] The lemon juice will cut through the creaminess of the celeriac, balancing the flavour of the purée.

[8] The butter will start to foam at about 130°C, turning hazelnut in colour at 150–155°C; i.e. the required beurre noisette stage.

Braised rabbit with mustard *Illustrated on previous page*

Serves 4–6

Preparation:
20 mins

Cooking:
45 mins–1¼ hours

Rabbit is probably the animal that polarises our two nations more than any other. The French look upon it as food, whereas to the British it is primarily a pet and therefore something that should not be eaten. At my family home in France, we had this dish almost every other Sunday. It is really very tasty and I hope I can persuade you to try it. Most good butchers and quality supermarkets now sell farmed rabbit.

2 small wild rabbits
    (800g–1.2kg) or 1 large
    farmed rabbit (1.5–2kg),
    jointed[1]
4 pinches of sea salt
4 pinches of crushed black
    pepper
1 rounded tbsp Dijon mustard
4 tbsp plain flour
50g unsalted butter
20ml olive oil
½ medium onion, peeled
    and cut into 6 wedges, or
    12 Griotte onions, peeled

6 garlic cloves, skin on
150ml white wine
1 tbsp white wine vinegar
150ml water
6 black peppercorns
2 sage leaves
1 tarragon sprig
1 bay leaf

To finish
1 tablespoon chopped parsley

To prepare the rabbit Preheat the oven to 120°C/Gas 1. Put the rabbit pieces into a large bowl and season with the salt and pepper. Add the mustard and turn the pieces to ensure each one is coated in a thin film of mustard. Scatter the flour on a plate. Dip each piece of rabbit in the flour to coat, patting off any excess.

To cook the rabbit In a large flameproof casserole dish over a medium heat, melt the butter and heat until lightly foaming. Sear the rabbit pieces in the hot butter, in batches as necessary, for 7–8 minutes, turning only as necessary to colour them all over[2].

Meanwhile, heat the olive oil in a small saucepan and sweat the onion and garlic over a medium heat for 10 minutes[3], seasoning lightly with salt and pepper after a couple of minutes. In a separate small pan, boil the wine for 30 seconds to reduce.

Add the wine vinegar to the rabbit and reduce the liquor down to a syrup[4]. Add the garlic and onion, reduced wine, water, peppercorns[5] and herbs. Stir, then cover with a lid and cook in the oven until tender, stirring occasionally. Allow 45 minutes for farmed rabbit; 1–1¼ hours for wild rabbit[6]. Taste and adjust the seasoning.

To finish the dish Using a slotted spoon, transfer the rabbit to a warmed dish. Place the casserole over a high heat to reduce the liquor by one-third. Pour the sauce over the pieces of rabbit and sprinkle with the chopped parsley. Serve with French beans, Swiss chard, braised lettuce or any other seasonal vegetable.

Variations Replace the rabbit with free-range or organic chicken or guinea fowl. Olives and sautéed wild mushrooms would be a lovely addition.

1   First get to know your rabbit! Most farmed rabbits come from France and the best label assurance scheme is Label Rouge. Ask your butcher to prepare and joint the rabbit for you, into small serving pieces.
2   For the best flavour I brown the rabbit slowly in butter, which must be sizzling on a medium heat and the pieces need to be in a single layer. As the meat browns, the juices leak out and begin to caramelise on the bottom of the pan; this sediment will richly flavour your sauce.
3   Gently cooking the onions converts their starch into sugar, sweetening them and enhancing the flavour.
4   It is important to reduce the vinegar right down. If it is under-reduced you will have a sauce that is too acidic.
5   Black peppercorns will release their spice gradually during the long cooking, so they are added at this stage.
6   Wild rabbit will take longer to tenderise. Cook until it just falls off the bone.

DID YOU KNOW?
Wild rabbits are smaller than farmed ones, but their flesh is tougher and needs longer cooking. You may find you prefer the texture and milder taste of farmed rabbit.

Pheasant Pithiviers

Serves 8–10

Preparation:
2 hours, plus
6 hours curing

Cooking: 15 mins,
plus 2 hours for
the confit

Special equipment:
cook's thermometer,
10cm and 14cm
pastry cutters

This dish takes its name from the town of Pithiviers in France, where it is thought to have originated. The filling is most often a sweet frangipane with stone fruit, such as cherry or plum, but a savoury Pithiviers is just as impressive. Here I am making it with pheasant – the entire bird is used so nothing is wasted. The legs are confit, the carcass is used for the sauce and the prime breast meat goes into the filling with the confit leg. It takes time to prepare, but is well worth the effort.

Planning ahead You can prepare the Pithiviers ready for the oven well in advance and freeze until needed. Bake from frozen, allowing an extra 5 minutes.

For the confit pheasant legs
2 pheasant legs and thighs
1 tbsp sea salt
1 tsp black peppercorns,
    crushed
1 garlic clove, peeled and
    crushed
½ bay leaf, chopped
2 thyme sprigs, leaves picked
    and chopped
2 juniper berries, crushed
600g duck fat, melted

For the sauce
1 tbsp duck fat
1 pheasant carcass, about 500g,
    chopped into 2cm pieces
¼ white onion, peeled and
    sliced
¼ celery stalk, sliced
1 flat mushroom, cleaned and
    sliced
150ml ruby port
150ml dry Madeira
200ml water
¼ tsp arrowroot, mixed with
    a little cold water

For the Pithiviers
2 pheasant breasts, skin on
sea salt and freshly ground
    black pepper
1 tbsp duck fat
150g white onion, chopped
    into 2cm pieces
2 juniper berries, crushed and
    finely chopped
1 thyme sprig, leaves picked
2 sage leaves
100g flat mushrooms, cleaned
    and sliced
100g cooked chestnuts,
    chopped[1]
30g dried cranberries
2 confit pheasant legs and
    thighs (from above), chopped
800g all-butter puff pastry[2]
2 eggs, beaten (for the eggwash)

To cure the legs Lay the pheasant legs on a tray, flesh side upwards, and scatter the salt, pepper, garlic, herbs and juniper berries evenly over them. Cover with cling film and leave to cure in the fridge for 6 hours[3].

To confit the legs Preheat the oven to 95–100°C/Gas ¼ (unless using the hob). Melt the duck fat in a 16cm saucepan or ovenproof cooking pot over a low heat and bring to 85°C. Meanwhile, rinse the pheasant legs to remove the cure ingredients and pat dry with a cloth. Immerse the legs in the hot duck fat. Cook for 2 hours in the oven or on the hob over a very gentle heat. The temperature of the fat needs to be maintained at 85°C (i.e. just under simmering point), so monitor it with a thermometer[4]. Using a slotted spoon, lift the legs out of the duck fat and allow to cool.

Once cooled, the meat will easily come away from the bone. Roughly chop it into bite-sized 2cm pieces and set aside.

To make the Pithiviers filling Lightly season the pheasant breasts and cut into 2cm pieces. Heat the 1 tbsp duck fat in a medium frying pan over a high heat and quickly colour the diced breast meat until golden brown. Remove with a slotted spoon and set aside in a bowl. Add the onion, juniper, thyme, sage and mushrooms to the pan and cook for 5 minutes or until slightly caramelised.

Take off the heat and add the chopped chestnuts, cranberries, browned pheasant breast and the chopped leg confit. Mix well, then taste and correct the seasoning. Cover and chill slightly, then turn the mixture onto a board and run a knife through it to mix and chop further. Refrigerate until required.

To make the sauce Heat the duck fat in a flameproof casserole over a medium heat and caramelise the chopped pheasant bones for 5 minutes until lightly browned. Add the onion, celery and mushroom and cook for 2 minutes. Spoon off the excess fat, turn up the heat and add the port and Madeira, scraping the bottom of the pan to deglaze. Let bubble for 30 seconds. Cover with the cold water, bring back to the boil and simmer for 15–20 minutes[5], skimming occasionally. Stir in the arrowroot to slightly thicken the sauce, then strain. Taste and correct the seasoning. Set aside or refrigerate until ready to serve.

To build the Pithiviers Cut the puff pastry into two pieces, one slightly bigger than the other. Roll out the smaller piece to a 2mm thickness and cut out 8–10 10cm circles. Roll out the other piece out to a 3mm thickness and cut out 8–10 14cm circles. Place the smaller circles on a large baking tray lined with greaseproof paper and brush the edges with beaten egg. Spoon 80g of the filling onto the centre of each one and cover with the larger circles. Gently press the pastry edges together, using the rounded edge of a cutter. Place in the fridge to rest for about 30 minutes[6].

To bake and serve Preheat the oven to 200°C/Gas 6. Make a small hole in the top of each Pithiviers to allow the steam to escape. Brush the top with beaten egg[7] and score lightly. Bake for 14–16 minutes until golden brown. Meanwhile, reheat the sauce. Serve the Pithiviers on warmed plates, pouring some of the sauce into the hole in the top and the rest around them. Caramelised apple wedges would be a good accompaniment. You can also serve the Pithiviers with a garnish of lightly poached prunes and chopped hazelnuts and walnuts, as illustrated.

Variation This would work just as well with duck, rabbit, guinea fowl, stewing beef or lamb or pork shoulder.

1   Good-quality ready-cooked chestnuts are available from most supermarkets.
2   You can buy very good puff pastry in the supermarkets, but do check it is all-butter and doesn't contain hydrogenated fats.
3   This is just a light curing to slightly season and flavour the pheasant legs. The salt draws moisture out of the meat and destroys bacteria. And, with the other aromatic curing ingredients, it seasons the meat and imparts a wonderful flavour.
4   This relatively low temperature (85°C) is crucial to the succulence of this dish. At this temperature there will be no bubbles breaking the surface. Although it seems a lot of duck fat, it is simply a medium to gently cook and flavour the meat, rather than permeate it.
5   This is just long enough to extract all the flavours from the carcass. Do not cook for any longer than this, or it will start to stew and the taste will be disappointing.
6   It is essential to refrigerate, or even better, part-freeze the pastry to allow it to rest and firm up before scoring. This allows for a neater, more accurate finish.
7   On baking, the egg wash will create a lovely shine and rich colour.

DID YOU KNOW?
The confit technique originates from southwest France, where everything is cooked in duck fat. There are two stages: first curing with salt and then cooking very gently in duck fat.

Pigeon de Bresse baked in a salt pastry crust

Serves 2
Preparation:
1½ hours, plus
making stock
Cooking: 20–30
mins, plus resting
Special equipment:
electric mixer with
dough hook
attachment

This is my best-known classic at Le Manoir. Be warned, it is quite a complex dish and requires a certain amount of skill, but I can assure you it is achievable at home and it will impress your guests. In the restaurant, when the sculptured squab wrapped in its salt pastry is brought to the table, there is always a small silence. As the squab is presented, the French waiter elegantly severs the head from its body in the good old-fashioned Republican way... la Guillotine! The squab may look like a Trafalgar pigeon, but it is in fact a bird with the most unctuous flesh and refined flavour.

Planning ahead Order your squabs well in advance. Ask your butcher to cut off the feet, wings and necks and save them (for the sauce). Get him to remove the wishbone (to make carving easier) and draw them, reserving the livers and heart.

1 tbsp rapeseed oil
2 squab pigeons, each about
   225g, cleaned and oven-ready

For the salt pastry crust
600g strong white flour
350g fine sea salt
5 organic/free-range egg whites
175ml cold water

To finish
eggwash (2 egg yolks beaten
   with 1 tbsp milk and a pinch
   of caster sugar)
handful of coarse sea salt
4 cloves
melted unsalted butter, for
   brushing

For the sauce
1 tbsp groundnut oil
20g unsalted butter
reserved squab neck, wings,
   livers and heart, chopped

1 shallot, peeled and finely
   chopped
100g flat mushrooms, cleaned
   and finely sliced
4 tbsp ruby port
4 tbsp dry Madeira
200ml brown chicken stock
   (see page 135)
2 tbsp whipping cream
sea salt and freshly ground
   white pepper

*For the cabbage garnish
(optional)*
½ pointed cabbage
100ml water
30g unsalted butter
sea salt and freshly ground
   black pepper

*For the mushroom garnish
(optional)*
200g fricassée of wild
   mushrooms (see page 136)

To prepare the squabs Heat the rapeseed oil in a large, heavy-based frying pan and sear the squabs over a medium-high heat for 3 minutes on each thigh and 1 minute on each breast[1]. Leave to cool completely.

To make the salt pastry[2] Combine the flour and salt in an electric mixer fitted with a dough hook. Mix at slow speed for 1–2 minutes, then add the egg whites and increase to medium speed. Finally, slowly add the cold water until the pastry just holds together. Take out the dough and shape into a ball.

To shape the pastry On a floured surface, divide the pastry into 2 portions, knead lightly until smooth and then flatten each piece into a round. Roll each out to a circle, about 28cm in diameter and 6–7mm thick. Using a small knife and a plate as a guide, trim each to a 23cm circle and set aside. Gather together the pastry trimmings and roll out to a 5mm thickness. Using a template, cut out 4 pastry 'wings' and set aside. Mould squab 'heads' from the trimmings, too.

To wrap the squabs Lay a squab, breast down, on each pastry circle and wrap to enclose completely, making sure there are no holes[3]. Dampen the pastry 'wings' and attach to the sides of the squabs. Brush the egg wash all over the pastry, except the bases. Sprinkle rock salt over the breasts. Lightly dampen the base of the pastry 'heads' and press firmly into place; use the cloves for 'eyes'. Glaze the head with egg wash. Place the squabs on a lightly oiled baking tray and put into the fridge to rest. Preheat the oven to 240°C/Gas 9.

To make the sauce Heat the oil and butter in a medium saucepan, add the squab necks and wings and sear over a medium heat for 3–4 minutes to colour lightly, adding the liver and heart for the final minute. Add the shallot and mushrooms and cook for a further 2 minutes. Add the port and Madeira to deglaze, scraping up all the caramelised juices from the bottom of the pan. Let bubble for 1 minute. Skim, then add the chicken stock and cream. Simmer for 10–15 minutes. Force through a fine conical sieve into a clean pan, pressing with a wooden spatula to extract as much flavour as possible. Season to taste and set aside.

To bake the pastry-wrapped squabs Bake for 20–22 minutes for medium, 18 minutes for medium-rare or 12 minutes for rare[4]. Leave to rest for 5 minutes.

To prepare the cabbage If serving, cut the cabbage half into quarters. Combine the water, butter, salt and pepper in a heavy-based pan over a medium heat, then add the cabbage. Cover and cook at a full boil for 3 minutes until tender[5].

To serve Sit these glorious squabs on a serving board and brush with melted butter. Bring the sauce back to the boil and pour into a sauceboat. Place the cabbage in a small serving bowl to one side of the pigeon and the mushrooms to the other, if serving. Present this spectacle to your guests.

Unfortunately the work doesn't stop here, as the squabs must be freed from their salt crusts – ideally in front of your guests. First cut off the head and then, with a spoon, following the inside of the wings, slide open the crust and free the squab by lifting it with a fork onto the carving board. If you are not confident, you can of course do this in the privacy of your kitchen[6].

Wrapping the squab in the pastry to enclose it completely.

Attaching the pastry wings to the sides.

The final assembly, ready for the head to be glazed before baking.

1 Do not season the birds; the salt crust will do it for you. The object is not to cook the squabs but simply to crisp them up and colour the skin to enhance their taste and appearance. This stage does, however, partially cook the legs, which require a longer cooking time than the breasts. It is important to allow the squabs to cool before wrapping them in the salt pastry.

2 The salt crust is not only for visual effect. It greatly enhances the taste and texture of the squab. Protected by the salt crust, the heat will permeate the meat without tensing it, so the meat remains meltingly tender. The juices and flavour are sealed in, creating a superb eating experience.

3 Ensure that the squab is completely wrapped and sealed within the pastry. If there are any holes in the salt pastry, it will greatly affect the cooking time. The build up of heat would not be the same as the hot air would escape and the bird would probably be extremely rare at the end of the cooking time.

4 Observe the cooking time precisely. The heat builds up slowly at first, but since it cannot escape, it intensifies during the final 5 minutes. Even as little as 2 or 3 minutes less or more cooking time could grossly under- or overcook the squabs. Only adjust the recommended cooking time if the dressed squabs weigh more or less than 225g.

5 This is a lovely little technique that can be used to cook nearly all types of vegetables quickly at the last minute. Over a high heat, the water will provide the steam and it also binds with the butter to create a very light emulsion.

6 Keep the carcasses as they will make an excellent sauce.

Spring & Summer Vegetables

At Le Manoir aux Quat' Saisons, as the name implies, each season defines the vegetables which are served to our guests. My gastronomy is essentially rooted in the soil and season. What I love about spring are the delicate colours and young, fresh flavours – barely formed. Summer brings with it an abundance of sweet, full-flavoured vegetables, and our vegetable garden changes almost weekly – as a new palette of colours and textures comes to its prime.

Le Manoir has not one garden but seven: the seventeenth-century water gardens; the Japanese tea house garden; a wild mushroom valley; a Southeast Asian garden; a Victorian herb garden; a wild flower garden; and last, but not least, my beloved French potager – the veg patch. We grow about seventy varieties of vegetables at any one time and they are subject to tasting trials – a democratic process, though I confess I do influence them a little!

Our lovely head vegetable gardener, Jo, and her team provide magnificent vegetables for the kitchens. I like to think that they inspire visitors to grow their own vegetables and herbs at home – even though that might be restricted to a window box.

I would like to share with you a great little secret for cooking vegetables; one that has served me well for many years. Place 200g vegetables, 10g butter, 50ml water, 2 pinches of sea salt and 1 pinch of pepper in a pot, ready to cook. When you are reaching the moment to serve your main course, simply heat the pot to the highest temperature and seal with a tight-fitting lid. Cooking time varies between 30 seconds and 5 minutes, depending on the vegetables you have chosen.

This technique will revolutionise your vegetable cooking. Due to the speed of the process, the vegetables will retain their colour, flavour and the majority of their nutritional content. The cooking water, butter and vegetable juices will form a light emulsion, lending a delicate sheen and taste. It is a much better cooking technique than steaming, and infinitely better than boiling, where both flavour and colour are lost, and the vitamins are destroyed by the prolonged heat.

Some vegetables, such as onions, benefit from gentle cooking, or 'sweating', which transforms starch into sugar and removes the bitterness. Contrast the sweetness of gently cooked onions with the harshness of a raw onion, for example, or cooked and raw garlic.

Of course, garlic plays an important role in my cooking. Apart from its flavour-enhancing qualities, it also has impressive health-giving properties. So, I'm delighted that in Britain we now seem to be eating almost as much of it as my compatriots across La Manche.

Watercress soup

Serves 4

Preparation:
10 mins

Cooking: 10 mins

Special equipment:
blender

Maman Blanc never used stock for soups, in the belief that the main ingredients should provide enough flavour. This recipe is no exception to her rule. This is a lovely fresh-tasting soup and the vivid colour of the watercress is well retained.

Planning ahead This soup can be prepared well in advance.

20g unsalted butter
¼ onion, peeled and diced
2 large bunches of watercress
   (200g each), stalks
   removed[1], washed
small handful of spinach (50g),
   stalks removed, washed
375ml boiling water

4 pinches of sea salt
pinch of freshly ground
   black pepper
375g ice

To serve (optional)
4 tbsp crème fraîche or Greek
   yoghurt

To make the soup Melt the butter in a large saucepan over a low heat, add the onion and sweat gently[2] for 3–5 minutes until softened and translucent. Turn up the heat, add the watercress and spinach and wilt for 2 minutes. Add the boiling water[3], season with the salt and pepper[4], and boil for 2 minutes only. Remove from the heat and immediately add the ice to stop the cooking process[5]. Purée the soup in a blender until very smooth.

To serve Reheat if necessary[6], then taste and correct the seasoning. Serve immediately, in a warmed tureen or individual bowls topped with a spoonful of crème fraîche or Greek yoghurt.

Variations Add a crushed clove of garlic to the soup base.

   A squeeze of lemon juice would heighten the flavour, but this will need to be added at the last minute or it will discolour the watercress.

[1] Watercress varies in its intensity of flavour. If your watercress is very peppery, cut off the entire stalk, but if it is mild, retain some of the stalk.

[2] The sweating process will convert the natural starches present in the onion into sugars, enhancing the flavour of the soup.

[3] Adding boiling water speeds up the cooking of the watercress and spinach, retaining the colour, flavour and vitamins.

[4] Season early on to allow the salt to permeate the ingredients, but do so sparingly and allow for the pepperiness of the watercress. You can always add more later.

[5] The addition of ice arrests the cooking process. This helps to retain the vivid colour of the watercress, as well as its texture, taste and nutrients.

[6] Reheat the soup briefly and at the last moment to keep its freshness.

Pistou soup

Serves 4
Preparation:
30 mins
Cooking: 10 mins
Special equipment:
blender

This hearty peasant soup – combining lots of fresh vegetables in a flavoursome broth – is truly delicious. There is some dispute over its origin, with both the French and Italians claiming it as their own. The pistou of Provence (a paste of garlic and basil), the foundation of this most renowned French soup, is similar to the Italian pesto. Pistou is probably derived from the old French word *pesto*, meaning pestle, to grind *l'ail* and *le basilic!* And let's not forget that Lombardy has been a kingdom of France many times throughout history.

Planning ahead The pesto can be prepared up to a week in advance and stored in a sealed jar in the fridge, with a thin film of olive oil over the surface to keep it fresh. The soup can be prepared a few hours in advance and finished at the last moment with pistou.

For the pistou
handful of basil leaves and
   stalks (30g)
4 garlic cloves, peeled and
   crushed
100ml extra virgin olive oil
pinch of sea salt
2 pinches of freshly ground
   white pepper

For the soup
4 tbsp extra virgin olive oil
½ medium onion, peeled and
   cut into 1cm dice
1 medium carrot, peeled and
   cut into 1cm dice
½ celery stick, cut into 1cm dice
½ small fennel bulb, cut into
   1cm dice
1 small courgette, cut into 1cm
   cubes

5 pinches of sea salt
pinch of freshly ground white
   pepper
700ml boiling water
50g freshly podded peas
   (optional)
60g freshly podded broad
   beans (optional)
60g French beans (optional)
1 medium tomato (skin on),
   diced
50g pistou (see above)
40g Parmesan, for grating

To serve
20 thin croûtes, rubbed with a
   cut garlic clove (see page 136),
   or a large handful of croûtons
   (see page 74, note 2)

To make the pistou Plunge the basil into a pan of boiling water and blanch for 3 seconds only, then remove and refresh in cold water[1]; drain well. Purée all the pistou ingredients in a blender. Taste and adjust the seasoning if necessary. Keep in a sealed container in the fridge until required, unless using straight away. (You'll need 50g for the soup.)

To make the soup Heat the olive oil[2] in a large saucepan over a medium-low heat. Add the onion, carrot, celery, fennel and courgette and sweat gently for 3–4 minutes[3], seasoning with salt and pepper.

Pour the boiling water[4] into the pan, then add the peas, broad beans and French beans, if using, and boil rapidly for 3–4 minutes. During the last minute of cooking, add the tomato, 50g pistou sauce and a generous handful of grated Parmesan. Taste and correct the seasoning if necessary.

To serve Pour the soup into a warmed tureen and grate over some more of the Parmesan. Place the croûtes or croûtons, Parmesan and grater on the table so guests may help themselves.

Variation Vary the ingredients as you wish, perhaps replacing one or more of the vegetables with coco beans, spinach, Swiss chard etc.

Any pasta or pulse would also be a great addition to this soup, transforming it into a main course. You'll need more garlic, of course...

1 Blanching the basil leaves for a few seconds and dipping them in cold water to stop the cooking will fix the chlorophyll, preventing discolouration, thereby ensuring the vivid green colour is retained. You will lose some of the perfume of the basil, but as there is so much of it you will still have a wonderful flavour. (You can prepare this sauce without blanching the basil, but it will oxidise and discolour within an hour.)

2 When cooking with olive oil, I generally use a good-quality refined oil, which can withstand a higher heat than extra virgin olive oil. However, for the cooking of this soup, I use an extra virgin oil as it imparts a wonderful flavour and it will only be heated gently.

3 By sweating the vegetables you are converting the starches into sugars, greatly enhancing the flavour of the soup.

4 I use boiling water to shorten the cooking time, which preserves the vivid colours, fresh taste and textures, and retains maximum nutrients. There is plenty of flavour from the vegetables and herbs so it is fine to use water rather than stock.

Comté cheese and chard tart *Illustrated on page 167*

*

Serves 8

Preparation:
30 mins, plus
1 hour resting

Cooking: 30 mins

Special equipment:
21cm tart ring
(2.5cm high),
baking stone
(optional), peel
(optional)

This dish is a tribute to the magnificent region of France where I come from. Comté is one of the finest cheeses in the world and it can be used in so many dishes. For this one, do not buy an aged Comté as it would be too salty; a one-year-old cheese would be just perfect. The tart is very simple. You do not need to pre-bake the pastry, just scatter the chard into the raw pastry case, pour in the filling, top with the grated cheese and bake.

Planning ahead The pastry case can be prepared up to half a day in advance and kept in the fridge ready to add the filling just before baking the tart.

For the shortcrust pastry
200g plain flour
100g unsalted butter, diced,
    at room temperature
pinch of sea salt
1 organic/free-range
    medium egg
1 tbsp cold water

For the filling
30g unsalted butter
2 medium Swiss chard stalks
    (200g), cut into 2cm batons
60ml water
sea salt and freshly ground
    black pepper
2 organic/free-range
    medium eggs
100ml whole milk
100ml whipping cream
5 rasps of nutmeg (optional)
200g Comté cheese, grated

To make the pastry Put the flour, butter and salt into a large bowl and rub lightly together using your fingertips until you have a sandy texture[1]. Make a well in the centre and add the egg and water. With your fingertips, gradually work the egg and water[2] into the flour and butter mixture; then at the last moment when the eggs have been absorbed, bring the dough together and press to form a ball[3].

Turn onto a lightly floured surface and knead gently with your palms for just 10 seconds. Break off 20-30g of dough, tightly wrap in cling film and refrigerate for later (to tuck in the dough). Flatten the remaining dough into a round, 2cm thick[4], and wrap in cling film. Refrigerate for 20-30 minutes before rolling out.

To roll out the dough Place in the middle of a large sheet of cling film, about 40cm square, and cover with another sheet of cling film, of similar dimensions. Roll out the dough to a circle, 3mm thick[5].

To line the tart ring Place the tart ring on a peel or flat tray lined with greaseproof paper. Take off the top layer of cling film and discard, then lift the dough by picking up the corners of the cling film and invert it into the tart ring, removing the cling film. Ease the pastry into the ring with your fingers and then tuck the dough into the edges using the little ball of dough, ensuring it is neatly moulded into the shape of the ring. Trim the edges of the tart by rolling a rolling pin over the top of the ring. Now, push the pastry edge gently up by pressing between your index finger and thumb all around the side of the tart ring, to raise the edge 2mm above the ring[6]. With a fork, lightly prick the bottom of the pastry case[7]. Place the tart case in the fridge for 30 minutes to relax and firm up the pastry[8].

Inverting the pastry round into the ring and peeling off the cling film.

Easing the pastry round into the tart ring.

A tightly wrapped ball of dough is useful for moulding the shape.

Using the ball of dough to tuck the pastry into the corners.

Rolling a rolling pin over the top of the ring to trim the edge.

Raising the pastry rim by pushing it up all the way around.

To prepare for baking Preheat the oven to 170°C/Gas 3. Place a baking stone or baking tray on the middle shelf of the oven.

To cook the Swiss chard Melt the butter in a medium saucepan over a medium-low heat, then add the chard batons, water and some seasoning. Stir, then cover and cook gently for 10 minutes until the chard pieces are soft and melting, but holding their shape. Drain and reserve.

To assemble and bake the tart In a large bowl, mix together the eggs, milk and cream and season with salt, pepper and nutmeg, if using. Scatter the chard pieces evenly over the base of the tart case.

Slide the tart directly onto the hot baking stone or tray in the oven and gently pour in the creamy egg mixture. Sprinkle the grated cheese over the top. Bake for 30 minutes until lightly souffléd and golden brown[9]. Leave to rest and cool slightly for 10 minutes before serving.

Variation In place of the chard and Comté cheese, you could use crumbled Roquefort and celery, tomato and goat's cheese, or pumpkin and spinach, topped with a handful of grated Comté.

~~~~~~

[1] For a successful pastry you need to have even distribution of butter within the flour, to give it flakiness. This is difficult to achieve if the butter is cold, so make sure it is at room temperature. Rub in delicately with your fingertips; do not try to knead at this stage.

[2] It is for you to judge the consistency of the dough. If it is too wet add a little flour; if too dry, add a little water. Flours differ in absorbency.

[3] Although hands are gentler and will give you a better pastry, you can make the pastry in a food processor, using the pulse button for no more than 30 seconds to bring the dough together (to avoid over-mixing).

[4] Flattening the dough before resting it in the fridge is much easier to do than once it is chilled. Resting makes the dough less elastic, more pliable and easier to roll. It also minimises shrinkage in the oven.

[5] Rolling the pastry between cling film is a great little secret. It makes life much easier as you can dispense with flour, which will make your pastry heavier; your work top will be cleaner; and you overcome the problem of sticking when you roll out the dough in a warm kitchen.

[6] By pushing the edge of the tart to 2mm above the ring, you are compensating for any slight retraction of the pastry during cooking.

[7] Pricking the base of the tart case allows the steam generated during cooking to escape, helping to keep the case flat and level.

[8] Allow the pastry to rest before you cook it, to minimise any shrinkage.

[9] The safest way to check that the base of your tart is cooked is to use a spatula to gently lift the tart to check the colour – it should be golden brown.

Crudités with dips

*
Serves 6–8

Preparation:
30 mins, plus
6 hours to crisp,
plus making dips

Special equipment:
mandolin (optional)

We are fortunate to have a garden that provides countless varieties of wonderful vegetables. With a few little dips you can create a real feast from vegetables picked from your garden, market, greengrocer or supermarket shelf. Local is best and this recipe is the embodiment of that simple philosophy. It's a real celebration of summer. Vary the vegetables according to what you have to hand.

Planning ahead The dips can all be made a day in advance. You will need to prepare the vegetables 6–12 hours ahead.

For the crudités
2 medium fennel bulbs, outer
   layer removed
4 large radishes or peeled
   long turnips
1 small mouli, peeled
1 small cucumber
2 medium carrots, peeled

For the dips
a selection from the following:
guacamole (see page 170)
hummus (see page 170)
smoked aubergine caviar
   (see page 171)
aïoli (see page 68)

For the garnish (optional)
fennel fronds

To prepare the vegetables Using a very sharp mandolin with guard, or a sharp large chef's knife, slice all the vegetables lengthways into 2mm thin strips. Wash in plenty of cold water.

To crisp the vegetables Plunge the vegetable strips into a large bowl of iced water and leave in the fridge for at least 6 hours, or up to 12 hours. The vegetables will absorb water, making them curl attractively and creating delicate structures.

To serve Arrange the curled vegetable strips in a bowl, garnish with fennel and accompany with the dips in bowls. You will find it easier to scoop up the tasty dips with the firmed-up vegetables.

Guacamole

Serves 4

Preparation:
10 mins

Special equipment:
blender

This Mexican dip is a delicious way to use avocado, an excellent source of vitamins, minerals and healthy monounsaturated fat.

1 large, ripe avocado (150g)	juice of ½ lime or ¼ lemon
2 tbsp olive oil	pinch of sea salt
2 tbsp cold water	2 pinches of cayenne pepper

To make the guacamole Blanch the avocado in boiling water for 2–3 seconds, then refresh in cold water to retain the colour. Halve, stone and peel the avocado and then cut into 1cm dice. In a blender, purée all the ingredients together on the slowest speed, increasing to the fastest speed and blitzing until you have a smooth dip. Taste and correct the seasoning if necessary.

Hummus

Serves 4

Preparation: 5 mins,
plus overnight
soaking

Cooking: 1 hour

Special equipment:
food processor or
blender

At home I always have hummus in the fridge. Spread onto toast or rye bread, or eaten as a dip with vegetables and olives, it makes a nourishing snack or starter. It is better to cook dried chickpeas for this recipe, rather than use tinned ones, which do not provide the same bite or full flavour.

200g dried chickpeas, soaked in water overnight	170ml extra virgin olive oil
90g tahini paste (sesame seed paste)	120ml water
2 garlic cloves, peeled and crushed	1 tsp cumin seeds, finely crushed or ground
	juice of 1 lemon, or to taste
	salt and cayenne pepper

To cook the chickpeas Drain the soaked chickpeas, place in a medium saucepan and pour on enough fresh cold water to cover by 3cm. Bring to the boil over a medium heat, then lower the heat and barely simmer until tender, about 1 hour. The cooking time will depend on the age of the chickpeas; if they have been stored for a while, they will take considerably longer. Once cooked, drain and allow to cool.

To make the hummus Put the chickpeas, tahini paste, garlic, extra virgin olive oil, water, cumin, two-thirds of the lemon juice and a little salt and cayenne pepper into a food processor or blender and process for 2 minutes. Taste and adjust the seasoning, adding more of the lemon juice if required. The hummus should have a pleasant acidity.

Smoked aubergine caviar

Serves 4
Preparation: 5 mins
Cooking: 15 mins
Special equipment:
blender

Chargrilling aubergine gives it a wonderful, gentle smoky flavour. Blending the smoky aubergine with Middle Eastern spices and good olive oil creates a fragrant dip – for crudités or to serve simply as a salad or part of a mezze platter.

1 ripe, large aubergine (500g)
1 small garlic clove, peeled
   and crushed
50ml extra virgin olive oil

2 tsp lemon juice
pinch of sea salt
pinch of freshly ground
   black pepper

To cook the aubergine Preheat the oven to 180°C/Gas 4. Char the aubergine by holding it with a pair of tongs over a gas flame, or grill for 5–10 minutes, until the skin blisters and blackens. Transfer to the oven and cook for a further 5 minutes. Allow to cool. The steam will help to separate the skin from the flesh, making peeling easier.

To make the dip On a board, peel the cooked aubergine, slice open lengthways and spoon out the excess water and seeds. Purée the aubergine flesh and garlic in a blender, adding the extra virgin olive oil little by little, until you have a rich, smooth and silky texture. Add the lemon juice to sharpen the flavour and prevent discolouration, then taste and correct the seasoning if necessary. Keep in a covered container in the fridge until needed.

Variation Toasted and ground cumin, fennel, caraway and/or coriander seeds can be added for a spicy flavour.

DID YOU KNOW?
You can easily dry aubergines. Finely slice them lengthways into 2mm slices, lay on a baking tray and dry in a preheated oven at 100°C/Gas ¼ for 2 hours. Truly delicious.

Spinach and quail's egg ravioli

Serves 4
(2 ravioli each)

Preparation: 1 hour, plus chilling, overnight resting, sauce and garnishes

Cooking: 4 mins

Special equipment: food processor, 1 plastic cylindrical mould (4cm in diameter, 4–5cm high) – I use a plastic drainpipe, cut to the required length, pasta machine, 6cm pastry cutter

One of my long-established classics, this dish is still highly popular at Le Manoir. It is visually stunning, all the textures are right, and the tastes are sophisticated, yet rustic and comforting at the same time. It takes time to prepare, but you can simplify it by using ordinary hen's eggs in place of quail's eggs and making fewer but larger ravioli (see variation).

Planning ahead The pasta dough can be made a day in advance. The spinach mix needs to be made and moulded a day ahead to firm up. The ravioli can be shaped a few hours in advance; keep on a plate dusted with semolina to prevent sticking.

For the spinach filling
800g large leaf spinach, stalks removed and washed
1 garlic clove, peeled and crushed
6 pinches of sea salt
2 pinches of freshly ground black pepper
20g unsalted butter
50g Parmesan, finely grated

For the ravioli pasta
250g pasta flour (type OO)[1]
1 tbsp water
5g sea salt
2 organic/free-range medium eggs, plus 1 egg yolk
1 tbsp extra virgin olive oil
pinch of saffron powder[2], mixed with 1 tbsp hot water (optional)

To assemble the ravioli
8 quail's eggs
1 tbsp white wine vinegar

For the sauce
240ml brown chicken stock, reduced by a quarter (see page 135)

For the garnish
40g wilted baby spinach leaves
80g fricassée of wild mushrooms (see page 136)
20g small croûtons (see page 74, note 2)
15g hazelnuts, toasted and lightly crushed (optional)

To make the spinach filling In a large bowl, mix together the spinach, garlic, salt and pepper. Place in a large pan and stir over a high heat for 1 minute until wilted. Tip the spinach into a large colander and leave to drain and cool, stirring occasionally. Squeeze out excess water[3] with your hands then chop the spinach, but not too finely as you want to retain some texture. Place in a bowl.

Melt the butter in a small pan and cook to the beurre noisette stage[4]. Add to the spinach with the Parmesan and mix well. Taste and adjust the seasoning. Cover and chill for 1 hour.

To mould the filling Divide the spinach mixture into 40g portions. Press one portion tightly into the cylindrical mould. Then using your finger, press the centre to create a little hollow (for the poached quail's egg to sit in). Repeat to create 8 spinach moulds. Refrigerate overnight to set firmly.

To make the pasta Place all the ingredients in a food processor and mix for about 1 minute until well blended and the dough is just coming together[5]. Turn onto a lightly floured surface[6] and knead for 5 minutes until perfectly smooth. Shape into a ball, flatten and wrap in cling film. Leave to rest[7] in the fridge for 1 hour.

To roll out the pasta Fix your pasta machine to the side of a table. Cut the pasta dough in half and flatten one portion with a rolling pin to the width of the

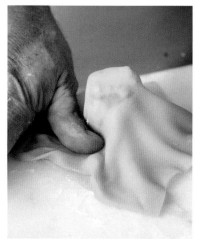
Releasing the spinach filling from the cylindrical mould.

Positioning the poached quail's egg in the created hollow.

Covering the filling with a larger pasta square.

Pressing down tightly around the ravioli to expel all air and seal.

Cutting out the ravioli using the 6cm cutter.

Removing the excess pasta from around the mould.

machine. Roll the pasta through the machine, on the thickest setting[8]. Seal the two ends together to make a conveyor belt and continue to roll the pasta, gradually narrowing the setting until the pasta reaches the thinnest setting for ravioli on your machine. Repeat with the other piece.

Cut eight 6cm pasta squares for the ravioli bases and eight 8cm squares for the tops. Layer them on a tray, separated by cling film. Reserve in the fridge.

To poach the quail's eggs Bring a shallow pan of water to the boil with the vinegar added. Lower to a simmer and poach the quail's eggs for 30 seconds. Remove with a slotted spoon and refresh in iced water; drain thoroughly.

To assemble the ravioli Lay the smaller pasta squares (for the bases) on non-stick baking paper to prevent them sticking. Nestle a poached quail's egg into the well in a spinach mould and place in the middle of a small pasta square. Drape a larger pasta square over the filling. With your thumb, tightly press down around the ravioli, to seal and expel all air. Using the 6cm pastry cutter, cut out the ravioli. Repeat to make 8 ravioli in total; leave on the paper until ready to cook.

To serve Bring a large pan of water to the boil and cook the ravioli for 4 minutes exactly[9]. Meanwhile, gently reheat the sauce and dress warmed plates with the wilted spinach, mushroom fricassée and croûtons. Drain the ravioli and place two on each plate. Sprinkle with the toasted nuts, if using. Serve with the sauce.

Variation Poach hen's eggs in place of quail's eggs and make 4 large raviolis, using 80g spinach mixture for each. These ravioli will take 5 minutes to cook.

1 For pasta you need a high gluten flour to give the dough elasticity. Durum wheat flour is by far the best, lending a wonderful texture to your pasta.

2 This tiny amount of powdered saffron lends a slightly richer colour without affecting the natural taste of the pasta.

3 If the spinach mixture is too wet, the ravioli will have a watery flavour and texture. If it is too dry, it will be fibrous.

4 The butter will start to foam at approximately 130°C, turning hazelnut colour at 150–155°C; i.e. the required beurre noisette stage.

5 All flours have different absorbency, so you will need to judge if your pasta is too wet and needs a bit more flour, or if it is too dry and needs a little extra water.

6 Use the minimum of flour when kneading the pasta, as it will be absorbed into the dough, making it drier and harder to work with.

7 The pasta needs to be rested, otherwise it is liable to shrink during cooking.

8 Don't stretch the pasta as you mould the ravioli, otherwise it will become too thin and is liable to tear. If this happens the ravioli will fill with water on cooking.

9 At a rolling boil, 4 minutes will cook the pasta perfectly, heat the spinach mixture and keep the egg to a soft poach with a runny yolk.

Tomatoes

Get to know your tomatoes. There are literally hundreds of varieties and you might have fun taste-testing a few, because in centuries past this fruit had aphrodisiac status! The French called it *pomme d'amour* (apple of love), while Italians still call it *pomodoro* (golden apple). But in this country, the tomato was believed to be poisonous until the turn of the eighteenth century. Today, however, Britain has one of the finest collection of tomatoes. The older 'heritage' varieties have enchanting names like Black Russian, Green Sausage and Sunblush.

Most of the tomatoes we eat are no longer grown outdoors or in soil, but hydroponically in heated greenhouses and fed on chemical nutrients. Is our love affair with the tomato being eroded? Should we grow our own in order to achieve the 'real' tomato experience? To me, it is impossible to imagine cooking without tomatoes. Not only are they incredibly versatile, they are also highly nutritious and contain the important antioxidant, lycopene.

At Le Manoir we are constantly conducting tasting trials, to establish which varieties are best suited to particular culinary purposes. Here are a few tips about choosing and cooking with tomatoes...

In common with other fruits, tomatoes will never reach their maximum flavour potential if they are picked before they have had time to fully ripen, so always buy 'vine-ripened' tomatoes and avoid keeping them in the fridge – their flavour doesn't benefit from the chill.

For sauces, the Roma plum tomato family and San Marzano are the best, because they are very fleshy, with relatively little juice and therefore low acidity. As long as they are ripe, they will cook down quickly and are perfect for a sauce. If possible, use an old-fashioned mouli rather than a blender to purée sauces – it gives a better texture. If the tomatoes are very ripe, don't purée them at all – just add garlic, a couple of basil leaves and olive oil.

When I was a child, my mother would send me out into the garden to pick Marmande whenever she wanted large tomatoes to bake and I still believe this is the best variety for baking. Try not to use a fan-assisted oven, as the forced, intense heat may split the skins.

For salads, I use Marmande, Coeur de Boeuf or Black Russian. The salad in this chapter is a lovely, simple celebration of the tomato, inspired by my mother. Make it an hour or so ahead and experience the exquisite jus created, which was the catalyst for my essence of tomato.

As for my tomato essence, cherry tomatoes that are sweet and juicy (and therefore high in acidity) are the ones to go for. At Le Manoir, I use a French variety grown from the Juno seed. Of the more widely available varieties, Santini and Piccolo are particularly good.

Tomato salad 'Maman Blanc'

Serves 4–6
Preparation:
15 mins,
plus 1 hour
marinating

Take advantage of good-quality produce and let it speak for itself. One of my most vivid childhood food memories is the wonderful smell and sight of huge, misshapen tomatoes lined up on the kitchen windowsill. Another is savouring the juices they formed as they marinated for this salad. We would fight over who would be first to dip their crusty bread into them. This recipe is one of the simplest to prepare, but you do need to use the right tomatoes.

800g tomatoes[1] (Coeur de Boeuf or Marmande), de-stemmed and cored
1 banana shallot, peeled and finely sliced
4 pinches of sea salt

1 tbsp Dijon mustard
2 tbsp warm water
4 tbsp extra-virgin olive oil
pinch of sea salt
2 pinches of freshly ground black pepper

For the dressing
½ garlic clove, peeled and crushed
1 tbsp white wine vinegar

For the garnish
6 basil and/or 6 flat-leaf parsley sprigs, leaves picked and torn or roughly chopped

To make the tomato salad Cut the tomatoes across into slices, about 5mm thick. Arrange them in a shallow oval serving dish, scatter over the sliced shallots and season with the salt. Set aside.

To make the dressing In a large bowl, mix together the garlic, wine vinegar, Dijon mustard and 1 tbsp warm water. Add the oil slowly, whisking constantly, then whisk in the remaining water to emulsify and thin the dressing[2]. Season with salt and pepper.

To assemble Spoon the dressing over the tomatoes and leave to marinate for about an hour[3] at room temperature. Scatter over the herbs to serve.

Variation Make double the quantity of dressing and use half of it to dress a small head of hearty lettuce, such as Little Gem, Batavia, Romaine or Escarole, to serve alongside the tomatoes.

[1] The success of this salad will depend on the ripeness and quality of the tomatoes.
[2] Alternatively you can make the dressing by shaking all the ingredients together to combine in a small jar with the lid on.
[3] A little miracle occurs during this hour. The salt will season and also lightly cure the tomatoes, creating a pool of wonderful jus at the bottom of the dish; this jus was the catalyst for my tomato essence recipe (see page 180).

Tomato essence

*

Serves 4
(makes 700–800ml)

Preparation:
10 mins, plus
3 hours macerating
and 2–3 hours
straining

Special equipment:
muslin cloth, food
processor

This dish has become one of the great classics at Le Manoir. It is simple in execution, yet delivers the best tomato experience you can ever imagine. The inspiration was Maman Blanc's tomato salad; the juices formed as the tomatoes marinate is one of the great tastes of my life and I always wanted to recreate it. Many attempts failed, but I finally achieved the result I was looking for. It is so simple, you *must* try it at home! The essence forms the base for several dishes – it can be served as a lovely cold soup, frozen for a granita, or turned into a sorbet or fragrant jelly. It also makes a superb risotto (see page 183).

Planning ahead The tomatoes ideally need to be macerated a day in advance and hung overnight to extract the essence.

2.3kg ripe cherry tomatoes, washed[1]

½ celery stick, washed and finely chopped[2]

1 small shallot, peeled and finely chopped

½ medium fennel bulb, finely chopped

1 garlic clove, peeled and finely sliced

2 thyme sprigs, leaves stripped and chopped

5g basil leaves, chopped

1 tarragon leaf

10g sea salt

10g caster sugar (optional)[3]

pinch of cayenne pepper

4 drops of Tabasco

4 drops of Worcestershire sauce

To make the tomato essence Combine all the ingredients in a large bowl and mix well. Now you will need to blitz the mixture in three batches (as a domestic food processor can only process 600–800g at a time). Blitz each batch using the pulse button for 2 seconds[4]. Return to the bowl, cover and leave to macerate at room temperature for 3 hours[5].

Spread a large double layer of muslin over a medium bowl (about 25cm) and fill with the chopped, macerated tomatoes. Tie up the muslin bag and suspend it above the bowl, which will collect the golden liquid as it drips through[6]. This will take 2–3 hours. Use the tomato essence as required. The pulp left in the bag can be used in other ways, in soups, sauces etc.

---

[1] To make a great tomato essence, you need to source the very best tomatoes. We use cherry tomatoes because they are sweeter. Ours come from France and are very juicy fruit, with a ratio of juice to flesh of about 50/50. A larger amount of juice will create more acidity, more volume and a better balance of flavour. All great tastes are mostly based on contradictions – sweet/acid etc.

2 Celery has a strong flavour. If you use more than suggested, you could unbalance the flavour of the essence.

3 Always taste your tomatoes before using them. At the start of the season they will need a little sugar to balance out the acidity, but as the season progresses and they have more exposure to the sun, their natural sugars will increase and you can omit the sugar.

4 Over-blitzing the tomatoes to a purée will break down the tomato skin and give a completely different, coarser flavour. It will also extract the red pigment, so the essence will be red, whilst we are looking to achieve a pale golden colour, which is the heart of the tomato.

5 The maceration is hugely important to enable all the flavours to mingle and fuse; 3 hours is the perfect amount of time.

6 The volume of the juices or essence will be proportional to the weight of the hanging crushed tomatoes. The heavier the hanging weight, the more juice you will produce. At Le Manoir, we can do up to 20kg per bag, but then we do use bed sheets to hang our essence! These hang for 24 hours to extract every drop; a small quantity will only need 2–3 hours.

Tomato risotto, summer vegetables

* *

Serves 4

Preparation:
40 mins, plus
making tomato
essence

Cooking: 30 mins

Special equipment:
muslin cloth

I was very happy when I first created this dish at Brasserie Blanc, as the guests immediately loved it. The tomato essence is the secret here – it gives the risotto both sweetness and fragrance. And, of course, there is that element of surprise; the risotto is gloriously white with an intense tomato flavour. Each pearly rice grain can be separated from the creamy unctuous risotto.

Planning ahead The tomato essence ideally needs to be made a day in advance and hung overnight.

For the risotto base
2 tbsp extra virgin olive oil
¼ white onion, peeled and
   finely chopped
½ garlic clove, peeled and
   crushed
200g carnaroli rice[1]
300ml hot water
4 pinches of sea salt
2 pinches of freshly ground
   white pepper
300g–400ml tomato essence
   (see page 180)

To finish the risotto
½ small fennel bulb, finely
   chopped
1 small courgette, cut into
   1cm dice
1 small carrot, peeled, cut into
   1cm dice and blanched for
   1 minute
100g freshly podded young
   peas (or frozen and defrosted)
20g Parmesan, finely grated
2 tbsp mascarpone
10 cherry tomatoes, halved
4 black olives (kalamata), cut
   into thirds (optional)

To garnish
2 tbsp mascarpone (optional)
baby salad leaves (optional)
coarsely ground black pepper

To cook the risotto Heat the extra virgin olive oil in a medium saucepan over a low heat and sweat the onion and garlic for about 2 minutes until soft. Stir in the rice and cook over a medium heat for 2 minutes until the grains appear shiny[2]. Stir in all of the water[3], bring to a gentle simmer and season with the salt and pepper. Cover and cook gently until all the water has been absorbed.

Now add three-quarters of the tomato essence[4]. Continue to barely simmer, covered, with one 'single' bubble breaking the surface, until the essence has been absorbed. There is no need to stir the risotto constantly.

To finish the risotto Now we need to impart creaminess and all the great risotto qualities to the dish. Add the remaining tomato essence, all of the vegetables, the

Parmesan and mascarpone. Cook the risotto, briskly stirring, for 5 minutes until the rice is *al dente*[5]. The vigorous stirring of the rice will help it cook evenly, extract the starch and lend the risotto a beautifully creamy consistency[6], whilst the vegetables cook to a perfect tender crunch. Add the cherry tomatoes and olives, if using. Taste and adjust the seasoning if necessary.

Divide the risotto among warmed plates and garnish with a spoonful of mascarpone and some baby salad leaves if you like. Finish with a sprinkling of coarsely ground black pepper.

Variation Any summer vegetables can be added or substituted to vary the textures and flavours. Tender broad beans, young pea shoots and baby spinach leaves are particularly good.

---

[1] I have chosen to use carnaroli rice, as it not only gives a good texture, it also has the best flavour of the risotto rices.

[2] This initial cooking stage is important as it ensures each grain of rice will be coated in a tiny amount of oil, preventing them from sticking together. It will also soften the rice a little.

[3] I have simplified the traditional risotto method, which calls for gradual addition of the liquid and constant stirring during cooking.

[4] We add the tomato essence last, to retain as much of its freshness as possible.

[5] Over-cooking the risotto takes only a minute or even less; you want your rice to be *al dente* – cooked but firm to the bite. The texture is as important as the flavour. It should have a little bit of bite left in the grain, so taste as you go and remember practice makes perfect.

[6] You will notice that we have not stirred our risotto until now. I developed this technique to spare you (and my chefs) the effort, and to get excellent results. At this stage, the grains will be fluffy but not starchy, and will still be slightly uncooked. If you break a grain of rice, it will be translucent on the outside but have an opaque core of uncooked starch. So it needs a brisk stirring over heat to extract the starch and turn into a risotto with a characteristic creamy texture.

Summer cherry tomato tart scented with basil *Illustrated overleaf*

Serves 2

Preparation:
20 mins, plus
30 minutes resting

Cooking: 15 mins

Special equipment:
peel (optional),
baking stone
(optional)

These are the perfect, easy individual tarts to make when tomatoes are at their peak. The ripeness and quality of the tomatoes are very important, so buy the best you can find. Similarly, good-quality puff pastry is a must. You can vary the topping as you like, perhaps adding your favourite pizza flavourings – anchovies, capers, roasted peppers etc.

Planning ahead The puff pastry rounds can be shaped in advance, placed on a baking sheet, covered and frozen or refrigerated.

For the tart bases
125g all-butter puff pastry[1]

For the filling
½ medium onion, peeled and finely chopped
3 tbsp extra virgin olive oil, plus extra for brushing
½ tsp thyme leaves
2 pinches of sea salt
pinch of freshly ground black pepper

about 30 cherry tomatoes[2], halved
6 baby mozzarella balls, thinly sliced
8 black olives, stoned and cut into thirds
8 basil leaves, roughly torn

To serve (optional)
pistou (see page 161)

To prepare the tart bases Cut the puff pastry into two equal portions and shape into balls. Roll each one out on a lightly floured surface to an 18–20cm round, 2mm thick[3]. Place the pastry rounds on a lightly floured tray and freeze for 5 minutes[4].

Transfer the pastry rounds to a peel or flat tray lined with greaseproof paper. Trim to neat 16cm discs, using a sharp knife and a plate as a guide. Run the tip of a knife around the edge of the pastry about 1cm in from the edge, making a shallow indent, to create a border. Place in the fridge and leave to rest for 30 minutes while you prepare the filling.

To prepare the onion In a small pan over a low heat, soften the onion in the extra virgin olive oil with the thyme leaves, salt and pepper for about 8 minutes; do not allow the onion to colour. Taste and adjust the seasoning if necessary, then set aside to cool.

To prepare for baking Preheat the oven to 230°C/Gas 8. Place a baking stone or baking tray on the middle shelf to heat up.

To assemble the tarts Take the puff pastry rounds out of the fridge. Spread with the onion mixture, within the border, and top with the tomato halves, packing them tightly together and overlapping them slightly[5]. Brush the tomatoes and the edges of the puff pastry with extra virgin olive oil and season with salt and pepper.

To bake the tomato tarts Carefully slide the tomato-topped puff pastry rounds onto the preheated baking stone or tray in the oven[6] and bake for 12 minutes.

Remove the tarts from the oven and distribute the sliced mozzarella and olives over the tomatoes. Bake for a further 2 minutes to melt the mozzarella, then remove and set aside to rest for 5 minutes.

To finish and serve Garnish the tomato tarts with torn basil and drizzle with a little extra virgin olive oil. Spoon over a little of the pistou, if serving, and hand the rest around separately.

[1] You can now buy 'all-butter' puff pastry. Avoid pastry made with margarine or hydrogenated vegetable fats, which contain unhealthy trans fats. You can prepare many discs of pastry and freeze them ready to pull out and use as required. One standard block will make two tarts.

[2] I find that cherry tomatoes are best for this tart, though the large Roma variety works very well too.

[3] Ensure that the pastry is no thicker than 2mm, or it may be undercooked and soggy.

[4] When you roll puff pastry thinly, it will become warm, elastic and more difficult to handle. Resting it in the fridge or freezer allows it to relax, cool down and firm up; it will then be very easy to cut.

[5] Ensure that the tomatoes and onion mixture are arranged within the border of the puff pastry, otherwise the sides will not rise up to encase the tomatoes and their wonderful juices.

[6] The hot baking stone or tray provides a direct heat which will seal and cook the base of the tart.

Tomato theme

Serves 4

Preparation:
2 hours, plus 2 days
straining/chilling/
freezing

Special equipment:
blender, 4 little jelly
moulds, ice-cream
machine, 4 shot
glasses

This is a celebration on one theme – the essence of tomato. Here I am serving it in four different ways – each has a different shape, texture and temperature. Each of the components can be served as a dish in its own right. Together, they deliver the ultimate tomato experience.

Planning ahead Two days ahead, make a double quantity of tomato essence if you're preparing all of the elements of this dish. Make the jelly a day in advance to allow it time to set. The granita should be frozen overnight. The sorbet can be prepared half a day ahead and churned an hour before serving. Chill 4 plates and 4 frosted sake glasses in the freezer an hour before the meal.

For the jelly
¾ sheet leaf gelatine (27x7cm)
100ml tomato essence
    (see page 180)
4 slivers of black olive
4 baby basil leaves
1 cherry tomato, quartered
20g tomato pips[1]

For the granita
200ml tomato essence
    (see page 180)
1 medium tomato, cut into
    4 petals, pips removed
    (reserve for the jelly),
    skinned

For the sorbet
400ml tomato essence
    (see page 180)
40g caster sugar
4 large basil leaves

For the essence cup
320ml tomato essence
    (see page 180)
12 baby basil leaves

For the cherry tomato garnish
4 cherry tomatoes, blanched
    for 10 seconds, refreshed
    and peeled
extra virgin olive oil, for
    brushing
4 sea salt flakes
pinch of crushed pepper

To make the jelly Soak the gelatine leaf in a shallow dish of cold water to soften for 5 minutes or so. In a small saucepan, heat a third of the tomato essence almost to a simmer and take of the heat. Drain the gelatine, squeeze out excess water, then add to the hot essence and stir until dissolved[2]. Stir this back into the remaining cold tomato essence.

Pour the liquid into 4 little moulds or ice cube trays to three-quarters fill them. Chill for about 5 minutes until the jelly starts to thicken slightly. Now add the garnish: olive slivers, basil leaves, tomato quarters and pips. Refrigerate to set.

To make the granita Pour the tomato essence into a suitable shallow container, seal and freeze overnight.

To make the sorbet Pour a quarter of the tomato essence into a small saucepan, add the sugar and dissolve over a low heat. Leave to cool and then add back to the remaining cold tomato essence. Transfer to an ice-cream machine and churn until the sorbet is just firm. Using 2 dessertspoons dipped in hot water, shape the tomato sorbet into quenelles and place on a well-chilled tray. Keep in the freezer until you are ready to serve[3]. Just before serving, blanch the basil leaves in boiling water for 2 seconds[4], refresh in cold water, drain and pat dry.

To serve Chill 4 serving plates (ideally rectangular) and 4 frosted shot glasses. De-mould the essence jelly and delicately arrange one on each chilled plate. Next to the jelly, place a quenelle of sorbet on a blanched basil leaf for support, so it doesn't slide. For the essence cups, pour the tomato essence into the frosted shot glasses and float the baby basil leaves on top. Scrape a spoon through the frozen granita to make beautiful large frozen flakes and place them gently on a tomato petal, again for support. Lightly brush each cherry tomato with extra virgin olive oil, season with a flake of salt and 2 or 3 grains of crushed pepper, then skewer on a cocktail stick and place on the plate. Serve immediately.

[1] The seeds of the tomatoes clump together in the centre of the fruit. Halve the tomatoes and extract the seeds with a teaspoon, keeping them in clumps.

[2] By heating only a small amount of essence to dissolve the gelatine, you will not lose the savour of the fresh essence.

[3] A savoury sorbet will never be quite as smooth as a sweet one because of the smaller quantity of sugar used. Once churned, this sorbet must be served within 2–3 hours as, due to its low sugar content, it will soon crystallise and harden.

[4] Blanching the basil leaves fixes the chlorophyll, so the vivid colour is retained.

DID YOU KNOW?
You don't have to serve all the elements of this dish; mix and match components as you like. Alternatively, serve singly as a canapé, or increase the quantity for a simple starter.

Spices & Chillies

This country has a well-integrated multicultural society and I am fortunate to have lived and worked here. We embrace tastes and textures from around the globe and this has influenced and enriched my style of food without undermining its Frenchness.

My travels have also played an important role in the food at Le Manoir. The exquisite dishes I have enjoyed in Japan, Malaysia, Thailand, Singapore and other far-flung destinations have inspired my cooking. At Le Manoir, we even have a Southeast Asian garden, where we grow aromatics, such as lemongrass, coriander and chillies.

Spices lend character to a host of dishes and, of course, every cuisine has its favourites. To intensify their flavour, toast spices in a dry frying pan over a gentle heat (at about 110°C) for 10 minutes to activate and release the natural oils. As they toast, the spices begin to release their fragrance. Avoid using a high heat or toasting for longer, as the spices are liable to burn. If they do so, they will impart an acrid and bitter taste to your finished dish.

To grind spices, you will need a good, large pestle and mortar with a rough inner surface. Besides being key to a lot of recipes, it is a beautiful object to have in your kitchen.

Chillies add heat and flavour to a host of dishes, but this is one ingredient you do need to get to know. Here at Le Manoir we have sampled over 40 varieties of chilli and have found that there is a vast difference in their heat and flavour. Generally, the smaller the chilli the hotter it will be. Little Thai Bird's Eye chillies, for example, are very fiery.

A good all-round red chilli is the Mexican Rio Grande (or 'snap nose'). Medium in length (7–8cm), it has a moderate heat and a subtle flavour, suited to our Western palates. Even moderate varieties of chilli need to be handled carefully as all chillies will irritate – rubbing your eyes while chopping chillies would be a big mistake! Always wash your hands with warm water and soap after preparing chillies.

Other exotic aromatics that feature in my dishes include lemongrass, galangal and kaffir limes. After numerous trials, we have found a variety of lemongrass that will grow in our herb garden and I use it to gently perfume many of my classic dishes.

Galangal, also known as Thai ginger, is bitter, but more subtly flavoured than the ginger we are familiar with. It is an important ingredient in Thai green curry paste, lending a sweet, herby, aromatic element to balance a typical salty, hot, acidic Thai curry.

Kaffir limes are very different from the limes we normally use. The tiny amount of juice they contain is intensely sour, but their zest is wonderfully fragrant and an excellent flavouring to use in exotic dishes.

Green papaya and pomegranate salad, chilli and lime dressing *Illustrated overleaf*

*

Serves 4
Preparation:
20 mins

This salad is inspired by my travels to the Far East, where I have enjoyed light, healthy, oil-free salads, such as this one from Thailand. It has the perfect balance of sweet, salty, sharp and herby tastes – and contrasting textures – making it one of my favourite simple dishes. As a bonus, the papaya is a nutrient powerhouse, making it the perfect raw food.

For the dressing
1 red chilli (ideally Rio Grande[1]), deseeded and finely chopped
2 garlic cloves, peeled and finely chopped
juice of 2 limes, or to taste
2 tbsp fish sauce, or to taste
2 tsp grated palm sugar[2], or to taste

For the salad
150g unripe green papaya[3]
⅓ cucumber (150g)
3 spring onions, finely sliced on the diagonal
handful of coriander, roughly chopped
handful of mint, spearmint or Vietnamese mint, roughly chopped, plus extra leaves to garnish
40g pomegranate seeds, pith removed (optional)[4]
60g unsalted peanuts, toasted in a dry pan[5] and roughly chopped

For the dressing In a small bowl, mix all the ingredients together until evenly combined; set aside[6].

To make the salad Halve and peel the papaya, then slice the flesh into fine 2mm strips and place in a large bowl. Halve the cucumber lengthways, scoop out the seeds and slice the flesh into fine strips. Add the cucumber to the papaya with the spring onions and chopped herbs. Scatter over half of the pomegranate seeds, if using, and two-thirds of the peanuts.

Toss the ingredients together with 3 tbsp of the dressing, then taste and add more of the dressing if required (or a little more lime juice, fish sauce and/or palm sugar to adjust the flavours). You are looking for an even balance of salty, sweet, acid and spicy.

To serve Pile the salad into a bowl, garnish with the reserved pomegranate seeds and toasted peanuts and finish with a few mint leaves.

Variations If you cannot find unripe papaya, you can substitute an unripe green mango, or any crunchy vegetable that can be cut into fine strips, such as carrot, celeriac, courgette or peppers, or you can use apple or firm pear.

For a more substantial, main course salad, add some quick stir-fried finely sliced chicken, duck, dried shrimps or grilled tiger prawns.

1. It is up to you how hot you make this dish. A Rio Grande chilli provides the dressing with a good chilli flavour and mild heat, but use whichever variety you prefer. Remember to wash your hands immediately after preparing chillies to avoid skin irritation and avoid touching your eyes until you have done so, or they will sting painfully.
2. Palm sugar can be found in the ethnic/oriental cooking section of most major supermarkets. It is commonly produced from the sap of date palm trees, but can also be made from the sap of the coconut tree. It tastes rather like light brown sugar, but with more rounded caramel and butterscotch notes.
3. Green papayas can be found at most Asian supermarkets.
4. You can make this salad without the pomegranate, but it lends a lovely crunchy texture and a vibrant contrasting colour.
5. Toasting the peanuts will release their natural oils, intensifying the flavour.
6. If you make the dressing too far in advance it will develop in intensity (rather like a tea bag) and overpower the flavours of the salad. If possible, make it just before assembling the salad.

DID YOU KNOW?
The hottest part of the chilli is not the flesh or the seeds, as it is generally thought to be. It is in fact the membrane holding the seeds together, so be careful to remove this.

Vegetable curry

*

Serves 4
Preparation:
20 mins
Cooking: 25 mins

My young development chef Kush cooked this superb curry for me. This is his adaptation of the spicing that his family has used for over 70 years. Spices are a wonderful catalyst of flavours and you will hardly need any salt in order to enjoy this curry.

Planning ahead This dish can be prepared a day in advance and simply reheated to serve. The spice blend can be made up to 2 days ahead, but for optimum flavour, prepare it on the day you make the curry.

For the masala (spice blend)[1]
5 cardamom pods
2 tsp coriander seeds
1 tsp cumin seeds
1cm piece cinnamon stick
12 black peppercorns
½ tsp fennel seeds
3 cloves

For the curry
40ml extra virgin rapeseed oil
10g fresh root ginger, peeled and finely chopped
1 garlic clove, peeled and finely chopped
1 large red chilli (such as Rio Grande), deseeded and finely chopped
1 medium onion, peeled and cut into 1cm dice
2 bay leaves

2 pinches of sea salt
1 medium courgette (150g), cut into 2cm dice
1 small aubergine (200g), cut into 2cm dice
200g cauliflower, cut into small 2–3cm florets
150g button mushrooms, halved
440ml tin coconut milk[2], warmed
100ml hot water
3 large plum tomatoes (200g), deseeded and cut into 2cm dice
small handful of curry or lime leaves (optional)
30g coriander leaves, chopped, plus extra leaves to garnish
juice of ½ lime

To prepare the masala (spice blend) In a small frying pan over a low heat, gently toast all the spices for 10 minutes until fragrant[3]. Tip the toasted spices into the pestle and mortar and grind to a fine powder[4]. Set aside.

To make the curry Heat the rapeseed oil[5] in a large saucepan over a medium-low heat. Add the chopped ginger, garlic and chilli and sweat gently for 2 minutes. Now add the onion, ground toasted spices, bay leaves and salt and continue to cook gently for 5 minutes.

Increase the heat to medium high, add the remaining vegetables (but not the tomato) and simmer gently, covered, for 5 minutes, stirring from time to time.

Add the warmed coconut milk and hot water, bring to a gentle simmer and cook for 6 minutes, stirring occasionally. Stir in the chopped tomatoes, with the curry or lime leaves if using, and cook for a further 5 minutes.

Finally, add the chopped coriander and lime juice[6], then taste and adjust the seasoning. Scatter over a few whole coriander leaves to garnish.

To serve Simply place the pan in the middle of the table so everyone can help themselves. Accompany with a bowl of steamed basmati rice and some warm naan bread. Spiced chickpeas or lentils would be an excellent side dish.

Variations Feel free to modify this traditional masala mix, by including other favourite spices, such as turmeric, saffron, star anise etc.

Vary the vegetables as you like – peppers, carrots, potatoes, sweet potatoes and okra all work well.

[1] Traditionally in India, the base for all curries would be a 'masala' or spice blend, ground from toasted whole spices. If the spices are whole, more of the freshness and aroma is retained and you are able to extract more flavour from the natural oils, which are not present in pre-ground spices.

[2] Coconut milk gives the curry a rich unctuous feel and lends a slight sweetness. The tinned coconut milk that we are familiar with in the West is not, as some assume, the juice from a fresh coconut, but rather the pulped and squeezed flesh of mature coconuts. Brands vary in consistency. This recipe calls for a relatively thick milk that is 'let down' by the added water and the juices from the vegetables during cooking.

[3] The spices must be toasted slowly over a low heat to extract as much of the natural oils as possible.

[4] Of course you can grind spices in a small spice grinder or coffee grinder, but I have found that the pestle and mortar is the best tool to use. Choose a heavy, deep mortar with a rough surface for best results.

[5] Traditionally this dish would be cooked in ghee, a form of clarified butter. However, it is very high in saturated fats and I prefer to use an unrefined extra virgin rapeseed oil. It may not be authentic, but I find that its subtle nutty characteristic lends itself well to the toasted spice flavour of the curry.

[6] Adding the fresh coriander and lime juice right at the end keeps their vibrant aromatic flavours, lifting the curry and cutting the richness of the coconut milk.

Slow-cooked marinated pork belly

Serves 4–6

Preparation:
30 mins, plus
2–12 hours
marinating

Cooking: 3 hours;
5½ hours if using
a sous-vide

Special equipment:
sous-vide (optional)

Fortunately we are now celebrating excellent rare pork breeds in this country, such as Tamworth, Middle White and Berkshire. A short time ago I presented the prestigious Derek Cooper Food and Farming Award to Richard Lutwyche, a gentleman who has devoted his life to rare breeds. So please try to source one for this recipe.

Pork belly lends itself beautifully to slow cooking. At Le Manoir, we marinate the pork in the spice combination below before cooking by sous-vide, but I have given a traditional slow-cooking option here too. Of course, you may wish to vary the spices.

Planning ahead The pork belly can be marinated and cooked a day in advance, ready to caramelise prior to serving.

1kg oven-ready pork belly, ribs
   removed

For marinating the pork
4g sea salt
1 lemongrass stalk, bruised[1]
   and halved lengthways
2 pinches of freshly ground
   white pepper
3 pinches of Chinese five-spice
   powder
15g new season's garlic, crushed
10g fresh root ginger, peeled
   and chopped
2 red chillies, deseeded and
   finely chopped

For cooking the pork
400ml cold water (or 200ml
   if using a sous-vide)
sea salt and freshly ground
   black pepper
dash of soy sauce (optional)
a little toasted sesame oil
   (optional)

For caramelising the pork
2 tbsp rapeseed oil

For the cabbage
350g pointed spring cabbage
20g unsalted butter
50ml water
pinch of sea salt
pinch of freshly ground
   black pepper

To marinate the pork Mix the marinade ingredients together and rub into the flesh side of the pork belly. Cover with cling film and set aside to marinate for at least 2 hours, or up to 12 hours in the fridge.

To cook the pork Preheat the oven to 150°C/Gas 2. Place the pork belly, skin side up, in a large flameproof roasting pot with a lid and spoon over the marinade. Add 200ml cold water and bring just to the boil over a medium-high heat[2]. Put the lid on and cook in the oven for 2½ hours or until tender. To check that it is cooked, push the blunt handle of a tablespoon through the belly; the meat should yield easily. Allow to cool.

Alternatively, if using a sous-vide, preheat the water bath to 85°C. Simply vacuum pack the pork belly with the marinade (no additional water is needed) and cook in the water bath for 5 hours. Remove from the water bath and allow to cool, then take out of the sous-vide bag.

Once cooled, place the pork belly between two baking trays, place a weight on top and refrigerate[3]. Strain and reserve the cooking juices.

To finish the cooking juices Add 200ml water[4] to the cooking juices. Bring the liquor to the boil, then taste and adjust the seasoning with salt and pepper. You can also add a little soy sauce and toasted sesame oil if you wish.

To caramelise the pork Preheat the oven to 180°C/Gas 4. Cut the pork belly into portions. Heat the rapeseed oil in an ovenproof frying pan over a medium heat and add the pork belly, skin side down. Crisp gently for 10–15 minutes, then turn the pork over and finish cooking in the oven for 10 minutes.

To cook the cabbage While the pork is caramelising, slice the cabbage into 5mm strips, rinse and place in a large saucepan with the butter, water and seasoning. Cover and cook over a medium heat for 5–7 minutes until tender. Drain off any excess liquor.

To serve Put the cabbage into a warmed large bowl or the roasting pot, place the pork belly on top and pour over a ladleful of the cooking juices.

───────────────────────────

[1] Bruising the lemongrass helps to release the natural oils. Simply bash firmly with a rolling pin to do so.

[2] When you are cooking in a low oven, it is important to bring the cooking liquor to the boil before the dish goes into the oven, otherwise it will take a long time to come up to temperature. With your oven set at 150°C, the pork will reach a temperature of around 84°C–87°C in the middle. This is sufficient to break down the collagen and fibrous tissues, making the pork beautifully tender, unctuous and juicy.

[3] Pressing the pork belly flattens it, which helps to achieve an even result when you caramelise the skin.

[4] The aromatics and pork will have created a very concentrated, strong jus. Adding water will thin it down and make it wonderfully palatable.

Sticky rice in coconut milk with mango

*

Serves 4
Preparation:
15 mins, plus
overnight soaking
Cooking: 20 mins

White and black glutinous rice are specific to Southeast Asia; their characteristic sticky texture is due to their high starch content. Here coconut milk adds flavour and creaminess, and mango is a natural partner. This dessert can be eaten hot or cold, but if serving cold, you may need to add a bit more coconut milk.

Planning ahead The rice is soaked overnight and improved by steaming the day before; reheat to serve. Prepare the mangoes an hour or so ahead; keep chilled.

For the sticky rice[1]
80g white glutinous
   (sticky) rice[1]
80g black glutinous
   (sticky) rice[2]
120ml tinned coconut milk
1 lemongrass stalk, bruised
25g sugar

To finish the rice
50g palm sugar, grated
juice of 1 lime

For the garnish
2 ripe mangoes
   (ideally Alfonso)
squeeze of lime juice

To soak the rice Put the black and white rice into separate bowls, pour 500ml water over each and leave to soak overnight[3].

To cook the glutinous rice The following day, put the black rice into a steamer over rapidly boiling water, cover and steam for 10 minutes. Add the white rice and steam for a further 15 minutes. Taste the rice – it should be sticky and slightly chewy; if it is not quite cooked, steam for a little longer. Meanwhile, simmer the coconut milk with the lemongrass for 2 minutes to infuse. Tip the cooked rice into a pan, strain in the coconut milk, add the sugar and stir to combine; set aside.

To prepare the mangoes Cut the mangoes lengthways in two, either side of the stone, then score the flesh in a criss-cross pattern, being careful not to cut through the skin. Turn inside out to create a 'mango hedgehog'. (Alternatively, you can simply peel and slice the mango.) Squeeze over a little lime juice[4].

To serve Stir the grated palm sugar and lime juice through the rice. Spoon into individual bowls and place the mango on the side.

[1] Glutinous white rice has been polished and the husk removed, making it stickier, as the starch is more easily released when cooked.
[2] Sweet and nutty, glutinous black rice or 'Indonesian black rice' is the whole grain.
[3] Pre-soaking the rice helps it to keep moist during steaming.
[4] Squeezing lime juice onto the mango flesh gives the flavour a little lift and helps to balance the richness of the coconut milk; it also deters discolouration.

Exotic fruit 'ravioli'

* * *

Serves 10

Preparation:
2 hours, plus
freezing

Cooking: 5 mins

Special equipment:
20 × 28cm Pyrex or
other tray (at least
2cm deep), sugar
thermometer, ten
7cm rubber dome
moulds, ice-cream
machine, 6.5cm
round cutter

One of Le Manoir's most elegant dishes, this dessert has Southeast Asian influences, yet its roots are definitely French. A dome of exotic fruits is glazed with a jellified passion fruit juice, giving the appearance of a ravioli. There are several components to this dessert, but each of them is straightforward enough to replicate in your own home. Make it for a very special occasion.

Planning ahead All the elements can be made a day or two in advance and kept in the freezer. Transfer the ravioli to the fridge 4 hours before serving to defrost slowly. Transfer the sorbet to the fridge 20 minutes before serving to soften.

For the panna cotta
450ml fresh pineapple purée
    (or quality pineapple juice)
130ml tinned coconut milk
6 egg yolks
50g caster sugar
4½ sheets leaf gelatine
    (27x7cm)
20ml white rum
20ml Malibu
juice of ½ lime
pinch of cayenne pepper

For the exotic fruit filling
100g fresh mango purée
    (or use shop bought)
10g sugar
juice of ½ lime
100g papaya flesh, cut into
    4mm dice
100g mango flesh, cut into
    4mm dice
100g pineapple flesh, cut into
    4mm dice
2 passion fruit, pulp extracted
4 mint leaves, finely chopped

For the glaze
2 sheets leaf gelatine (27x7cm)
30g sugar
2 tbsp water
200ml fresh passion fruit pulp
    or juice, strained

For the coconut jus
320ml tinned coconut milk
45g caster sugar
½ tsp vanilla syrup (see page 9)
    or best vanilla extract
3 kaffir lime leaves, finely
    chopped

For the coconut sorbet
100g sugar
100ml water
300ml tinned coconut cream
200ml tinned coconut milk
50ml Malibu
juice of 1 lime

For the garnish
spun sugar lattices (optional,
    see page 229)
finely grated zest of 1 lime

To make the panna cotta Line the 20 × 28cm tray with non-stick baking paper. Tip the pineapple purée and coconut milk into a saucepan, bring to the boil over a medium heat and let bubble for 10 seconds.

Dipping the frozen 'ravioli' in the passion fruit glaze.

Lifting and turning the ravioli to allow excess glaze to drip off.

Meanwhile, in a bowl, whisk together the egg yolks and sugar. Slowly pour a third of the hot pineapple mixture onto the eggs, whisking as you do so, then pour back into the saucepan. Cook over a low heat, stirring all the time, until the mixture registers 87°C on a sugar thermometer[1].

Meanwhile, soak the gelatine leaves in a shallow dish of cold water to soften for a few minutes[2]. Remove the panna cotta mixture from the heat. Drain the gelatine leaves and squeeze out excess water, then add to the hot mixture, stirring to dissolve. Pass through a fine sieve into a bowl set over a larger bowl of iced water to cool quickly.

Once cooled, add the rum, Malibu, lime juice and cayenne pepper. Pour the mixture into the prepared tray to approximately a 1cm depth and place in the freezer to harden.

To make the exotic fruit filling In a large bowl, combine the mango purée, sugar and lime juice, then stir in the diced fruit, passion fruit and mint. Divide among the 10 rubber moulds to one-third fill them. Level with the back of a spoon.

To assemble Cut out 10 discs of panna cotta jelly, using the 6.5cm cutter, and position on top of the exotic fruit mixture. Place in the freezer (the 'ravioli' need to be completely frozen before glazing).

To make the glaze Soften the gelatine in cold water (as above). Dissolve the sugar in the water in a pan over a medium heat and add the passion fruit pulp or juice. Bring just to the boil, then take off the heat. Drain the gelatine, squeeze dry and add to the passion fruit syrup, stirring to dissolve. Leave at room temperature[3].

To glaze the ravioli Once set, de-mould the ravioli onto a wire rack with a tray underneath to catch any drips of jelly. One at a time, spear an upside-down ravioli on a cocktail stick and dip in the glaze for about 3 seconds to form a 2mm thick passion fruit gelée coating right up to the panna cotta base. Invert onto a tray and leave to defrost slowly in the fridge or place back in the freezer once glazed[4].

To make the coconut jus In a medium saucepan, combine the coconut milk, sugar and vanilla syrup. Place over a low heat, add the kaffir lime leaves and allow to infuse for 10 minutes. Take off the heat and leave to cool. Pass through a fine sieve, taste for sweetness and reserve in the fridge.

To make the sorbet In a small pan, dissolve the sugar in the water over a medium heat, bring to the boil and let bubble for 10 seconds. Meanwhile, combine the coconut cream and coconut milk in a large bowl. Pour on the hot sugar syrup, whisk together and add the Malibu and lime juice. Churn in an ice-cream machine for about 1 hour until thick. Reserve in the freezer.

To dress the plate Using a spatula, place a ravioli in the centre of each shallow serving bowl. Foam the coconut jus, using a hand blender, and spoon around the ravioli. Place a spun sugar lattice on top of each ravioli, if using; otherwise make a small indent in the centre of the ravioli. Crown with a scoop of coconut sorbet and a dusting of lime zest[5]. Serve at once.

1 It is essential to keep stirring this custard mixture, otherwise the egg will begin to cook and set on the base of the pan.

2 Gelatine must be rehydrated in cold water, never in hot water as it would simply dissolve. Make sure it is well drained before adding it to a mixture, as excess water will dilute the mix and may affect the setting. Note that the high acidity of the pineapple juice will restrict the setting capacity of the gelatine. Here we are using just enough gelatine to set the coconut panna cotta to a melting texture.

3 For dipping, you need to keep the jelly at an oily consistency, so don't refrigerate it otherwise it will set firm. This is because as you dip the frozen moulded fruits into the jelly, it will quickly cool and thicken. Before dipping the ravioli, microwave the jelly for 3–5 seconds and stir until it regains an oily consistency.

4 At this stage you can either transfer all the glazed ravioli to the fridge for 4 hours to defrost slowly or keep those you don't need now in the freezer for up to a month, ready for another occasion.

5 To moderate the harshness of fresh lime zest, mix the grated zest of 4 limes with 50g caster sugar and dry out in a low oven at 100°C for 2 hours. Store for up to a week in an airtight container.

Autumn & Winter Vegetables

As a young chef, I dreamt of having a small place with an enormous garden, but I certainly never envisaged I'd end up in such a huge place with a garden to match – no less than 27 acres. Excited by the opportunity, I set myself the challenge of producing as many vegetables as possible in the gardens at Le Manoir throughout the year.

Of all the important moments in the garden, there is one particular instant that I truly love: when autumn turns to winter. First you can smell it – an earthy scent rising from the vegetation, musty and rich, the unmistakable scent of slow decay. Then you can see it in the plants' structure, with their leaves and stalks collapsing around them. Battalions of brassicas stand up tall in their green jackets, welcoming the winter. Above the dark earth fat pumpkins shine bright, and deep underneath the soil, life is at work: root vegetables swell, waiting for the pot.

To capture the glorious tastes of these autumn and winter vegetables, I would like to share with you a few of my culinary secrets, to create those comforting, rustic dishes that we all crave in the cold weather.

One of my favourite cooking techniques is pot-roasting. Here is a miniature recipe: heat your oven to a very low temperature, not exceeding 150°C/Gas 2. Place 700g mixed, peeled root vegetables, 40g butter or olive oil and 4 pinches each of salt and pepper in an ovenproof pot, and roast for about an hour. No additional liquid is added to the cooking pot, which makes this technique different from braising; the juices released by the vegetables will be enough to steam them. It will turn the oldest root into a sweet, tender treat, as the starches within the vegetables are transformed into sugar, a process which is called 'sweetening'.

Beetroot is one of my favourite vegetables. It often features in my winter salads and I use it to make a delicious risotto. A word of advice: wear plastic gloves and protective clothes when you prepare beetroot, as this vegetable leaves a stain on clothes and hands.

To ensure even cooking, simmer rather than boil beetroot, to allow the heat to permeate slowly. Test by inserting a small knife into the middle; it should meet with minimal resistance.

For maximum flavour, go for larger beets; the same applies to other roots, such as carrots and parsnips, as these will have a better taste. I love cooking with turnips, and you'll find on page 222 a recipe for a delicious turnip gratin. My favourite turnip variety is one that my Papa introduced me to, and it is called Navet de Croissy: a long, thick, creamy white root, with a mild but distinct flavour.

Chicory, walnut and Roquefort salad

Serves 4
Preparation: 5 mins

Roquefort is generally regarded as the king of blue cheese, although Stilton and other British blue cheeses such as Cashel Blue, Barkham Blue and Blue Vinney could be great substitutes in this dish. To me, chicory – with its crunchy texture and beautiful bittersweet taste – is one of the best winter salad leaves. There are many varieties, but white and red make a most striking combination. Should you wish, you can use other winter salad leaves instead, such as lamb's lettuce, frisée and escarole.

1 firm, ripe pear or apple
4 small chicory bulbs,
   quartered lengthways
1 celery stick, finely sliced
100g walnuts, roughly
   chopped[1]
80g Roquefort cheese[2], chilled
2 tsp finely chopped chives

For the Roquefort dressing
50g Roquefort cheese[2],
   at room temperature
20ml warm water
1 tbsp white wine vinegar
2 tbsp extra virgin olive oil[3]
pinch or two of freshly ground
   black pepper

To prepare the dressing In a large bowl, using a spatula, cream the Roquefort cheese to a smooth paste. Add the warm water[4] and wine vinegar and whisk until smooth, then gradually whisk in the olive oil. Season to taste with pepper[5].

To assemble the salad Halve, core and finely slice the pear or apple. Place in a salad bowl with the chicory, celery and walnuts. Crumble in two-thirds of the Roquefort, add the dressing and toss gently. Crumble the remaining Roquefort over the salad and sprinkle with chopped chives to serve.

Variations Try adding some garlic croûtons or grilled bacon lardons, or a handful of prunes, raisins or dried apricots for contrast.

[1] Walnuts are the perfect companion to most cheeses and Roquefort is no exception. They do, however, turn rancid quite quickly, so buy little and often.

[2] Roquefort is probably one of the oldest cheeses in the world. It is a raw ewe's milk cheese, matured in caves in the Aveyron region of France. The mould penicillium found in these caves gives it its distinctive flavour, aroma and blue veining. The flavour, based on salty acid, is awesome. The cheese for the salad will be easy to crumble if it is chilled.

[3] Use your best olive oil for your dressings.

[4] Whisking a little warm water into the creamed Roquefort will help to create a smooth emulsion.

[5] Due to the saltiness of the Roquefort no additional salt is needed in this recipe.

Warm salad of leeks, Jerusalem artichokes and winter leaves

Serves 4
Preparation:
10 mins
Cooking: 15 mins
Special equipment:
steamer

At home in France, we used to call this *salade du pauvre*, as Jerusalem artichokes were normally only consumed by livestock. It is a shame that these knobbly tubers have not become more popular, as they are truly delicious. Combined with leeks and winter leaves, they make an inviting winter salad.

Planning ahead You can prepare this salad up to 2 hours in advance.

4 medium leeks, outer layers
  removed
4 Jerusalem artichokes (320g)
squeeze of lemon juice
60g mixed winter leaves, such
  as mache and frisée

For the dressing
1 tbsp Dijon mustard
1 tbsp white wine vinegar
2 tbsp water
3 tbsp extra virgin rapeseed oil
sea salt and black pepper
1 tsp chopped chives
1 tsp chopped chervil

To prepare the leeks and artichokes Slice the leeks into short lengths on the diagonal and wash well. Peel the Jerusalem artichokes, immersing them in cold water with the lemon juice added as you do so[1], then slice each one into 4 pieces. Place the leeks and Jerusalem artichokes in a large steamer over boiling water, cover tightly and steam over a high heat for 15 minutes.

Check that the leeks are cooked[2]; they should be soft and melting but still retaining some texture. If necessary, cook for a further 5 minutes. Remove from the heat and set aside while you make the dressing.

To make the dressing In a small bowl, mix together the mustard, wine vinegar and water. Gradually whisk in the rapeseed oil, adding it in a steady thin thread to emulsify into the dressing. Season, add the herbs, taste and adjust as necessary.

To assemble the salad In a bowl, toss the steamed vegetables in half of the dressing. Check the seasoning. Arrange the vegetables on a platter or individual plates, scatter over the salad leaves and then drizzle with the remaining dressing.

[1] Jerusalem artichokes will oxidise quickly and discolour as you prepare them. To prevent this, keep covered in water acidulated with a squeeze of lemon.

[2] A member of the onion family, the leek needs to be cooked thoroughly to be digestible and tasty. To check, simply pierce the leek with the tip of a sharp knife; the blade should go through with minimal resistance – you should not feel the layers. Or better still, taste a little piece.

Beetroot risotto Illustrated overleaf

Serves 4

Preparation:
40 mins

Cooking: 30 mins
for the beetroot,
plus 25 minutes for
the risotto

Special equipment:
blender or food
processor

I created this dish for Brasserie Blanc a few years ago, using some magnificent freshly harvested beetroots from the garden. It was very well received in the restaurant and guests still love it today.

Planning ahead The beetroot garnish and beetroot juice can be prepared a day or two in advance.

For the beetroot garnish
400g beetroot
800ml water
1 tsp salt
4 tbsp balsamic vinegar
5g unsalted butter
4 pinches of freshly ground
    black pepper

For the beetroot juice
200g beetroot, peeled and
    finely chopped
500ml beetroot cooking liquor
    (from the garnish, above)

For the risotto
½ banana shallot, peeled and
    finely diced
15g unsalted butter

4 tbsp red wine vinegar
150ml red wine (ideally
    Cabernet Sauvignon)
250g carnaroli rice[1]
550ml beetroot juice (see left)
3 pinches of sea salt
pinch of freshly ground
    black pepper

For the garnish (optional)
30g Parmesan cheese
oil for deep-frying
20g beetroot slices, 1mm thick
5g flat-leaf parsley sprigs

To finish the risotto
40g Parmesan cheese, grated
40g unsalted butter
50ml beetroot juice (see left)

To prepare the beetroot garnish Peel the beetroot[2], cut them in half and place in a medium saucepan. Add the water and salt, bring to the boil and simmer for 30 minutes until soft. Remove from the heat, strain off the juice and reserve both the juice and beetroot. Leave the beetroot until cool enough to handle.

Meanwhile, boil the 4 tbsp balsamic vinegar in a small saucepan to reduce down by half.

Cut the beetroot into 1cm dice and return to the cleaned pan. Add the butter, reduced vinegar, pepper and a pinch of salt and cook, stirring occasionally, for 3 minutes or until the beetroot is nicely glazed. Set aside.

To prepare the beetroot juice In a blender or food processor, blend the chopped raw beetroot with the reserved beetroot cooking liquor for 1 minute. Strain the juice through a fine sieve and discard the pulp. This will produce approximately 600ml juice; set aside 50ml of this to finish the risotto.

To cook the risotto In a large saucepan over a medium heat, gently soften the shallot in the butter for 2 minutes. Add the wine vinegar and reduce until thick and sticky. Meanwhile, boil the wine in a separate pan to reduce to 100ml[3].

Add the rice to the shallot and stir to coat the grains evenly. Add the boiled wine, 550ml beetroot juice and the seasoning and bring to the boil. Stir once and leave at a very gentle simmer for 20 minutes[4].

To prepare the garnish (if using) While the rice is cooking, preheat the oven to 220°C/Gas 7, grate the Parmesan onto a non-stick baking tray and bake for 6 minutes. Heat the oil to 140°C. Deep-fry the beetroot slices[5] for 3 minutes until crisp, then drain on kitchen paper. Deep-fry the parsley for 30 seconds; drain well.

To finish the risotto After 20 minutes, when the rice has absorbed most of the cooking liquid, start to stir vigorously and cook until *al dente*[6], adding the grated Parmesan, butter, fresh beetroot juice[7] and diced beetroot garnish.

To serve Divide the risotto between warm bowls and finish with deep-fried beetroot slices and parsley sprigs, and Parmesan crisps, if required.

[1] Carnaroli rice, cultivated mainly in the Piemonte region of Italy, is my preferred rice for risotto. It has a good flavour and excellent texture.

[2] The beetroot are peeled to release as much juice and colour into the water as possible; this liquor will be used later to cook the risotto.

[3] By boiling the wine you are removing most of the bitter alcohol taste, leaving the fruity, acidic characters.

[4] Making a risotto in the traditional way – stirring it constantly during cooking – is laborious. Instead, I cook the rice in two stages, first barely simmering without stirring to cook the grains, then stirring vigorously to extract the starch and lend the characteristic creaminess to the risotto. It is much easier, but during the slow simmering you must keep the heat low – just one bubble breaking the surface.

[5] If preferred, instead of deep-frying, the beetroot can be dried in a low oven at 100°C for 4 hours.

[6] Over-cooking the risotto only takes 1–2 minutes, so check frequently from this point. The rice needs to be *al dente* – cooked but firm to the bite. At this stage the outer starch is softened whilst the inner starch remains firm. The Italians refer to the soul or *anima* being intact.

[7] This small amount of juice added at the end of cooking will give the risotto a burst of fresh beetroot flavour.

Winter vegetable salad *Illustrated on previous page*

Serves 4
Preparation:
20 mins
Cooking: 1½ hours
Special equipment:
ovenproof sauté
pan, blender,
steamer

This is lovely way to cook and present our autumn produce and the dish is very flexible, so you can use whatever is available and local, making the salad as simple or as sophisticated as you like.

Planning ahead All elements of this dish can be cooked up to half a day in advance and finished to serve.

For the roasted pumpkin discs
2 tbsp olive oil
160g peeled, deseeded
    pumpkin, cut into 8 discs
sea salt and freshly ground
    black pepper

For the pumpkin purée
10g unsalted butter
200g peeled, deseeded
    pumpkin, cut into 2cm dice
1 tsp hazelnut oil

For the beetroot
2 candy beetroot, cleaned
2 golden beetroot, cleaned
1 ruby beetroot, cleaned

For the sauce
100ml port
100ml red wine

For the mushroom fricassée
15g unsalted butter
½ garlic clove, peeled and finely
    chopped
100g assorted wild mushrooms
    (chanterelles, ceps,
    trompettes de mort etc.)[1],
    cleaned and trimmed and
    halved or quartered if large
5g flat-leaf parsley, chopped
squeeze of lemon juice

For the garnish
100g young spinach
1 tsp butter
2 tbsp water
8 deep-fried parsnip ribbons
    (optional)
12 deep-fried sage leaves
    (optional)

To cook the pumpkin discs Preheat the oven to 170°C/Gas 3. Heat the olive oil in a medium ovenproof sauté pan over a medium heat and caramelise the pumpkin discs all over for 1–2 minutes. Season with salt and pepper and finish cooking in the oven for 7–10 minutes until tender[2]. Leave to one side until needed.

To cook the pumpkin purée In a medium saucepan over a medium-low heat, melt the butter and add the diced pumpkin, with a little seasoning. Cover with a tight-fitting lid and cook gently, stirring regularly to ensure the pumpkin does not stick to the bottom. When it begins to break down and release its moisture, uncover and cook off as much of the liquid as possible, stirring all the time. Transfer the pumpkin to a blender and purée until smooth, adding the hazelnut oil to finish. Taste and correct the seasoning.

To cook the beetroot Steam the beetroot until tender[3]. Drain and leave until cool enough to handle, then peel whilst still warm. Quarter or halve according to size and season with salt and pepper.

For the sauce Meanwhile, simmer the port and red wine together in a saucepan until reduced by two-thirds and thickened[4].

Shortly before serving Reheat the beetroot and the pumpkin discs in the oven for 8–10 minutes. Warm the pumpkin purée in a small pan.

To cook the mushroom fricassée At the last moment, heat a small sauté pan over a high heat, add the butter, then the garlic and cook briefly for 10 seconds. Add the wild mushrooms, except trompettes, and cook for 30 seconds. Add the trompettes[5] with a pinch each of salt and pepper and cook for 1 minute, then stir in the parsley and lemon juice.

To prepare the garnish Briefly wilt the spinach in an emulsion of the butter and water; keep warm.

To serve To dress the plates, spoon the pumpkin purée into the middle of each plate and spread it across the plate. Arrange the beetroot, pumpkin and spinach on top of the purée and scatter the wild mushrooms around. Spoon the red wine and port reduction over and around the warm salad. Garnish with a few deep-fried parsnip ribbons and crisp sage leaves, if you wish.

Variations Vary the vegetables according to the season. Try replacing the beetroot, pumpkin and onions with carrots, celeriac, Jerusalem artichokes, new season's garlic cloves, butternut squash, Grelot or small red Thai shallots.

[1] Use seasonal mushrooms: morels and St. George mushrooms in the spring; girolles and black trompettes in the summer; ceps during the autumn and chanterelles during the winter. Many varieties can be found all year round, such as oyster mushroom, enoki, shiitake etc.

[2] This slow method of cooking the vegetables ensures all the starches are converted into sugars, giving maximum flavour and a soft melting texture.

[3] The time taken to steam the beetroot is proportional to their size. Larger beetroot could take an hour to cook through.

[4] Reduce the wines until they coat the back of your spoon. Taste and add a little caster sugar if the concentrated tannins of the wines become too overpowering.

[5] If the trompettes are added too early they will release their juices and discolour the fricassée.

Gratin turnip dauphinoise

*

Serves 6

Preparation:
15 mins

Cooking:
1 hour 10 mins

Special equipment:
22cm gratin dish,
mandolin

Seriously satisfying, this is a take on one of the truly great potato dishes. Layers of potato and turnip are cooked in a rich garlic cream to delicious effect. It goes well with any roast, but is especially good with beef. The variety of the potatoes is important – I have found Desirée and Belle de Fonteney to be very successful.

Planning ahead The gratin can be cooked an hour before the meal and reheated for 20 minutes before serving.

500ml whipping cream
10 pinches of sea salt
2 pinches of freshly ground
    black or white pepper
2 garlic cloves, peeled and
    crushed

5 medium Desirée potatoes
    (550g), washed
6 large turnips (550g), washed
50g Gruyère cheese, grated
    (optional)

To infuse the cream In a small saucepan over a medium heat, bring the cream to a simmer. Add the seasoning and crushed garlic, remove from the heat and set aside to infuse while you prepare the vegetables.

To prepare the vegetables Preheat the oven to 160°C/Gas 3. Peel the potatoes and turnips, pat dry and cut into fine (2mm) slices, using a mandolin[1].

To assemble the dish Layer half of the potato and turnip slices in a large gratin dish, then pour on half of the warm cream through a strainer. Layer the remaining vegetable slices on top, making sure you finish the gratin with a layer of potatoes only[2]. Strain the remaining cream over and press the potato slices gently with the back of a spoon to ensure the cream is evenly distributed.

To cook the dish Cover with foil and bake in the oven for 40 minutes. Remove the foil and sprinkle the grated cheese, if using, evenly over the surface. Bake, uncovered, for a further 30 minutes or until the top is golden brown and the vegetables are just cooked through[3]. Leave to stand for 5 minutes before serving.

[1] We don't wash the potatoes after slicing them, as the starch present will help to bind the layers together.
[2] The starch in the potatoes will give you a golden caramelisation. If, instead, the top layer was turnip slices, they would dry out and curl up.
[3] To test if the gratin is cooked, insert the tip of a sharp knife in the middle; it should meet with little resistance (you shouldn't be able to feel the layers).

Summer Fruits

Anne-Marie has been the head gardener at Le Manoir for many years but she still recalls her first day as a young apprentice back in 1984. A member of staff drove her to a pick-your-own farm a few miles away and said, 'Pick as much as you can and I'll be back to collect you in 3 hours.' Laden with raspberries and strawberries, she was at the farm gates at the designated time. She was still waiting 2 hours later and phoned reception. 'Oh, that will be RB,' she was told. 'He can be forgetful.'

I've never stopped apologising for failing to collect her, and she's never stopped reminding me of it. However, pick-your-own farms have served me well, and there are many benefits of buying local produce: it's close to home and the fruit is fresh, ripe and invariably cheaper.

I love raspberries, yet until recently I didn't understand how Scotland, so often windswept, cloudy and cold, produced the finest Britain has to offer. In fact, it is precisely because of the weather and long hours of daylight that the berries are superior. In heat, raspberries ripen too quickly and their flavour does not have time to develop fully. But in Scottish raspberry-growing areas temperatures rarely go above 22°C, which is perfect for this fruit.

In search of the finest raspberry varieties, I recently visited Scottish farms in Blairgowrie and discovered three jewels: Glen Ample, Glen Doll and Autumn Bliss (which can be picked until late November). They were outstanding and will soon be plentiful at Le Manoir.

Raspberries and other soft fruits make easy desserts. They are splendid enough to serve on their own, with cream or crème fraîche, or you can pour Champagne over them and let it foam enticingly. Alternatively you can churn them with sugar to make a superb sorbet.

Sugar is not the only flavour catalyst for fruits – a few chopped herbs, a dash of lemon juice or a pinch of cayenne will also enhance flavour (and reduce the sugar needed).

Another useful tip: fruits that are liable to oxidation – peaches, apples, pears and bananas, for example – can be prevented from discolouring by sprinkling the peeled and cut surfaces with lemon juice.

You can dry summer berries to create an extraordinary garnish for desserts. To prepare, simply halve raspberries or quarter strawberries and lay them on a baking tray lined with silicone paper. Place in the oven, preheated to 100°C, for about half an hour. Use them just as they are, or powder the dried fruits with a little sugar and sprinkle over a dessert, or include within it – to add magnificent texture and flavour.

And, in your cupboard, keep a bottle of kirsch, which is distilled from cherries. A drop or two sprinkled over red fruits will bring yet more sunshine to your guests.

Raspberry sorbet

*

Serves 4

Preparation:
10 minutes,
plus 30 minutes
macerating and
20–30 minutes
churning

Special equipment:
blender, ice-cream
machine

You must invest in a sorbetière or ice-cream machine for your kitchen – you will reap the benefits. Summer fruits and berries can be gathered or bought during the summer when they are plentiful, stored in the freezer and turned into delectable clean-tasting, refreshing sorbets throughout the year.

600g raspberries, washed[1]
100g caster sugar[2]
squeeze of lemon juice

To macerate the fruit Place the raspberries in a bowl and sprinkle with the caster sugar and lemon juice. Mix together and set aside to macerate[3] for 30 minutes at room temperature.

To purée the fruit Purée the raspberry mixture in a blender and pass it through a fine non-reactive sieve into a bowl, pressing the pulp in the sieve with the back of a ladle to extract as much juice as possible.

To freeze Pour the raspberry purée into the ice-cream machine and churn until frozen[4]; this will take 20–30 minutes depending on your machine. Reserve in the freezer until ready to serve[5].

Variation Replace the raspberries with strawberries, blackcurrants, blueberries, apricots, peaches, Granny Smith apples, Blood oranges, rhubarb etc., adjusting the sugar according to the fruit.

A sorbet can be served as an accompaniment to many other desserts, or with meringue, or on a biscuit or sponge base.

[1] The fruit must be perfectly ripe to give maximum flavour and colour.
[2] The less sugar you put in, the fresher your sorbet, but the firmer it will be. This is the minimum amount of sugar needed to give a smooth texture.
[3] Macerating the fruit with sugar and lemon juice will enhance its flavour by up to 20 per cent.
[4] If you do not own an ice-cream machine simply freeze the purée in a shallow container, beating vigorously 2 or 3 times during freezing to break down the ice crystals and ensure a smooth-textured result.
[5] The best sorbets are from fresh fruit, freshly puréed and taken straight from the machine, as they will have an unctuous texture. If the sorbet is to be stored in the freezer, then soften it slightly in the fridge before serving, so it is not rock hard.

Summer fruits steeped in wine, basil and mint

*
Serves 4
Preparation:
30 mins, plus
6½–12 hours
macerating
Cooking: 10 mins
Special equipment:
2–3cm melon baller

Another classic at Le Manoir, which is also served at Brasserie Blanc. The refreshing taste of red fruits steeped in Monbazillac with minty, peppery and citrus flavours makes a delightful simple dessert for a warm summer's day.

Planning ahead The summer fruits can be prepared 6–12 hours in advance. The spun sugar lattice can be made up to an hour ahead, but no sooner.

For the macerated fruit
230g raspberries[1], washed
160g strawberries[1], hulled,
    washed and halved
100g blackberries[1], washed
20g caster sugar
12 spearmint leaves
6 basil leaves
6 lemon verbena leaves[2]
    (optional)
½ Charentais melon

For the liquor
250ml Monbazillac
    or dessert wine
90ml Cabernet Sauvignon
    or other red wine
40g caster sugar
4 turns of freshly ground black
    pepper
1 tsp best vanilla extract or 2 tsp
    vanilla syrup (see page 9)
100ml water

For the spun sugar lattice
(optional)
100ml water
300g caster sugar
pinch of finely grated lemon,
    lime or orange zest
pinch of finely shredded herbs
    (julienne), such as mint,
    lemon verbena or basil
pinch of dried raspberries
    and/or dried strawberries,
    finely chopped[3]

To serve
mint or lemon verbena sprigs
100ml chilled pink champagne

To macerate the fruit In a large bowl, combine all the berries, sugar and herbs. Toss gently to mix and leave to macerate for 30 minutes.

To prepare the liquor Pour both wines into a small saucepan and add the sugar, pepper and vanilla. Place over a medium heat to dissolve the sugar, then bring to the boil and boil for 1 minute[4]. Turn off the heat and add the cold water. Set aside to cool down to approximately 40°C[5].

Add the wine mixture to the macerated fruit. Using your melon baller, scoop the melon into 12 balls and add them too. Cover and refrigerate for at least 6 hours, or up to a day.

To make the sugar lattice If required, an hour or less before serving[6], pour the water into a medium saucepan, add the sugar and let it absorb the water for 1–2 minutes. Then dissolve over a medium heat, bring to the boil and cook to a dark golden caramel[7]. Remove from the heat and dip the base of the pan in cold water briefly to stop the cooking. Allow the caramel to cool down and thicken a little before making your lattice.

Using a fork, thread caramel onto a tray lined with greaseproof paper, using a back and forth motion to make a large square. Sprinkle the citrus zest, herbs and chopped dried fruit evenly over the threads. Thread caramel over the top at right angles to the first layer, creating a latticework that encases the flavourings. Leave until set, then carefully break into 4 squares. (Or you can thread the caramel over the back of a ladle to create a lovely dome; once set, de-mould and repeat to make 3 more lattices, re-warming the caramel slightly to melt if necessary.)

To serve Transfer the fruit and liquor to a large glass serving bowl or individual bowls. Pour a little pink Champagne[8] into each bowl and garnish with the mint sprigs. At the last moment, carefully position the spun sugar lattice, if using, on each serving.

Variations Many other fruits can be used, for example wild strawberries, blueberries, redcurrants, blackcurrants and peaches.

1 The secret to this dish is to use the freshest, ripest berries you can find. In Britain, we have some excellent varieties. Look for Glen Doll, Glen Ample and Autumn Bliss raspberries; Mara de Bois and Marshmallow strawberries; and Loch Ness blackberries. You can now find these on supermarket shelves. If the fruit is not quite ripe enough you can compensate for this by first macerating them with a little sugar for 1 hour.

2 Lemon verbena will add a lovely depth of flavour to your soup, giving off a citrus perfume. It can easily be grown in the garden or in a windowbox.

3 To dry berries and other fruits, such as pears and apples, slice and place on a tray lined with greaseproof paper in a low oven at 60°C to dry overnight. The moisture will be driven off leaving the fruit with an intense flavour and crunchy texture; berries will be rich ruby in colour.

4 Boiling wine drives off the alcohol to give a rounder flavour, but you cannot remove all of the alcohol, so this is not the best dessert to give to young children.

5 The wine needs to be warm, rather than hot, to stimulate the exchange of flavours between the herbs, the pepper, the fruit and the wine; 40°C is the perfect temperature. If the soup is too hot it will cook the fruits.

6 Humidity is the enemy of caramel lattices, as it will soften them and cause them to collapse. This is why they must be made shortly before serving, or no more than an hour ahead and kept in an airtight container.

7   When you dissolve sugar, it will try to re-crystallise, which will ruin your caramel. To prevent this happening, always use a totally clean pan, never stir the sugar when it is boiling, and have a pastry brush with a small pot of water ready to brush down any crystals that form on the side of the pan during boiling. If you do manage to crystallise your sugar (as I have done many times), swirl the pan to incorporate the crystallised sugar into the mass and continue to cook the caramel – the flakes should dissolve. If you wish, you can replace 30 per cent of the sugar with liquid glucose, which will help prevent crystallisation and increase the density of the caramel, making it more pliable.

8   When the dry Champagne is added to the sweet fruit and juice it will create a foam of pink bubbles, which finishes this dish beautifully, adding a little festive touch. The remainder will be much appreciated by your guests…

DID YOU KNOW?
My general rule about cooking with wine is to avoid spending over £5 per bottle. I have seen some wonderful expensive Pinot Noir and Cabernet Sauvignon murdered by boiling. What you are looking for is a deep, richly coloured Cabernet Sauvignon or Merlot. Pinot Noir wines are usually too light and delicate.

Peaches poached in white wine with mint, basil and citrus flavours

Serves 8

Preparation:
10 mins,
plus 6–18 hours
infusing and
freezing
Cooking:
15–20 mins

This is the perfect dessert to serve when peaches are at their peak, at the height of the summer. The white-fleshed peaches from France and Italy are the best.

Planning ahead The peaches and granita can be prepared up to 18 hours ahead.

8 firm, ripe peaches
120g caster sugar
600ml water
400ml dry white wine
1 vanilla pod, split lengthways,
  or 1 tsp best vanilla extract or
  vanilla syrup (see page 9)

1 orange, cut across into
  2–3mm slices[1]
1 unwaxed lemon, cut across
  into 2–3mm slices[1]
4 basil sprigs
8 peppermint sprigs, plus an
  extra sprig to garnish

To poach the peaches Place the peaches in a single layer in a saucepan in which they fit quite snugly. Add the sugar, water, wine and vanilla. Top with the orange and lemon slices. Cut a round of greaseproof paper the diameter of the saucepan and cut a hole in the centre to let steam escape; lay over the peaches[2].

Place over a medium heat to dissolve the sugar and bring to the boil. Reduce the heat to a gentle simmer and cook for 15–20 minutes until tender[3]. Turn off the heat and leave the peaches to cool in their own liquor.

To infuse the peaches Roughly chop the herb sprigs and immerse in the cooking liquor. Leave to infuse in the fridge for at least 6 hours.

To make the granita Pour half the liquor into a shallow freezerproof container and freeze until firm. Return the peaches in the remaining liquor to the fridge until ready to serve.

To serve Using a slotted spoon, remove the peaches to a plate and carefully peel off the skin. Place the peaches in a glass bowl and pour on the liquor. Top with the orange and lemon slices, vanilla pod, if using, and mint sprig. Using a fork, scrape the granita into little glass dishes to serve alongside the peaches.

[1] Ensure that the lemon and orange slices are cut very thin, so they can be eaten.
[2] This greaseproof paper 'cartouche' will help keep the peaches submerged in the liquor and ensure an even cooking.
[3] Peaches are delicate. If subjected to high heat or boiling, their texture will be ruined, so cook them very gently. To check if a peach is cooked, look for tiny bubbles escaping from the stalk end. Once these cease, the peach is ready.

Pain perdu and warm summer fruits

*

Serves 4

Preparation:
10 mins,
plus 20 minutes
macerating

Cooking:
10 mins

Pain perdu, or 'lost bread', is another vivid childhood memory. At home, Maman Blanc would put all the dried bread into an earthenware bowl. Once it was full, she would add a mixture of milk, sugar and eggs and bake it all together – so the *pain perdu* would never be lost. Obviously today we are not victims of post-war economy and have the luxury of using brioche, which you can buy in bakers and good supermarkets, or better still, bake your own (see page 50). Of course, you can use bread, but brioche is so much nicer and an affordable little luxury, I feel.

For the macerated fruits[1]
100g strawberries, hulled,
    washed and halved
100g raspberries, washed
1 tsp caster sugar

For the pain perdu
2 organic/free-range large eggs
50g caster sugar
100ml whole milk
2 tsp kirsch, rum or Cognac
    (optional, but lovely)
1 tsp best vanilla extract or
    vanilla syrup (see page 9)
4 slices of brioche, 2cm thick,
    crusts removed and halved or
    quartered diagonally
40g unsalted butter

For the caramel sauce
2 tbsp water
50g caster sugar
30g cold unsalted butter, diced
2 tsp kirsch or Cognac

To macerate the fruits Put the strawberries and raspberries into a large bowl, sprinkle with the sugar and toss lightly. Set aside to macerate for 20 minutes.

To prepare the pain perdu In a large bowl, beat the eggs and sugar together, then incorporate the milk, alcohol, if using, and vanilla. Add the brioche slices and leave for 4–5 minutes to allow them to absorb the egg mixture. With a large, wide spatula carefully lift the brioche slices from the bowl and reserve on a tray.

To fry the soaked brioche Preheat the oven to 120°C/Gas 1. Melt the butter in a large frying pan over a medium heat. When it is foaming[2], fry the brioche slices, in batches if necessary, for 2–3 minutes on each side to a rich golden brown colour. Lift the brioche slices from the pan with a wide spatula and place on a baking tray. Place in the oven for 5 minutes or so while you prepare the caramel and warm the fruit.

To make the caramel sauce Put the water into a medium frying pan, add the sugar and allow it to stand and absorb the water for 1–2 minutes. Then dissolve over a medium heat, bring to the boil and cook to a very pale blond caramel[3]. Lower the heat and stir in the diced butter.

To warm the fruit Add the strawberries and raspberries to the caramel sauce with the kirsch[4] and cook gently for 30 seconds to soften the fruits and create the delicious juices[5].

To serve Remove the hot brioche slices from the oven and divide them between 4 warmed plates. Spoon the warm berries and red fruit syrup around the brioche and serve.

Variations Replace the berries with apples, peaches, plums or cherries.
   Although it is best to use fresh berries, you can substitute good-quality frozen fruit.

[1] Macerating is derived from the Latin word for 'made soft/soaked'. Sprinkling the berries with sugar will soften them, releasing their juices and enhancing their flavour.

[2] The butter will start to foam at about 130°C. At about 150–155°C it will go hazelnut colour. This is the perfect stage to caramelise the brioche slices. If the butter becomes too hot, it will burn.

[3] Here you want a light caramel; if you cook the caramel until dark, the flavour will be intense and it will overpower the fruit. When the caramel reaches the right stage, quickly stir in the cold butter and this will stop the caramel cooking. It will also create a shiny emulsion.

[4] You can use either kirsch or Cognac, but I think kirsch is best!

[5] Cook the fruits briefly and gently – they are delicate and will soon lose texture and freshness.

Fig tart

✳ ✳

Serves 6

Preparation:
25 mins, plus 1 hour resting and
30 minutes cooling

Cooking: 50 mins

Special equipment: blender or food processor, 20cm tart ring, baking stone (optional), peel (optional)

I wanted to created a fig tart without cream or milk, as seems appropriate to Provence and the Mediterranean, where these fruits grow profusely. After a number of trials, I came up with this recipe, which I am particularly pleased with. The black figs *Les Violettes de Solliès*, from Solliès Pont in Provence, are the best variety to use.

Planning ahead You can prepare this dessert a few hours in advance. There will be enough pastry to make two tarts; freeze one portion for later use.

For the sweetcrust pastry
250g plain flour
75g icing sugar, plus extra
    to dust
pinch of sea salt
120g unsalted butter, diced,
    at room temperature
2 organic/free-range medium
    egg yolks
1–2 tsp cold water

For the filling
150g blackcurrants (fresh or
    frozen)
150g semi-dried figs, stalks
    cut off
100g best-quality fig jam[1]
10–12 small fresh figs (ideally
    black figs from Provence)

For the glaze
50g fig jam

To make the sweet pastry In a large bowl, mix together the flour, icing sugar and salt. Add the butter and, using your fingertips, lightly rub it in, lifting the mixture as you do so, until it reaches a sandy texture. Create a well in the centre and add the egg yolks and water. With your fingertips, in little concentric circles, work the liquid ingredients into the flour mixture until evenly combined and clumped[2], then bring the dough together and press to form a ball[3].

Break off 20-30g of dough, tightly wrap in cling film and refrigerate for later (to tuck in the dough). Shape the remaining dough into a cylinder, cut in half[4] and flatten each piece to a round, 2cm thick[5]. Wrap each portion in cling film. Refrigerate for 20–30 minutes before rolling out (or freezing one for later use).

To roll out the dough Place the rested dough in the middle of a large sheet of cling film, about 40cm square, and cover with another sheet of cling film, of similar dimensions. Roll out the dough to a circle, 3mm thick[6].

To line the tart ring Place the tart ring on a peel or flat tray lined with greaseproof paper. Take off the top layer of cling film and discard, then lift the dough by picking up the corners of the cling film and invert it into the tart ring, removing the cling film. Press the dough onto the base and inside of the ring with the little ball of dough, ensuring it is neatly moulded into the shape of the ring.

Summer Fruits 237

Trim the edges of the tart by rolling a rolling pin over the top of the ring. Now, push the pastry gently up by pressing between your index finger and thumb all around the rim, to raise the edge 2mm above the ring[7]. Prick the base of the pastry case[8]. Refrigerate for 30 minutes to rest and firm up the pastry.

To pre-bake the pastry case Preheat the oven to 170°C/Gas 3. Place a baking stone or baking tray on the middle shelf of the oven. Slide the pastry case directly onto the hot baking stone or tray in the oven and par-bake for 25 minutes. Remove from the oven and allow to cool.

To make the filling While the pastry case is in the oven, crush the blackcurrants[9] and place in a bowl. Purée the semi-dried figs in a blender or food processor and add to the blackcurrants with the fig jam. Mix well and then spread evenly in the pastry case. Cut the fresh figs into quarters and arrange in a rosette on top.

To cook the tart Bake for 25 minutes or until the pastry is crisp and deep golden. Set aside to cool to room temperature. For the glaze, warm the jam in a small pan and brush over the fig quarters. Serve the tart cut into slices, dusted with icing sugar and accompanied by a bowl of crème fraîche.

[1] You do not want a jam that is overly sweet. Of the various fig jams I have tried, La Confiture à l'Ancienne gave the best balance of sweet and fruit.

[2] Do not over-mix the pastry, as this will make the dough elastic and cause it to retract during cooking.

[3] Although hands are gentler and will give you a better pastry, you can make the pastry in a food processor, using the pulse button for no more than 30 seconds to bring the dough together (to avoid over-mixing). A few seconds too many and your pastry will be over-mixed and brittle once cooked.

[4] There will be enough pastry to make two tart cases but it isn't practicable to make a smaller quantity. Freeze the other half for another occasion.

[5] During chilling the dough will firm up, so if it is shaped into a ball it will be difficult to roll out. Flatten the dough into a disc before putting in the fridge and you will find it much easier to roll. Resting makes the dough less elastic, more pliable and easier to work with. It also minimises shrinkage in the oven.

[6] Rolling the pastry between cling film avoids the problem of it sticking and enables you to manage without flour, which makes your pastry heavier.

[7] By pushing the edge of the tart to 2mm above the rim, you are compensating for any slight retraction of the pastry during cooking.

[8] Pricking the base of the tart case with a fork allows steam generated during cooking to escape, helping to keep the case flat and level.

[9] Lightly crush the blackcurrants in a food processor or defrost and roughly chop with a chef's knife. Blackcurrants bring a touch of magic to this dish, introducing an element of sharpness and supporting the fig flavour.

Blackcurrant charlotte

**

Makes 2;
each serves 6

Preparation: 1 hour,
plus making
sabayon and
4½ hours setting

Cooking: 15 mins

Special equipment:
electric mixer,
piping bag and
8mm plain nozzle,
two 16cm cake
rings (4cm high),
blender or food
processor

Many great chefs have created recipes especially for beautiful women, noble kings and queens, and other heads of state. The renowned French chef Carême devised this dessert to honour Queen Charlotte (1744–1818), wife of George III. For convenience, I have given quantities for two charlottes; one can be frozen for another occasion.

Planning ahead This dessert can be made a day ahead and kept in the fridge, or frozen for up to a month.

For the sponge
4 organic/free-range
   medium eggs, separated
2 tsp lemon juice
80g caster sugar
80g plain flour, sifted
40g icing sugar, sifted, for
   dusting

For moistening the sponge
60g caster sugar
140ml water
4 tsp kirsch or eau-de-vie

For the mousse
1.5kg blackcurrants
100g caster sugar
1 tbsp water
4 sheets leaf gelatine (27x7cm)
600ml prepared sabayon (see
   page 21)

For the blackcurrant glaze
2 sheets leaf gelatine (27x7cm)
250g blackcurrants
40g caster sugar
100ml water

For the sponge Preheat the oven to 190°C/Gas 5. Line a large baking tray (or two smaller trays) with greaseproof paper. On the paper, draw two 14cm circles (for the bases) and two 10 x 25cm oblongs (for the sides)[1], then turn the paper over.

Using an electric mixer on full power, whisk the egg whites[2] with the lemon juice and half the caster sugar to form soft peaks. Gradually whisk in the rest of the caster sugar and continue to beat until firm. Turn the speed to low, add the egg yolks and carry on beating until well mixed in. Remove the bowl from the machine then, using a spatula, gently fold in the sifted flour[3]; do not over-mix.

To pipe the sponge Put the sponge mixture into a piping bag fitted with the 8mm nozzle and for each oblong, pipe a continuous line of adjoining sponge fingers onto the paper-lined tray, side by side, from one end of the stencilled oblong to the other, going right to the edges (see overleaf). Pipe the remaining mixture over the stencilled discs, to make two 14cm sponge rounds (see overleaf).

To bake the sponge Dust the sponge with icing sugar, leave for 5 minutes and then dust again[4]. Bake in the oven for 8–10 minutes until cooked and lightly coloured. Leave to rest for 15 minutes, then peel away the paper.

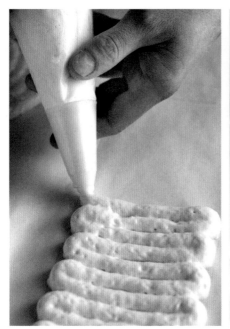

Piping the sponge fingers, which will form the sides of the charlottes.

Piping the mixture in a continuous spiral to form a round for the base.

To line the cake rings Stand each cake ring on a board. Cut each sponge oblong in half lengthways and use the strips to line the inside of each cake ring, with the crust facing outwards and the wavy edges at the top. Carefully position a sponge disc in the bottom of each sponge-lined ring[5].

To moisten the sponge In a small pan, dissolve the caster sugar in the water and bring to the boil. Add the kirsch and remove from the heat. Using a pastry brush, evenly soak the sponge discs with the flavoured syrup.

To make the blackcurrant mousse In a medium pan, gently cook the blackcurrants with the sugar and water for 5 minutes, then purée in a blender or food processor and pass through a sieve into a bowl; you will need 600ml purée for the mousse.

Soak the gelatine leaves in a shallow dish of cold water to soften for a few minutes. In a medium pan, bring a third of the blackcurrant purée to the boil and take off the heat. Drain the gelatine leaves and squeeze out excess water, then add to the hot purée and stir until melted. Stir into the remaining blackcurrant purée and allow to cool to room temperature[6].

To assemble the charlotte In a large bowl, carefully fold the blackcurrant mixture into the sabayon, using a spatula. Pour the mousse into the sponge-lined moulds to three-quarters fill them and smooth the surface with a small palette knife. Refrigerate for 4 hours to set.

To make the blackcurrant glaze Soften the gelatine leaves in cold water as above. In a small saucepan, simmer 200g of the blackcurrants with the sugar and water for 5 minutes, then remove the pan from the heat. Drain the gelatine leaves and squeeze out excess water, then add to the hot blackcurrant mixture and stir until melted. Press through a fine sieve into a bowl to extract a clear liquid glaze. Cool down. Scatter the reserved 50g blackcurrants on top of the charlottes and spoon over the glaze. Place in the fridge for about 5 minutes to allow the glaze to set. (Freeze one of the charlottes at this stage for another occasion.)

To serve Using a knife dipped into hot water, carefully cut the charlotte into portions. Vanilla ice cream would be a delicious accompaniment.

Variations For a quicker mousse, replace the sabayon with whipped cream.

All sorts of fruits could be used in place of blackcurrants. Try blackberries, strawberries, raspberries or blueberries; these are all sweeter than blackcurrants, so you will need to reduce the amount of sugar in the mousse accordingly.

1   These measurements are important, as the sponge strips and discs will need to fit the cake ring exactly. Turning the paper over ensures your pencil marks will not be in contact with the sponge.
2   Whisking the egg whites traps tiny air bubbles inside the protein network and gives lightness to the sponge. Avoid over-whisking, which turns the egg whites grainy, so they lose volume, eventually separating into a dry froth and a runny liquid. At this stage they cannot be rectified.
3   Incorporating the flour is best done with the help of a friend who can sift in the flour while you fold. Take care to avoid knocking out the air you've incorporated during whisking.
4   The first coating of icing sugar on the sponge will melt a little bit. The second will not; instead it will form a nice shiny, crunchy crust on baking, which will also give some strength to the sponge strips.
5   Pack the sponge base and side tightly together to make sure the blackcurrant filling won't run out.
6   Ensure that the mixture is cold before adding it to the sabayon, as a hot mix would melt the sabayon.

Apples

For many years I had a deep yearning to grow a magnificent orchard, championing our own apple varieties and celebrating their heritage.

The apple is not an indigenous fruit: it came originally from China, and there are some 8,000 varieties. If you ate an apple a day it would take you almost a quarter of a century to work your way through all the varieties!

The Royal Horticultural Society is able to tell us so much about the apple tree's history, the soil that's best for it, and how it should be cultivated. But my interest lies in the taste and how different apples behave in cooking.

For the past eight years, with the help of respected experts, I have been working on the creation of a culinary orchard at Le Manoir. Sadly, so many of our orchards have been lost, so it's an epic journey of rediscovery.

The orchard will be home to ancient varieties from Oxfordshire, Berkshire and Buckinghamshire, other British apples and those from across the Channel. It will have about 6,000 fruit trees in total. I see it as a harmonious marriage – a sort of arboreal celebration of the *entente cordiale*.

For this project, I have tasted more than 600 varieties and made copious notes about each one. It's enabled me to establish the best culinary uses for specific varieties.

Interestingly, a stored apple will often taste better than its freshly picked counterpart, as it has had time to mature. If you take a number of apples from a tree and store them at room temperature, tasting them every few days, you will notice the difference. Some experts say that Christmas is the best time to eat an apple.

Here are some of my favourites for specific uses, few of which are found in supermarkets:

DESSERT Cox's Orange Pippin (and most Cox's), Egremont Russet, Royal Jubilee, Sweet Society, Oxford Yeoman and Orleans Reinette.

SAUCE OR PURÉE Adams Pearmain, D'Arcy Spice, Golden Nobel, Discovery, Blenheim Orange, Temptation and Devonshire Quarrenden.

BAKING WHOLE Adams Pearmain, Blenheim Orange, Cox's Orange Pippin, D'Arcy Spice, Annie Elizabeth and Lord Burleigh.

TARTS Adams Pearmain, Blenheim Orange, Cox's Orange Pippin, Captain Kidd, Crimson Cox, Egremont Russet, Royal Jubilee, Sweet Society, Orleans Reinette, D'Arcy Spice and Cheddar Cross.

TARTE TATIN Braeburn, Granny Smith, Crimson Cox, Cox's Orange Pippin, Winter Gem, Winston, King Russet and Jonagold.

By the way, in this country, the Bramley is widely regarded as the best cooking apple, but I strongly disagree. Yes, it is full of juice and acidity, so it breaks down quickly under the heat – it purées in 17 seconds, to be precise. However, the Bramley is so acidic that it requires double the amount of sugar.

Apple tart 'Maman Blanc'

** **

Serves 6

Preparation:
20 mins, plus
45 mins resting

Cooking: 30 mins

Special equipment:
18cm tart ring,
baking stone
(optional), wooden
peel (optional)

In my book, Maman Blanc makes the best apple tart. It takes its roots from simplicity. The secret lies in choosing the right apple, with a great flavour and the right balance of acidity and sweetness. The varieties I have suggested to use here will fluff up and caramelise beautifully, filling your kitchen with an enticing apple aroma. I sometimes pour a light custard into the tart towards the end of cooking – it is simply divine, so do try it (see variations). I also make this tart using other fruits, notably plums, apricots and cherries.

For the shortcrust pastry
200g plain flour
100g unsalted butter, diced,
    at room temperature[1]
pinch of sea salt
1 organic/free-range
    medium egg
1 tbsp cold water

For the apple filling and glaze
3 dessert apples, such as Cox's
    Orange Pippin, Worcester,
    Egremont Russet, Braeburn
15g unsalted butter
15g caster sugar
1½ tsp lemon juice
7g Calvados (optional)
icing sugar, for dusting

To make the shortcrust pastry Put the flour, butter and salt into a large bowl and rub together delicately using your fingertips until the mixture reaches a sandy texture[1]. Create a well in the centre and add the egg and water. With your fingertips, in little concentric circles, work the liquid ingredients[2] into the flour and butter mixture; then at the last moment when the eggs have been absorbed, bring the dough together and press to form a ball[3].

Turn onto a lightly floured surface and knead gently with the palms of your hands for 10 seconds until you have a homogeneous dough; do not overwork it.

Break off 20–30g dough, wrap separately and chill. Wrap the remaining dough in cling film and flatten it to about a 2cm thickness. Leave to rest in the fridge for 20–30 minutes[4].

To roll out the dough Place the rested dough in the middle of a large sheet of cling film, about 40cm square, and cover with another sheet of cling film, of similar dimensions. Roll out the dough to a circle, 2–3mm thick[5].

To line the tart ring Place the tart ring on a wooden peel or flat tray lined with greaseproof paper. Lift off the top layer of cling film from the pastry and discard, then lift the dough by the lower cling film and invert it into the tart ring, removing the cling film. Press the dough onto the base and inside of the ring with the little ball of dough, ensuring that the pastry is neatly moulded into the shape of the ring. Trim the edge of the pastry by rolling a rolling pin over the top of the ring.

Now, push the pastry gently up by pressing between your index finger and thumb all around the edge of the tart ring, to raise the edge 2mm above the ring. With a fork, prick the bottom of the pastry case[6]. Place in the fridge for about 20 minutes to relax the pastry.

To prepare for baking Preheat the oven to 220°C/Gas 7. Place a baking stone[7] or baking tray on the middle shelf of the oven.

To assemble the tart Peel and core the apples and cut each one into 10 segments. Lay the apple segments closely together and overlapping in a circle in the base of the tart case. In a small pan, melt the butter and sugar, then remove from the heat and mix in the lemon juice and Calvados, if using. Brush this mixture over the apple slices and dust liberally with icing sugar.

To bake the tart Using the peel or board, slide the tart directly onto the preheated baking stone or tray in the oven and cook for 10 minutes. Turn the oven down to 200°C/Gas 6 and bake for a further 20 minutes until the pastry is light golden in colour and the apples are beautifully caramelised. Leave the tart to stand for about 30 minutes before serving, until barely warm. To de-mould, remove the ring and slide the tart onto a large, flat plate. Dust with icing sugar to serve.

Variation For a creamy filling, whisk 1 medium egg with 50g caster sugar and 100ml whipping cream to make a light custard and pour into the tart 10 minutes before the end of cooking.

[1] For a successful pastry you need to have even distribution of butter within the flour, to give it flakiness. This is difficult to achieve if the butter is cold, so make sure it is at room temperature. Rub in delicately with your fingertips; do not try to knead at this stage.

[2] At this point it is for you to judge the consistency of the dough. If it is too wet add a little flour; if too dry add a little water. Flours differ in their absorbency.

[3] Alternatively, you could make the pastry in a food processor, using the pulse button to bring the dough together.

[4] Because you have worked the gluten in the flour, the dough is elastic at this stage. Resting it in the fridge makes the dough more pliable and easier to roll. This will minimise shrinkage in the oven.

[5] Rolling the dough between cling film enables you to roll it very thin without using flour. You then discard the top layer, using the bottom cling film to pick up the pastry. As you place the pastry in the tart ring ensure the cling film is uppermost.

[6] Pricking the base will help the distribution of heat and thorough cooking.

[7] A common problem is an undercooked, soggy base – the result of insufficient bottom heat. Using a bottomless tart ring and a baking stone overcomes this, as there is an instant transfer of heat from the hot baking stone to the pastry base.

Apple and blackberry crumble

Serves 6–8

Preparation:
15 mins, plus
cooling

Cooking: 30 mins

Special equipment:
30cm round gratin
dish

For centuries it seems the French have generally poo-pooed all English culinary efforts, past and present. But today things are changing, with one single stroke of the humble crumble breaking through the French resistance! Today everyone seems to be 'crumbling' in France.

Planning ahead You can prepare the crumble topping a day in advance and keep it in a sealed container in the fridge. The fruit compote can also be prepared a day ahead and kept in the fridge, ready to be baked under the crumble topping.

For the crumble topping
120g plain flour
60g caster sugar
60g demerara sugar
120g unsalted butter, cut into
  2cm pieces, at room
  temperature

For the apple and blackberry compote
20ml water
80g caster sugar
600g apples, such as Cox's,
  Discovery, Golden Pearmain,
  Golden Noble, Blenheim
  Orange, Orleans Reinette,
  James Grieve
60g cold unsalted butter, cut
  into cubes
230g blackberries

To make the crumble Preheat the oven to 200°C/Gas 6. Sift the flour into a large bowl, add both sugars and stir to combine. Now lightly rub in the butter pieces, using your fingertips, until you have a light breadcrumb texture; this will take about 4 minutes[1].

To bake the crumble Scatter the crumble topping directly onto a baking tray and cook in the oven for 15 minutes until lightly coloured[2]. Tip onto a plate and set aside to cool.

To cook the apples Put the water into a large saucepan, spoon the sugar evenly over and leave for 1–2 minutes to allow it to absorb the water . Meanwhile, peel, halve and core the apples and cut them into 2–3cm dice; set aside.

Over a medium-high heat, cook the sugar syrup to a very pale blond caramel[3], then stir in the butter off the heat. Add the diced apples, return to a medium-low heat and cook for 8–10 minutes[4].

To assemble the compote Stir the blackberries into the hot apples and then remove from the heat. Immediately tip the fruit and juices into the gratin dish. Set aside to cool down[5].

To assemble and finish Scatter the crumble mixture over the cooled fruit to form an even layer, about 1cm thick. Bake the crumble in the oven for 10 minutes. Serve hot or warm, with vanilla ice cream.

1. Do not overwork the crumble; lift it with the tips of your fingers and rub it lightly between them. Avoid compressing the mixture, otherwise you will end up making a dough.

2. Traditionally crumble is spooned directly on top of the cooked filling and then baked, but I find the steam generated by the fruit makes the topping pasty and heavy, with only the surface being crusty. It is also indigestible, as the flour isn't properly cooked. Instead I precook the crumble and finish baking it atop the fruit to a crusty, crumbly, dry finish.

3. Do not let the caramel darken, or it will overpower the fruit. When the caramel reaches the pale blond stage, immediately add the butter, which will stop the cooking and create an emulsion, giving richness to the dish.

4. The time will vary according to the variety of apples you are using.

5. Cooling the fruit in the gratin dish before topping with the crumble helps to keep the crumble crunchy (as it is steam rising from hot fruit that makes it soggy). This method should give you a perfect crumble experience.

Baked apple with caramel sauce *Illustrated overleaf*

Serves 6

Preparation:
15 mins

Cooking:
35–40 mins

Special equipment:
apple corer, 20cm
oval baking dish

This is one of my simplest desserts and it is truly delicious, provided you choose your apple variety carefully. You need a full-flavoured apple with a good texture, a variety that doesn't collapse into a heap on baking. I have found some of the best baking apples to be Adams Pearmain, Annie Elizabeth, Cox's Orange Pippin, D'Arcy Spice, Discovery and Golden Nobel, but if you are able to find some, the queen of Russets, Reine de Reinette, is the best overall for this dish. Please do not use imported Pink Lady apples.

Planning Ahead You can par-cook the apples three-quarters of the way through and finish them in the oven when ready to serve.

For the baked apples
4 large apples, such as Reine de
    Reinette, Cox's Orange
    Pippin or Discovery
60g unsalted butter, melted
60g caster sugar

For the caramel sauce
1 tbsp water
50g caster sugar
80ml apple juice
½ tsp arrowroot, mixed with
    a little cold water
1 tbsp Calvados or cider
    (optional)

For the garnish (optional)
15g pistachio nuts
10g almond flakes
15g bread, diced
15g icing sugar

To prepare the baked apples Preheat the oven (without fan) to 170°C/Gas 3. Wash the apples and pat dry. Using a small knife, trim a slice off the base of each apple so that it will sit upright. Now make a small incision through one side of each apple, slightly above and beyond the core. Push the apple corer up through the base of the apple as far as the incision and then twist it to release the core. (Alternatively, you could leave the apples whole.)

Brush the apples with the melted butter and roll in the caster sugar to coat all over. Brush the baking dish liberally with butter and sprinkle with sugar, then stand the apples in the dish. Bake for 35–40 minutes until the apples are tender but still holding their shape[1]. Set to one side.

To prepare the garnish[2] If serving, toss the pistachios, almond flakes and bread cubes in the icing sugar and scatter on a small baking tray. Toast in the oven for 8–10 minutes until lightly caramelised.

To make the caramel sauce While the apples are in the oven, put the water into a large saucepan, spoon the sugar evenly over and let it absorb the water for 1–2 minutes. Now bring to the boil and cook to a dark golden caramel[3]. Add the apple juice[4] and bring back to the boil. Thicken with the arrowroot, then remove from the heat and stir in the Calvados or cider, if using.

To serve Place a baked apple on each warmed plate and pour on the caramel sauce. Scatter the garnish, if using, around. This dish is delicious on its own, or you could serve it with custard or ice cream.

[1] The cooking time will vary according to the size, variety, crop (early or late) and how long the apple has been stored for.

[2] For the garnish, you can toast any mixture of nuts (Brazils, pecans, walnuts, hazelnuts etc.), along with some seeds (sunflower, pumpkin or sesame) if you like. You can also add some dried fruits (such as cranberries, blueberries, raisins and/or golden sultanas) and a pinch of ground spice (cinnamon, nutmeg, allspice etc.).

[3] Taking the caramel to a golden brown shade is important; it will have a deeper, richer flavour. If it is too light or blond it will be too sweet and ruin the dish.

[4] Be careful when you add the apple juice to the hot caramel, as it will splutter violently and is hot enough to cause burns.

DID YOU KNOW?
The power of a fan-assisted oven can be too much for baked apples, causing the skins to split. If possible, switch the fan off and allow the heat to penetrate the apples slowly.

Baked apples in a semolina soufflé
Illustrated on previous page

Serves 4

Preparation:
25 mins

Cooking:
25–30 mins for apples; 25 mins for soufflé

Special equipment:
28 x 23cm oval or 25cm round baking dish (7cm deep)

I adore this comforting pudding, which my mother used to bake often when I was a child. It is very easy to prepare and looks so inviting. The contrast of the fruity baked apples and soft melting soufflé is most appealing. Try trickling a little maple syrup over the tops of the apples as you serve it; children will love it.

Planning ahead The apples must be pre-baked. The semolina soufflé base can be prepared half an hour in advance and kept warm in a bain-marie, ready to whisk up the egg whites and incorporate just before baking.

For the baked apples
4 apples, such as Reine de Reinette, Cox's Orange Pippin or Discovery, stalks intact
60g unsalted butter, melted
60g caster sugar

For preparing the baking dish
10g unsalted butter, melted
20g caster sugar

For the soufflé
500ml whole milk
2 drops of vanilla syrup (see page 9) or vanilla extract
80g caster sugar, plus extra for sprinkling
70g semolina
70g sultanas
4 organic/free-range medium eggs, separated
8 drops of lemon juice
10g unsalted butter

To finish
icing sugar, for dusting

To prepare the apples Preheat the oven (without fan) to 170°C/Gas 3[1]. Wash the apples and pat dry. Brush the apples with the melted butter and roll in the caster sugar to coat all over. Place on a greased baking tray and bake in the oven for 25–30 minutes, according to ripeness, until almost tender and still holding their shape. Set aside.

To prepare the dish Meanwhile, grease the baking dish with the melted butter, then sprinkle with the caster sugar. Wipe the rim of the dish with a damp cloth to clean it[2].

To make the soufflé Heat the oven to 190°C/Gas 5. Pour the milk into a saucepan, add the vanilla and bring to the boil. Lower the heat and add 60g of the sugar, the semolina[3] and sultanas. Simmer for about 3 minutes until thickened, whisking constantly to keep it smooth. Transfer to a large bowl, sprinkle with a little sugar to prevent crusting, and let cool slightly, for 2–3 minutes[4].

In a clean bowl, whisk the egg whites with the lemon juice until soft peaks form and then slowly add the remaining 20g caster sugar, whisking constantly. Continue to whisk to stiff peaks.

Mix the egg yolks into the semolina soufflé base, then briskly whisk in a third of the whisked egg whites to loosen the mixture. Now carefully fold in the remaining egg whites with a spatula or large metal spoon[5].

To bake the soufflé Pour the mixture into the prepared baking dish and embed the baked apples in it. Dab a knob of butter on top of each apple and sprinkle caster sugar evenly over the surface of the pudding. Bake for 25 minutes or until the soufflé is risen and golden.

Serve at once, sprinkled with icing sugar.

Variations Replace the baked apples with cherries, peaches or plums. Stone the fruit, halving peaches and plums, then macerate with a few pinches of sugar and 1 tbsp eau-de-vie: kirsch for cherries, pêche for peaches, mirabelle for plums; this softens the fruit slightly.

[1] If you are able to turn off your oven fan, do so to reduce the risk of the apple skins splitting.

[2] This will stop the soufflé sticking to the rim and enable it to rise evenly.

[3] Here semolina is replacing the traditional pastry cream in a soufflé, epitomising true home cooking.

[4] The soufflé base must be warm when you incorporate the egg whites to ensure a smooth result, but it must not be too hot or it will cause them to collapse. You need to get the temperature right.

[5] As you fold in the egg whites, delicately cut and lift the mixture with the spatula or spoon to ensure there is a minimum loss of volume and lightness.

DID YOU KNOW?
The force of the fan in a fan-assisted oven can accelerate the cooking by as much as 20 per cent.

Tarte tatin

Serves 6

Preparation:
20 mins, plus
freezing pastry and
cooling

Cooking: 1¼ hours

Special equipment:
20cm tarte tatin
dish[1]

We owe a great deal to the two elderly spinsters, the Tatin sisters, who invented this amazing, sensuous dessert. All the elements of pleasure are here: the dark caramel, the sweet and acidic taste of the apple, the crisp pastry. Serve with the finest crème fraîche (full-fat, please) or a scoop of good-quality vanilla ice cream to fully appreciate it.

For the best results, cook the tarte tatin a day in advance and keep it in its mould – the pectin in the apples will gel and bind them together. Simply reheat it, then turn out and serve.

Planning ahead Cook the tart a day in advance and leave in the tin. Reheat in the oven for 20 minutes at 150°C/Gas 2 an hour before serving.

For the tatin base
300g all-butter puff pastry[2]

For the filling
40ml water
100g caster sugar

900g (about 6) dessert apples,
  such as Braeburn, Cox's
  Orange Pippin or Adams
  Pearmain
90g unsalted butter, 60g
  chilled and diced, 30g melted

To prepare the pastry Roll out to a 3mm thick round on a lightly floured surface and cut a 24cm circle, using a plate as a guide. Lightly prick all over with a fork. Wrap in cling film and freeze.

To prepare the fruit and caramel Preheat the oven to 180°C/Gas 4. Put the water into the tatin dish, spoon the sugar evenly over and let it absorb the water for 1–2 minutes.

Meanwhile, peel, quarter[3] and core the apples. Over a medium-high heat, cook the sugar syrup to a golden brown caramel[4], then stir in the 60g diced chilled butter off the heat.

To assemble the tarte tatin Arrange the apple quarters very tightly[5] in a circle around the edge of the dish first, rounded side down, then fill in the middle in a similar fashion (see overleaf). Gently press with your hands to ensure there are no gaps. Brush the fruit with the melted butter.

To bake the tarte tatin Cook in the oven for 30 minutes, then take out the dish. Place the disc of frozen puff pastry[6] on top of the tatin and tuck in the edges down the side of the dish. With a knife, prick a few holes in the pastry to allow steam to escape.

Bake in the oven for a further 40–45 minutes until the puff pastry is golden brown and crisp.

To serve Allow the tarte tatin to cool at room temperature for about 1 hour before de-moulding if you decide to eat it immediately, though it is best kept until the following day and reheated before serving.

To de-mould, simply run a knife around the edge of the dish and invert onto a large serving plate, deep enough to contain the juices.

Variation Other fruits such as mango, quince and pears can be used for this dish, but apples are my favourite.

1. The best dish to use is an Emile Henry tarte tatin dish – a flameproof ceramic dish especially designed for the purpose. It can be easily upturned, making it perfect for de-moulding the tatin.
2. You can buy very good puff pastry in supermarkets, but do check it is all-butter and doesn't contain hydrogenated fats.
3. For the ultimate tarte tatin, don't quarter your apples. Just halve, core and cut a sliver off the rounded base of each half, so they won't slide in the dish. Stand the apple halves upright in the dish, packing them firmly. You will need 12 apples.
4. Here you want a golden brown caramel; if it is too dark, the flavour will overpower the fruit, and if it is too pale, it will be overly sweet and insipid.
5. It is important to pack the apples in the dish as tightly as possible, to get in as much fruit as possible.
6. As you apply the frozen disc of puff pastry, it will quickly defrost and you will easily be able to tuck in the edges. Puff pastry at room temperature would end up in a sticky mess.

  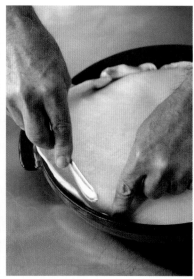

| Arranging a circle of apples around the edge of the tatin dish. | Packing the apples in tightly to ensure there are no gaps. | Tucking the edge of the pastry down the side of the dish. |

Puddings

Sophie Grigson is a superb cook, gifted food writer and a dear friend. When she invites me for lunch I don't say no.

One day I arrived early to discover her preparing an extraordinary 'Sussex pond pudding'. As I watched, I became alarmed by the richness of the ingredients. Sophie layered the pudding bowl with a crust made of flour and suet, then filled it with butter and sugar. Then she buried a whole lemon in it, sealed it with more suet pastry, wrapped it in paper and set it to steam on the hob for 3½ hours.

If I was anxious, there was no need to be. The pudding was absolutely delicious: the crust was moist and gold, the melted butter and sugar had bonded into a perfect syrup and the lemon pervaded all beautifully. I'm afraid to say, I ate it all...

British puddings – sweet or savoury – may be starchy, but I am a big fan. Sophie's dish is on my list of favourites, along with bread and butter pudding, sticky toffee pudding and Christmas pudding.

Every year I make my own Christmas pudding to take to my family in France. On the 25th we have our traditional Christmas log, *bûche de Noël*, followed by my Christmas pudding and a glorious brandy butter.

In other French homes, it might be another British classic, as these puddings are gaining a reputation on the other side of the Channel.

After 600 years the French have discovered crumble. There are crumbles on the menus at small bistros and on 3-star Michelin menus. The crumble is a great traditional British dessert, although I must confess to preparing it differently. To ensure a fully cooked, crisp crumbly topping, I first cook the crumble mix in the oven, then layer it on top of the fruit and finish it the oven.

In this chapter you'll also find my recipe for rice pudding. This dessert became the subject of fierce debate between me and my chef pâtissier Benoit Blin, after he claimed that his mother does the best rice pudding. As far as I was concerned Maman Blanc's rice pudding was undoubtedly the finest.

A rice pudding battle was declared, him in his kitchen, me in mine. We both practised for a week to perfect the puddings, but on tasting decided they were equally divine. It was a draw, though Benoit knows it wasn't really...

A general rule with puddings: you have to be precise. The difference of a mere 10g of flour can turn success into drama. So, take your time to measure accurately. Sometimes weighing scales can be a little out, so it's worth checking them with a weight.

By the way, before serving a pudding at a special lunch or dinner party it's a good idea to practise on your long-suffering family and trusted friends. They will forgive you.

Strawberry crumble

Serves 4

Preparation:
10 mins, plus 1 hour
freezing

Cooking: 10 mins

Special equipment:
food processor, 8cm
pastry cutter

A traditional English dessert... perfected by the French! I cook the crumble topping separately from the fruit, so it stays crisp, light and delicate. You can vary the fruit with the seasons, adjusting the cooking time accordingly – apples, pears, apricots, plums and rhubarb all make lovely crumbles.

Planning ahead Make the crumble discs a day ahead; store in a sealed container.

480g strawberries
60g caster sugar
2 tbsp water
30g unsalted butter
1 tsp lemon juice
1 tbsp kirsch (optional)

For the crumble
80g plain flour
50g caster sugar
20g brown sugar
55g unsalted butter

To serve (optional)
raspberry sorbet (see page 226)

To macerate the strawberries Halve the berries, place in a bowl and sprinkle with half of the sugar. Set aside[1] while you prepare the crumble.

To make the crumble In a food processor, pulse all the ingredients together to a light crumbly texture, then press together and cut into 2–3cm cubes. Place on a small baking tray, cover and freeze for 1 hour until solid.

   Preheat the oven to 190°C/Gas 5. Pulse the cubes of dough in a food processor to break into small pieces of crumble. Spread evenly on a baking tray to a 5mm thickness and bake for 7 minutes until golden brown[2]. While still warm and pliable, cut out 4 discs with the 8cm cutter. Bake these for a further 3 minutes.

To prepare the berries Put the water into a large, heavy-based saucepan, add the remaining 30g sugar and leave for a few minutes, then dissolve over a medium-high heat and cook to a very pale blond caramel. Immediately add the butter[3], then the strawberries, lemon juice and kirsch, if using. Heat for 30 seconds.

To serve Divide the warm strawberries between individual dishes and top each serving with a crumble disc. Add a scoop of raspberry sorbet, or vanilla ice cream, or a dollop or crème fraîche if you prefer.

[1] Macerating the fruit with sugar draws out the juices, creating a wonderful coulis. It also heightens the flavour of the fruit by at least 30 per cent.

[2] Pre-cooking the crumble ensures the gluten in the flour is cooked out and makes the crumble topping lighter and more digestible.

[3] The butter emulsifies with the sugar to create a wonderful glaze for the fruit.

Rice pudding

*

Serves 8

Preparation:
10 mins

Cooking: 1 hour,
plus 1–2 hours
standing

Special equipment:
2 litre shallow
baking dish

This is a timeless classic. In France, almost every mother has her own recipe, which will have been handed down through the generations and, of course, hers is always the best. On its own it is wonderful, but it's also delicious served with poached pears or peaches in vanilla syrup.

Prepare ahead Make the rice pudding an hour or two in advance.

1700ml full-fat milk[1]
100g caster sugar
2 tbsp vanilla syrup (see page 9)
   or 2 tsp best vanilla extract
150g short-grain pudding rice[2],
   washed and drained

To finish
icing sugar, for dusting,
   or 50g caster sugar to
   caramelise the top

For the initial cooking Put the milk, sugar, vanilla and rice into a large saucepan over a medium heat and bring to the boil. Turn down to a gentle simmer and cook for 30 minutes, stirring from time to time[3]. During the last 5 minutes, stir slowly and continuously to prevent the rice from sticking. At this stage it will be three-quarters cooked.

To finish cooking in the oven While the rice is simmering, preheat the oven to 150°C/Gas 2. Pour the rice into the baking dish and bake for 30 minutes. Leave to stand in a warm place for 1–2 hours[4]. Sprinkle with icing sugar to serve.

Or to caramelise and serve cold Allow the baked pudding to cool completely. Preheat the grill to high and sprinkle the caster sugar evenly over the surface of the pudding, using a sieve. Place under the grill for 2–3 minutes to caramelise, then leave to cool for 10 minutes before serving.

Variation Spread jam or fruit compote in the baking dish before adding the rice.

[1] The ratio of rice to milk is roughly 1:10. It may sound incredible but the rice will absorb about 6–8 times its own weight.
[2] Short-grain or pudding rice has a higher starch content than normal long-grain rice which thickens the pudding and lends the characteristic creamy texture. Washing the rice under cold water removes any starch particles from the surface of the rice grains, which would make the pudding too thick.
[3] The gentle cooking and occasional stirring of the rice will help to develop the natural starches and thicken the milk, giving it a wonderful creamy texture.
[4] Never serve straight from the oven. The rice pudding needs to rest and further develop its creamy texture.

Bread and butter pudding

*

Serves 4

Preparation:
15 mins, plus
50 minutes soaking

Cooking:
30–35 mins

Special equipment:
1.3–1.5 litre oval
baking dish

It seems every nation in Europe claims this dish to be their own – the French version is *pain perdu*, the Swiss *brotauflauf*, the Germans *ofenschlupfer*... Regardless, it remains one of our best-loved home puddings.

Planning ahead Cook the pudding a couple of hours before it is needed.

380ml double cream
380ml milk
½ tsp best vanilla extract or
    vanilla syrup (see page 9)
4 organic/free-range
    medium eggs
2 egg yolks
180g caster sugar

pinch of sea salt
30g unsalted butter, diced, plus
    extra to grease
80g sultanas, soaked in sugar
    syrup for 30 minutes[1]
200g bread or brioche[2]
icing sugar, for dusting

To make the custard In a saucepan, bring the cream, milk and vanilla to the boil, then take off the heat and let stand for a minute. In a large bowl, whisk the eggs, egg yolks, sugar and salt together, then whisk in the hot creamy milk. Set aside.

To assemble the pudding Butter the baking dish, pour in a layer of custard and scatter over the sultanas. Cut the bread or brioche into 5mm thick slices. Dip into the pan of warm custard to soak, then layer in the baking dish, overlapping the slices and building up layers to fill the dish. Let stand for 20 minutes or so, to allow the bread to fully absorb the liquid. Reserve the rest of the custard.

To bake the pudding Preheat the oven to 170°C/Gas 3. Top up the dish with the remaining custard[3] and dot the butter on top the pudding. Stand on a baking tray and cook in the oven for 30–35 minutes until the custard is lightly set.

To serve Preheat the grill to high. Dust the surface of the pudding with icing sugar twice to get a good covering and then place under the hot grill for a few minutes to glaze. Add a final sprinkling of icing sugar before serving.

Variations Any dried fruit can be added instead of, or in addition to the sultanas. Dried cherries soaked in kirsch are particularly delicious.

[1] Soaking the sultanas in sugar syrup (made by dissolving 50g caster sugar in 50ml boiling water) will soften and plump up the fruit.

[2] Traditionally, this is made with leftover pieces of dry bread, but brioche lends a lovely richness.

[3] It is important to immerse the bread in the custard to ensure the pudding will be luscious and moist.

Caramelised pears baked in a thin brioche crust

** **

Serves 4
Preparation: 2 hours
Cooking:
10–12 minutes
Special equipment:
four 6cm metal ring
moulds (4.5cm high)

I am so completely in love with this recipe, yet this dessert is celebrating its 27th anniversary as a classic at Le Manoir. Its success is largely determined by the quality and ripeness of the pears. They must be perfectly ripe, barely needing to be cooked.

Planning ahead The charlottes can be can be assembled ready to bake a day in advance and refrigerated, or frozen for up to a week.

For the charlottes	*For the caramel*
5 ripe pears, such as Williams Red, Comice, Doyenne du Comice or Beurre Hardy	2 tbsp water
	100g caster sugar
	100ml whipping cream
60g unsalted butter, plus extra to grease	1 tbsp Poire William eau-de-vie
	pinch of freshly ground black pepper
1 long brioche	
30g caster sugar	juice of ¼ lemon

To make the caramel Put the water into a large, heavy-based saucepan, pour the sugar evenly over and leave for a few minutes to allow the water to be completely absorbed. Dissolve over a medium-high heat and cook the sugar syrup to a golden brown caramel[1]. Pour in the cream, taking care as it will splutter as it cooks down to a beautiful butterscotch sauce. Add the eau-de-vie, pepper and lemon juice. Keep warm.

To prepare the pears Peel all of the pears. Halve and core two of them, then cut out a round from the middle of each half using the 6cm ring mould; these 4 pear rounds will form the tops for the puddings. Save all the pear trimmings for the filling. Core and chop the remaining 3 pears into 2cm pieces and mix with the pear trimmings.

To cook the pear tops and diced pear for the filling Add the pear tops and chopped pear to the caramel, and let simmer, covered for 3–4 minutes until tender. Using a slotted spoon, remove the pear tops and pieces from the pan to a clean tray and allow to cool. Strain the caramel through a fine sieve into a bowl. Reserve the pears and sauce in the fridge until needed.

To prepare the brioche Lightly grease the ring moulds with softened butter and stand on a baking tray. Cut the brioche lengthways into 5mm thick slices. Cut four 20 x 6cm rectangles and four 6cm discs from the slices to form the bases of the charlottes.

In a large frying pan, heat the butter until foaming. Lay 2 brioche rectangles and 2 discs in the pan and cook for 2–3 minutes on each side until golden. Immediately line the sides of two of the greased rings with the fried brioche rectangles, pressing the overlapping join to seal. Now slide a fried disc into the ring and press it down to form the base. Repeat with the remaining brioche slices and discs, using them to line the other 2 moulds.

To assemble the charlottes Preheat the oven to 170°C/Gas 3. Fill the brioche-lined rings with your caramelised pear pieces, packing them down tightly and evenly with a spoon[2]. Refrigerate until needed.

To bake the charlottes Carefully slide off the metal rings and delicately roll the charlottes in caster sugar to coat the side. Slide the rings back over the charlottes and bake for 10–12 minutes. Meanwhile, gently heat your caramel sauce in a small pan over a low heat to simmering point and reheat the pear tops.

To serve Remove the charlottes from the oven, place on serving plates and lift off the rings. Position the pear tops, pour the caramel sauce around the charlottes and serve. For an elegant presentation, place a quenelle or neat scoop of vanilla ice cream next to the charlotte and sprinkle with crushed or chopped pistachios.

Variation For a simple dessert, cook 4 peeled, cored and halved pears in the caramel and serve on toasted or pan-fried brioche slices.

---

[1] Here you want a golden brown caramel; if it is cooked until dark, the flavour will overpower the fruit. If it is cooked too little, it will be overly sweet and insipid. When the caramel reaches the right stage, quickly stir in the cream and this will stop the caramel cooking. It will also create a shiny emulsion, lending richness.

[2] At this stage the charlottes can be refrigerated for up to a day or frozen for up to a week. If frozen, simply defrost in the fridge and finish as above.

DID YOU KNOW?
The finest homegrown pears are available from the end of October until December. In my view, the best varieties are Passe-Crassane, Williams Red, Comice, Doyenne du Comice and Beurre Hardy. I am sorry, the English are coming soon.

Steak, kidney and oyster pudding

**

Serves 4–6

Preparation:
35 mins, plus
making stock and
3 hours soaking

Cooking: 5 hours

Special equipment:
1.8 litre pudding
basin

When I first came to England, I found that the best way to get to know the language was to read recipes by esteemed cookery writers. My favourites were Constance Spry and Jane Grigson. I came across this recipe, which seemed peculiar to me. Why would you use one of the prime cuts of meat and cook it for 5 hours? How can you mix oysters and kidneys? And make a dough of suet and flour? Mon Dieu! But I cooked the dish with good humour and my French smugness was soon put to the test. As the pudding steamed, the kitchen was filled with heavenly aromas. I couldn't wait to try the dish. It was magnificent, so much so that I ate the whole pudding by myself...

Planning ahead You will need to soak the kidneys 3 hours ahead and allow 5 hours for steaming.

For pre-soaking the kidneys
300g calf's or ox kidneys,
   cleaned
500ml water
500ml milk
10g salt

For the suet dough
300g self-raising flour
2 pinches of sea salt
150g suet, chopped
200ml cold water
   (approximately)

For the filling
700g rump steak
300g calf's or ox kidneys (from
   left)
4 pinches of sea salt
4 pinches of freshly ground
   black pepper
2 tbsp plain flour
1 medium white onion, peeled
   and sliced
180g large field mushrooms,
   cleaned and sliced
150ml red wine (ideally
   Cabernet Sauvignon)
150ml brown chicken stock
   (see page 135)
8–12 plump oysters, shucked,
   juices reserved (optional)

To prepare the kidneys Soak in the water and milk with the 10g salt added for 3 hours[1]. Drain thoroughly and set aside.

To make the suet dough In a large bowl, stir all the dry ingredients together to combine, then, using a wooden spoon, gradually mix in enough cold water to make a firm dough[2].

Roll out the dough to a large circle, 5–7mm thick, and cut a quarter segment out of it. Shape this quarter into a ball and reserve for the lid[3].

Line the pudding basin with the three-quarter circle of dough, pressing the join together and leaving some overhang at the rim. Put to one side.

To make the filling Cut the steak and kidneys into 3cm pieces, season with the salt and pepper and coat with the flour. Mix with the onion and mushrooms. In a small pan, boil the wine to reduce by one-third[4], then mix with the stock.

To assemble the pudding Spoon the steak and kidney mixture into the lined pudding basin, adding the oysters with their juices, if using. Ensure the filling is tightly packed and the oysters are evenly distributed. Carefully pour in the wine and stock mixture to almost cover the filling.

Roll out the reserved ball of dough to a round for the lid and position over the pudding. Seal with the overhanging pastry, using a little water to act as glue and pressing the edges together well[5].

Cover the pudding basin with a pleated sheet of foil[6] and secure tightly under the rim with string, looping a handle over the top of the pudding.

To cook Place the pudding basin in a steamer[7] and cook for 5 hours, no more, no less. Your mouth will start watering after 3 hours, but you must resist! Serve the pudding straight from the basin, with marrowfat peas and crusty bread.

Variation If you are not a fan of offal, simply replace the kidneys with an extra 300g beef; the pie will be equally delicious.

[1] Soaking the kidneys beforehand will draw out any blood and bitterness. Make sure they are well drained before you use them.

[2] The amount of water needed will depend on the absorbency of your flour. If you add a little too much water you can rectify it by adding a little extra flour.

[3] Cutting a portion out for the lid in this way will make it easier to line the basin.

[4] By boiling the wine you are evaporating some of the alcohol, removing the harsh bitterness and leaving the intense fruity qualities of the wine.

[5] Ensure you make a watertight seal or the cooking liquor will leak out.

[6] Pleating the foil allows room for the pudding to rise slightly.

[7] Alternatively, stand the basin on an upturned saucer in a large saucepan and pour in enough boiling water to come halfway up the side of the basin, then put the lid on. Check the water level from time to time and top up as necessary with boiling water.

Cakes & Pastries

The mere mention of cakes and pastries whisks most of us straight back to our childhood. You might have enjoyed apple turnovers, Eccles cakes, Bakewell tarts and Victoria sponges. On the other side of the Channel, I looked forward to chocolate éclairs, tarte au citron, and macaroons.

The macaroon – the French national emblem of pâtisserie – has an interesting history. When Catherine de Medici married Henri II in 1533, she arrived in France with her own regiment of chefs and pâtissiers who, in turn, brought their own kitchen secrets and recipes. Catherine is hardly remembered, yet macaroons have survived her. Still today, they are the ultimate sweet treat.

There were other indulgences chez Blanc. On Saturdays my mother always baked a tart filled with pears, apples, plums or cherries, according to the season. The four fruit trees stood behind our house and I loved the Montmorency cherry tree, both in full blossom and when it was fruiting; I could see branches bending under the weight of thousands of cherries – little bright jewels, sharp and delicious, perfect for the tart.

On Sundays, after church and before lunch, my grandmother, a renowned cook, would arrive with a galette, my grandfather beside her clutching a bottle of one of his distilled concoctions. They were truly happy days.

Every section of the professional kitchen is enjoyable but I have to say Pastry is my favourite. Richly rewarding, it is the final challenge: the cook's last chance to win smiles from the guests.

There are rules to follow. For instance, when baking, read and re-read your recipe before scaling the ingredients. Ensure that the oven is preheated and once the cakes or pastries are in the oven, keep the door closed to prevent heat loss. A substantial heat loss can have disastrous effects – flat, soft choux buns for example.

The temperature in a standard domestic oven can drop by as much as 20°C when the oven door is opened for as little as 5 seconds. To counteract this, preheat your oven 10–20° higher than stated in the recipe, then turn it down to the required temperature once the item has been inside for a few minutes.

Having your ingredients at the correct temperature is critical when making cakes and pastry. It is much better to work with pastry dough when it is chilled, as this will make it less sticky and easier to roll and shape; chilling also prevents shrinkage. On the other hand, when making cakes and macaroons, to achieve the perfect texture, all the ingredients must be at room temperature before you start. If they are taken straight from the fridge you won't be able to mix them satisfactorily.

Lemon cake

Makes 12 slices

Preparation:
15 mins, plus
cooling

Cooking: 50 mins
– 1 hour

Special equipment:
26 x 9cm non-stick
loaf tin, cook's
thermometer

Perfect for afternoon tea, this has been served at Le Manoir for the past 25 years.

Planning ahead You can make the cake in advance; the glaze will prevent it from
drying out. Have all the ingredients at room temperature before you start.

butter, to grease
5 organic/free-range
    medium eggs
300g caster sugar
140ml double cream
finely grated zest of 3 lemons
25ml dark rum
pinch of sea salt

80g unsalted butter, melted
240g plain flour
½ tsp baking powder

For the glaze
50g apricot jam, warmed
finely grated zest of 1 lemon,
    plus 3 tbsp juice
150g icing sugar

To prepare the cake Preheat the oven to 180°C/Gas 4. Lightly grease the loaf tin
and line with greaseproof paper[1]. In a large bowl, whisk together the eggs, sugar,
cream, lemon zest, rum, salt and melted butter. Sift the flour and baking powder
together, then whisk into the egg mixture until smooth.

To bake the cake Spoon the mixture into the loaf tin and gently level the surface.
Bake for 50 minutes – 1 hour, turning the tin around halfway through cooking.
To test the cake, insert a small knife into the middle – if it comes out clean, the
cake is cooked. Turn out onto a wire rack[2] and leave to cool for 10 minutes.

To glaze Lightly brush the cake all over with the warm jam[3]. Leave for 5 minutes.
Mix the lemon zest and juice with the icing sugar in a small pan and warm over
a low heat to 35°C[4], until smooth. Brush the lemon glaze evenly over the top and
sides of the cake[5] and leave for a few minutes to set.

   Place the cake on a baking tray in the oven, turn off the heat and leave for 3–5
minutes to dry the glaze – it will become translucent. Allow to cool before slicing.

Variations Replace the lemons with other citrus fruit, such as oranges or
grapefruit, using marmalade in place of the apricot jam.

[1] Leave some paper overhanging the sides when you line the tin; this will enable
   you to lift out the cake by the paper, making it easy to de-mould.
[2] Do not leave your cake to cool in the tin, as this would prevent the steam from
   escaping, making your cake heavier.
[3] Brushing the cake with jam creates a barrier, so the lemon glaze is not absorbed.
[4] If the glaze is any hotter, it will re-crystallise, losing its shine and crispness.
[5] The lemon glaze must be even and thin; if it is too thick it will run in the oven.

Chocolate macaroons

Makes 25–30

Preparation:
30 mins, plus
cooling

Cooking: 8 mins

Special equipment:
electric mixer, cook's
thermometer, large
piping bag, 8mm
plain nozzle

Although created in France way back in the sixteenth century, macaroons continue to mesmerise us. They are the little black dress of pâtisserie and a blissful treat. Still today, they remain a standard-bearer of a fine pâtissier.

Prepare ahead The macaroons are best made the day before and kept in an airtight container in the fridge, ready to assemble. Be careful not to squash them as they are very fragile. The ganache should also be made a day in advance.

For the macaroon paste
60g pure chocolate
(cacao paste)[1]
185g icing sugar
185g ground almonds
2 organic/free-range medium
egg whites

For the Italian meringue
185g caster sugar
50ml water
2 organic/free-range medium
egg whites
½ tsp lemon juice

For the ganache
100g good-quality dark or
white chocolate
100ml whipping cream

To make the macaroon paste Preheat the oven to 170°C/Gas 3, placing a baking tray on the middle shelf to warm up[2]. Melt the chocolate in a heatproof bowl over a pan of simmering water, making sure the bowl is not touching the water. Stir until smooth and remove from the heat.

In a large bowl, combine the icing sugar, ground almonds and egg whites and warm briefly in a microwave for about 10 seconds. Using an electric mixer, mix together to form a smooth paste, then fold in the melted chocolate[3].

To make the Italian meringue In a small saucepan over a medium heat, dissolve the sugar in the water, then cook over a high heat until the sugar syrup reaches 120°C[4]. Meanwhile, using an electric mixer on medium speed, whisk the egg whites with the lemon juice to firm peaks. Lower the speed[5] and pour in the hot sugar syrup. Increase the speed to high and continue to whisk for 2–3 minutes.

To pipe and cook the macaroons While still warm, fold the Italian meringue into the macaroon paste until evenly combined – the mixture should have a ribbon consistency[6]. Spoon into the piping bag fitted with the 8mm nozzle.

Pipe the mixture into 3cm rounds on baking trays lined with non-stick baking paper, spacing them at least 2cm apart[7]. Carefully slide the macaroons on the baking paper onto the preheated baking tray and cook for 8 minutes. Leave to cool and firm up on the baking trays for 5 minutes before transferring to a wire rack to cool completely.

To make the ganache Finely chop the chocolate and place in a heatproof bowl. In a medium saucepan over a medium-high heat, bring the cream just to the boil. Immediately take off the heat and slowly pour onto the chocolate, whisking constantly. Continue whisking until the chocolate is melted and the ganache is smooth, then leave to cool. Place in a piping bag until needed.

To finish Pipe about 1 tsp ganache onto the flat side of a macaroon and sandwich together with the flat side of another macaroon. Repeat to pair the rest. Store in a single layer in a sealed container in the fridge until needed.

Variations Omit the chocolate from the macaroon paste and flavour the filling with any of the following:

LEMON: Colour the macaroon paste with 8 drops of natural yellow food colouring; use lemon-flavoured cream or lemon curd for the filling.

RASPBERRY: Colour the macaroon paste with 8 drops of natural red food colouring; use good raspberry jam for the filling.

PISTACHIO: Colour the macaroon paste with 8 drops of natural green food colouring; use pistachio paste for the filling.

COFFEE: Flavour the plain macaroon paste with 2 tsp coffee extract. For the filling, bring 40ml whipping cream to the boil in a small pan, take off the heat and stir in ½ tsp instant coffee granules to dissolve. Add 40g finely grated milk chocolate and stir until smooth. Let cool before using.

VANILLA: Keep the macaroon paste plain. For the filling, beat 60g soft unsalted butter with 120g sifted icing sugar and ½ tsp best vanilla extract until smooth.

[1] This is 100 per cent pure chocolate, with no added sugars or cocoa butter. It is available from specialist suppliers.

[2] By preheating the baking tray, you will kick-start the cooking of the macaroons, giving extra rise and creating the 'collarette'. This gives the macaroons a good, firm texture and a pleasing shape, especially when sandwiched together.

[3] The melted chocolate needs to be at 50°C. If it is any hotter, it will seize when it is added to the macaroon paste.

[4] The sugar syrup needs to be at 120°C in order to partially cook the whipped egg whites. This is the 'soft boil stage'; i.e. when a little of the sugar syrup dropped into a cup of cold water will form a soft ball.

[5] It is essential to reduce the speed of the mixer to low, to avoid the hot syrup being sprayed out of the machine and potentially burning you.

[6] The 'ribbon stage' is when a spoonful of the mixture lifted and then drizzled back into the bowl sits in a ribbon on top of the mixture, before slowly fading in. It is important to get this stage right. You do need to knock out a little of the air to get a consistent, beautifully dense texture. Over-mix and the macaroons will have a cracked finish. Under-mix and they will rise too much and have a dull finish.

[7] Don't pipe the macaroons close together as they will expand slightly on cooking.

Galette des rois

*

Serves 4–6

Preparation:
20 mins, plus
2 hours chilling

Cooking: 45 mins

Special equipment:
20cm and 22cm
metal rings or
plates, peel
(optional), baking
stone (optional)

In France this dessert is traditionally served just once a year at Epiphany, on 6 January, to honour the Three Kings, or at least that is the tradition... Most likely it was instigated by an opportunistic pâtissier seeing a profitable market. It is customary to hide two little figurines in the almond cream. The children – or adults – who find them become King and Queen for the day and have all of their wishes realised. Folklore aside, this is a delectable dessert and it's remarkably easy, as the almond cream takes only minutes to make and you can buy the puff pastry.

Planning ahead The dessert can be prepared a day in advance and reheated to serve, but it is best cooked within an hour or two of serving.

For the puff pastry
400g all-butter puff pastry,
   ready rolled (in 2 sheets)[1]
½ egg yolk, beaten

For the glaze[2]
1 organic/free-range medium
   egg, plus ½ egg yolk
1½ tsp single cream

For the almond cream
75g unsalted butter, at room
   temperature
75g icing sugar
75g ground almonds
1 organic/free-range medium
   egg, plus 1 egg yolk
1 tbsp dark rum or Cognac

To cut out the pastry Using metal rings or plates as guides, cut out a 20cm round from one pastry sheet for the base, and a 22cm round from the other for the top. Place on a tray and refrigerate for a minimum of 1 hour[3].

To make the almond cream In a large bowl, whisk the butter, icing sugar, ground almonds, whole egg, egg yolk and rum or Cognac together to a smooth paste. Cover and refrigerate until ready to assemble.

To make the galette Spoon the almond cream onto the centre of the puff pastry base. Using a palette knife, spread the cream evenly over the pastry, leaving a clear 2cm margin around the edge.

   Brush the pastry rim with beaten egg yolk and carefully drape the other puff pastry circle neatly over the top. Press the pastry edges gently together to seal and expel all air, using your fingers and thumb. Cover loosely with a sheet of greaseproof paper and refrigerate or freeze for 1 hour to firm up the pastry before finishing[4].

To finish the galette Preheat the oven to 180°C/Gas 4 and place a baking stone or baking tray inside to heat up. Using a sharp knife, trim the edge of the galette to neaten. With the back of the knife, crimp the edge of the pastry all around[5].

For the glaze Lightly beat the egg, egg yolk and cream together until evenly blended. Brush the galette with the glaze.

Now, using the back of a knife, score a spiral of curved rays starting from the centre of the galette and extending right to the edge. (Alternatively, you could simply criss-cross the top of the galette with the knife.)

To bake the galette Carefully slide the galette onto the preheated baking stone or tray in the oven and bake for 45 minutes until the pastry is crisp and golden brown. Carefully lift the galette onto a wire rack and leave to rest for 5 minutes before serving.

Variations Scatter grated lemon or orange zest or arrange some pan-fried sliced pears, apples or quince on top of the almond cream before applying the top pastry round. Some grated chocolate and/or chopped nuts sprinkled on top of the almond cream would be delicious, too.

1   You can now buy 'all-butter' puff pastry. Avoid pastry made with margarine or hydrogenated vegetable fats which contain unhealthy trans fats.
2   This is the ultimate glaze – the cream helping to give that immaculate gloss.
3   If you roll out a block of pastry then you must rest it to prevent shrinkage during cooking. Resting it in the fridge for an hour will make it much easier to work with.
4   Please work with cold pastry. If the pastry is warm when you score it, you will compress all the layers of dough and butter and the pastry will not rise, so it must be chilled first.
5   Crimping the edge of the pastry will completely seal the galette and also give an attractive presentation.

Crème patissière

Makes 600ml

Preparation:
10 mins, plus
cooling

Cooking: 8 mins

Crème patissière is the easiest of all creams, as the flour makes it completely stable. It has many uses – as a filling for cakes and éclairs, as a lining for fruit tartlets, and as a base for soufflés, for example.

Planning ahead This pastry cream can be made up to 2–3 days in advance and kept covered in the fridge.

500ml whole milk
1 tbsp vanilla syrup (see page 9)
    or 1 tsp best vanilla extract
6 organic/free-range medium
    egg yolks

75g caster sugar, plus extra
    for dusting
25g plain flour
20g cornflour

To make the crème patissière Put the milk and vanilla into a heavy-bottomed saucepan, bring to the boil and simmer very gently for about 5 minutes. Take off the heat and let cool for 30 seconds.

Meanwhile, in a large bowl, whisk together the egg yolks and caster sugar until they turn a pale straw colour, then whisk in the flour and cornflour. Pour on the milk, whisking continuously[1], then pour back into the pan. Whisking constantly[2], bring back to the boil over a medium heat and cook for 1 minute.

Pour the crème pâtissière into a bowl. Cover the surface with a light dusting of caster sugar to prevent a skin from forming and leave to cool.

[1] When you are making custards or pastry creams, always pour the hot milk/ cream mixture onto the cold beaten eggs before returning to the heat to cook through. If you reverse this process you are in danger of scrambling the eggs before the sauce has had a chance to thicken.

[2] Constant whisking is important to get rid of any small lumps and keep the crème patissière smooth.

Chocolate éclairs

**

Makes 10
Preparation:
40 mins, plus
cooling
Cooking:
25–30 mins
Special equipment:
2 piping bags,
1.5cm and 5mm
plain nozzles

Chocolate éclairs are among the world's most famous pastries and they are certainly one of my great favourites. Choux pastry is really very easy to make, so do give it a try. It also translates into so many wonderful desserts – gâteau saint-honoré, profiteroles and my pièce montée croquembouche (see page 291).

Planning ahead You can prepare, cook and freeze the éclairs in advance; defrost 1 hour before needed, then fill and glaze them. You can also pipe the éclairs and freeze them uncooked; bake directly from the freezer, adding an extra 5 minutes to the cooking time. The crème patissière can be made 2–3 days in advance and kept in the fridge.

For the choux pastry
65ml water
65ml whole milk
55g unsalted butter, at room
    temperature
1 tsp caster sugar
pinch of fine sea salt
100g plain flour
4 organic/free-range medium
    eggs, beaten

For the filling
450ml crème patissière, at
    room temperature (see left)
20g good-quality dark
    chocolate
15g cocoa powder

For the glaze
200g white fondant[1]
12g cocoa powder
1–2 tsp water

To prepare the choux pastry Preheat the oven to 180°C/Gas 4. Put the water, milk[2], butter, sugar and salt into a small saucepan and bring to the boil over a high heat. Take off the heat, immediately tip in the flour and quickly stir with a wooden spoon until completely smooth.

Return to a medium heat and cook for about 1 minute until the mixture comes away from the side of the pan[3]. Remove from the heat and gradually whisk in the beaten eggs until you have a smooth, dropping consistency[4].

To pipe and bake the éclairs Spoon the mixture into a large piping bag fitted with a 1.5cm plain nozzle and leave to cool and stiffen slightly, for about 5 minutes; this will make it easier to pipe.

Line a large baking tray with greaseproof paper. Pipe 10 large éclairs, each about 15cm long, onto the paper, spacing them well apart to allow them room to expand. Bake in the oven for 25–30 minutes[5] until golden brown, then transfer to a wire rack and leave to cool.

To make the filling Have the crème patissière ready in a bowl. Melt the chocolate in a bowl over a pan of simmering water. Pour the melted chocolate into the crème patissière, add the cocoa powder and whisk to a smooth consistency. Transfer the filling to a piping bag fitted with a 5mm nozzle. Using the tip of the nozzle, pierce the underside of the éclairs in 4 places along their length and gently fill each éclair evenly.

To make the glaze In a wide saucepan over a low heat, gently warm the fondant to make it easier to work with[6]. Stir in the cocoa powder and water until evenly combined. One at a time, dip the top of each éclair into the mixture to glaze, lift vertically and wipe off excess from the lower end with the back of your finger[7]. Place on a board or rack and allow to set in the fridge before serving.

Variations Pipe small choux buns, 8–12g, and cook for 20–25 minutes. Large choux buns will take 25–30 minutes.

Flavour the crème patissière with a little extra vanilla or coffee extract instead of chocolate and keep the fondant for the glaze white.

For classic *choux à la crème*, fill large choux buns with crème Chantilly, dust with icing sugar and serve with chocolate sauce.

[1] You can now buy fondant in specialist cake decorating shops. White fondant is a solution of sugar and water, cooked and pumelled as it cools to incorporate air. It is this process that gives the fondant its white colour and shine.

[2] It is customary to use all water in a choux pastry, but adding some milk gives a softer texture, which I prefer. Using all water will give you a drier, crustier finish.

[3] When the choux paste starts to come away from the side of the pan you know you have evaporated enough water from the mixture.

[4] It is important to add the eggs slowly, to ensure they are incorporated evenly. It will also be easier to judge the texture. You are looking for the mixture to just drop from the spoon, not run off it; you may not need all of the egg to reach this stage. The eggs add flavour and colour, and help to lift the choux on baking.

[5] As the choux pastry cooks, the moisture escapes as steam, which helps to puff out the choux, giving it lift and lightness; the dry heat of the oven will create a crust. Do not bake more than one batch at a time, or the amount of steam they generate will cause your pastry to crack.

[6] For the correct consistency, the white fondant must be used at 35°C (body temperature). If it is hotter, you will lose the shiny finish to your glaze. Regulate the heat of the glaze by placing it back on a low heat and stirring to regain the correct thickness.

[7] Alternatively, you can pipe the glaze on top of the éclairs, using a piping bag fitted with a 1.5cm flat nozzle.

Pièce montée croquembouche

***

Serves 15

Preparation:
2 hours

Cooking: 40 mins

Special equipment:
2 piping bags, 5mm
and 1cm nozzles,
silicone liner, 23cm
loose-bottomed
cake tin, 6cm and
7cm pastry cutters,
30cm plastic ruler,
30cm cake ring,
cake board, piping
bag fitted with a
2–3mm nozzle

A splendid cake that can stretch from table to ceiling, croquembouche is served at all French feasts, be it a wedding (where it is decorated with white sugared almonds), a baptism (blue sugared almonds for the boys, pink for the girls) or a birthday. It is a sweet mountain of hundreds of light choux pastries, filled with pastry cream and held together with crunchy caramel. At weddings, models of the happy couple are placed on top; some might find this kitsch, but sentimental souls will approve. I can still remember sitting at the table as a child, waiting patiently for this amazing dessert to be carried in, a round of applause greeting its arrival. Expect your fortunate guests to be just as impressed.

Planning ahead The crème patissière and nougatine can be made the day before. Keep the pastry cream in the fridge. Store the nougatine in an airtight container. You can assemble the pièce montée up to 6 hours in advance – any more than this and the humidity will soften the caramel.

For the choux pastry
130ml water
130ml whole milk
110g unsalted butter, at room
    temperature
2 tsp caster sugar
2 pinches of fine sea salt
200g plain flour
8 organic/free-range medium
    eggs, beaten

For filling the choux buns
900g crème patissière, at room
    temperature (see page 286)
60ml Cointreau

For the nougatine
350g flaked almonds
480g fondant[1]
320g liquid glucose[1]
40g chilled unsalted butter,
    diced

For the caramel
960g fondant[1]
120g liquid glucose[1]

For the royal icing (optional)
80g organic/free-range egg
    whites (about 2 medium)
1 tbsp lemon juice
400g icing sugar

For the garnish
200g almonds, sugared
about 75g nibbed sugar

For the choux pastry[2] Preheat the oven to 180°C/Gas 4. Prepare the choux pastry, using the above-listed quantities and following the method on page 287.

To pipe and bake the choux Scoop 150g of the choux pastry into a small piping bag fitted with a 5mm nozzle. Scoop the rest into a large piping bag fitted with a 1cm nozzle. Line 2 large baking trays with greaseproof paper. Using the larger nozzle, pipe 80 small choux buns (about 10g each) onto the paper. With the smaller nozzle, pipe 8 'S' shapes, each 10cm tall. Bake for 20–25 minutes until golden brown, transfer to a wire rack and leave to cool. Pierce a hole in the underside of each choux bun with the tip of a nozzle.

To make the filling In a large bowl, whisk the crème patissière until smooth and incorporate the Cointreau. Pour into a piping bag and fill each choux bun through the hole in the base. Reserve the choux buns in the fridge until needed.

To make the nougatine Preheat the oven to 170°C/Gas 3 and roast the almonds on a tray for 8 minutes; keep warm. Lower the setting to 140°C/Gas 1. In a large saucepan over a medium heat, combine the fondant and glucose and cook for 10–15 minutes to a golden brown caramel. Stir in the butter and mix to emulsify, then add the toasted almonds, take off the heat and mix well. Pour onto a warm tray lined with a silicone liner or greaseproof paper and cover with a sheet of greaseproof paper. Using a rolling pin, flatten to a 5mm thickness[3].

To shape the nougatine base Take half the nougatine and, using scissors, roughly cut out a 30cm circle and place in the cake tin. Using a clean cloth, press the nougatine onto the base and sides, right up to the edge of the tin. Trim off any excess with the scissors and thin down the edge of the nougatine by rubbing it with your thumb. Trim off any excess, keeping it even. Carefully remove from the tin and leave to cool. (The trimmings can be re-used by warming through in the oven, rolling to 5mm and shaping as required).

To make the nougatine discs[4] Take half of the remaining nougatine and cut one disc with the 6cm cutter and another with the 7cm cutter. Set aside to cool.

To make the fang shapes From the remaining warm nougatine, cut 3 strips to the same dimensions as your 30cm plastic ruler. Using a large cook's knife, cut 10 triangles from each of these and set aside to cool.

For the caramel In a small saucepan over a medium heat, cook the fondant and the glucose to a dark golden caramel[5]. Immediately immerse the base of the pan in cold water for 1 minute[6]. As the caramel cools it will start to thicken[7].

To assemble the dessert One at a time, dip the top of each choux bun in the caramel to coat and dip half of the caramel-topped buns into the nibbed sugar to decorate. Place the buns caramel side down on a non-stick silicone liner to cool. Pierce the 'S' shape choux buns with the point of a small knife and dip the rounded side in the caramel to glaze; leave to cool.

Turn the nougatine base upside down to create a platform. Now one by one, taking the largest buns first, lightly dip the edge of the choux bun in the caramel, turn 90° and lightly dip again. Place the dipped choux buns on the edge of the nougatine base with the flat side of caramel facing out. Continue until you have completed a full circle around the rim of the base. Build another layer of buns on top of your first circle. Continue building the buns in a pyramid until you only have a gap wide enough to fit the large nougatine disc over. Affix this with a little of the caramel. Now affix 'S' shaped choux buns around the lower part of the pyramid and on the nougatine disc. Affix the smaller disc of nougatine on top.

For the fang shapes Place the large cake ring over the pièce montée and affix the fang shapes to the nougatine base with the tip facing out, so the tip of the fang is resting on the edge of the cake ring. Repeat until you have completed a circle all around the pièce montée. Leave to cool for 1 minute, then wrap a clean cloth around the ring and carefully lift the pièce montée out and onto a cake board.

For the royal icing Using an electric mixer, whisk together all the ingredients until you reach firm peaks. Spoon into a piping bag fitted with the fine nozzle.

To finish Decorate the pièce montée with the royal icing and affix some sugared almonds around, by first dipping them in the caramel.

1 Making caramel with fondant and liquid glucose rather than just sugar makes it more elastic and ensures it won't crystallise. You can buy fondant and liquid glucose in specialist cake decorating shops.

2 For detailed advice on making choux pastry, refer to notes 2–5 on page 288.

3 At this stage you can lightly mark the nougatine into four with the edge of a knife, leave it to cool, then break into 4 pieces and store in an airtight container for up to 1 month. Use as required to crumble up and sprinkle over mousses, ice creams and other desserts, or re-melt in the oven, cool slightly and cut out shapes.

4 If your nougatine becomes too cool and brittle to cut into shapes at any stage, simply place back in the oven for 2–3 minutes to gently warm through and make it more pliable, then continue.

5 Don't be tempted to take the caramel off the heat too early. Here you need a dark caramel – to add some bitterness to the dish and balance the sweetness. If it is too pale it will be too sweet. Also, the darker the caramel the more stable it will be (as the water content reduces on boiling). This is important as you need to make the pièce montée several hours in advance. If the caramel is too pale it will soften and your pièce montée will collapse.

6 Dipping the pan in cold water arrests the cooking and prevents the caramel from over-darkening. Take care, as the water will boil violently as you dip the base of the very hot pan in it.

7 To check the consistency, lower a spoon into the caramel and lift it out so the caramel pours from the spoon back into the pan. You should have a steady unbroken stream of caramel from spoon to pan. Now it should be thick enough to stick the buns to each other. If the caramel gets too thick and begins to firm up, place the pan back on the hob to warm slightly and regain the desired consistency.

Chocolate

There is a universal appreciation of chocolate. We love it because it is smooth, sweet, silky, rich, comforting and instantly gratifying. Surely, the expression 'melt in the mouth' must have been created for chocolate. Just put a piece onto your tongue and it will melt, because the temperature of the mouth equals the melting point of chocolate. There is no effort required.

Chocolate contains a small amount of mood-enhancing phenethylamine –a mild aphrodisiac. It is also a good source of antioxidants, which have valuable health-giving properties. But to reap the benefits, you need to buy good-quality chocolate with a high cocoa solid content.

The nation is really starting to appreciate chocolate with 60–70 per cent cocoa solids, and to use it in cooking. But be aware that a high cocoa solid content doesn't necessarily guarantee quality. It may contain '70 per cent or more cocoa solids' but if that cocoa is of poor quality it will never make good chocolate. Do look at the label, but trust your taste-buds to make the ultimate judgement.

As with apples, there are the eaters and the cookers... and a lot of rubbish to avoid. It is not necessary to re-mortgage the house to buy chocolate, but if you choose the sweet, cheap stuff then that's precisely how your chocolate mousse will taste.

When it comes to cooking with chocolate, you do need to handle it reasonably carefully. To melt chocolate, chop it first, then place in a bain-marie or heatproof bowl over a pan of gently simmering water, making sure the bowl isn't touching the water. If chocolate is over-heated, it will turn grainy, 'seize' and become unusable, although it is not quite as delicate as you might think. It can go to 95ºC before the cocoa solids start graining. Above 102°C it will burn. If you are very careful, you can melt chocolate in a heavy-based pan over a low heat.

When you blend melted chocolate into a mixture, such as a mousse, ensure that the chocolate is at a minimum of 40°C. This will ease the mixing process. Barely heated chocolate will not mix well, because the cocoa butter will seize up. Quickly mix a third of the whisked egg whites into the hot chocolate first, rather than all at once. This prevents the chocolate from cooling and solidifying.

Tempering is a technique that gives chocolate a beautiful, shiny surface and a fine, crackling texture – perfect for delicate moulded shapes, for example. To temper chocolate, first chop the chocolate, then melt two-thirds of it to 55°C. Immediately add the remaining third and stir until you reach a temperature of 32°C. The chocolate is now at the perfect stage to spoon, spread or paint, as for my chocolate cups (on page 305).

Chocolate mousse 'Maman Blanc'

*

Serves 4

Preparation:
20 mins, plus
6 hours chilling

Special equipment:
electric mixer

This is the lightest, most delicious chocolate mousse I have ever tasted – melt in the mouth, instantly gratifying and inexpensive to make. Simplicity is the essence. Such is the genius of Maman Blanc.

Planning ahead Prepare half a day in advance and refrigerate to set.

165g good-quality dark
   chocolate (at least
   70 per cent cocoa solids),
   roughly chopped

8 organic/free-range medium
   egg whites
¼ tsp lemon juice
20g caster sugar

To make the chocolate mousse Melt the chopped chocolate in a large heatproof bowl over a pan of simmering water[1]. In the clean, dry bowl of an electric mixer, whisk the egg whites with the lemon juice on a medium speed, until they form soft peaks[2]. Then switch to high speed and gradually whisk in the sugar[3]. Continue to whisk until you reach firm peaks. Take a third of the egg whites and briskly whisk them into the hot melted chocolate[4], then immediately fold in the remaining egg whites using a large spatula[5].

To finish Pour the mousse into individual serving bowls or glasses and leave to set in the fridge for a minimum of 6 hours before serving[6].

Variation This mousse can be baked in ramekins in a preheated oven at 200°C/ Gas 6 for 3 minutes and served warm. Simple and delicious.

[1] To avoid overheating, make sure the bottom of the bowl is not in direct contact with the simmering water. At 90°–95°C cocoa solids begin to solidify and grain.

[2] See notes on page 17 for detailed advice on whisking egg whites.

[3] There is a very little sugar in this recipe as the chocolate will provide some. If using a chocolate with a higher cocoa solid content you will need to add more sugar to the mousse. Always taste all your ingredients before you start.

[4] Adding the cold egg whites to the warm chocolate must be done quickly and briskly because you are adding a cold mass (egg whites) to a hot mass (chocolate) and there is a risk that the cocoa butter within the chocolate will solidify, leaving you with a lumpy, grainy mousse.

[5] Don't over-mix at this stage or you will lose air and lightness, resulting in a much heavier mousse. And you may lose up to 20 per cent of the volume.

[6] Between 6 and 12 hours is the ideal setting time. Beyond 12 hours the mousse will be much heavier, as the cocoa butter within the chocolate will set and firm up the mousse.

Chocolate fondant

* *

Serves 6

Preparation:
20–30 mins, plus at least 1 hour chilling

Cooking: 15 mins

Special equipment:
sugar thermometer,
electric mixer, six
4cm fondant rings
(5cm high)

This is a dessert close to my heart, which has been adapted by many chefs all over the world. As I watched my mother making chocolate mousse in her kitchen, some splashed onto the hob and I noticed it had formed a crust, but was still molten on the inside. This sent me on many trials to perfect the chocolate fondant as we know it today. There are two stages to cooking the fondant. The first creates a crust around the liquid chocolate; the second completes the cooking of the fondant, leaving you that delectable, melting centre.

Planning ahead The caramel centre, if required, needs to be prepared the day before to allow it time to set. You can also make the fondant a day in advance and do the first stage cooking.

For the fondant
80g good-quality dark
   chocolate (70 per cent
   cocoa solids), chopped
80g unsalted butter
2 organic/free-range
   medium eggs, plus
   1 egg yolk
45g icing sugar, sifted, plus
   extra to dust
16g arrowroot, sifted

For lining the moulds
15g unsalted butter, softened
15g caster sugar
15g cocoa powder

For the caramel centre (optional)
200ml double cream
25ml liquid glucose
15g muscovado sugar
60g caster sugar
pinch of sea salt
½ tsp lime juice

For the chocolate sauce and pistachio garnish
2 tbsp milk
90ml whipping cream
80g dark chocolate (70 per
   cent cocoa solids), chopped
100g pistachio nuts,
   roughly chopped

To make the caramel centre If you decide to do so, you will need to prepare this a day ahead. In a medium saucepan over a medium-low heat, bring the cream, liquid glucose[1] and muscovado sugar slowly to the boil, dissolving the sugar.

In a separate small saucepan, cook the caster sugar to a light brown caramel. Add the cream mixture to the caramel, bring to the boil and cook to 102°C, as registered on a sugar thermometer. Remove from the heat, add the salt and lime juice[2] and leave to cool. Pour into 20g moulds and freeze overnight.

To make the fondant Melt the chocolate and butter in a heatproof bowl over a pan of simmering water[3]. Using an electric mixer, whisk the eggs, egg yolk and icing sugar together on low speed for 1 minute to begin with and then on full speed for 2 minutes[4] until light and aerated. Now reduce the mixer speed to low

and incorporate the melted chocolate and butter mixture. Add the arrowroot[5] and whisk to distribute evenly and emulsify.

To prepare the moulds Brush the inside of the fondant rings with softened butter. Mix the caster sugar and cocoa together and use to coat the inside of the rings. Stand them on a tray lined with non-stick baking paper. Pour the fondant into the moulds to three-quarters fill them. Press a caramel insert, if prepared, into the middle of each and smooth the fondant over the top. Refrigerate for at least 30 minutes, up to a day.

For the first cooking stage Preheat the oven to 230°C/Gas 8. Bake the fondants for 7 minutes until the top has just formed a crust[6]. At this stage they will be fragile as the centre will be liquid chocolate. Leave to cool for 2 minutes. Refrigerate for at least 30 minutes.

To make the chocolate sauce In a medium saucepan, bring the milk and cream to the boil, then take off the heat and stir in the chocolate. Continue to stir until melted and you have a smooth chocolate sauce.

For the second cooking stage and to serve Lower the oven temperature to 180°C/Gas 4. Reheat the fondants for 8 minutes precisely – they will be plump and crusty on the outside and full of liquid chocolate and caramel, if used, on the inside. Place a fondant in the middle of each plate, carefully ease off the ring[7] and dust with icing sugar. Pour the chocolate sauce around and scatter over the crushed pistachios. Serve at once.

Variation Replace the caramel centres with cherry ganache. Bring 200ml milk, 65ml water and 42g liquid glucose to the boil. Take off the heat and stir in 240g chopped plain chocolate (66 per cent cocoa solids) to melt. Add 70g chopped griottine cherries (Morello cherries macerated in kirsch). Freeze in 20g moulds.

---

[1] The density of the glucose will give a smoother texture, with only half the sweetness of sugar. You can buy liquid glucose in most good supermarkets.

[2] Both lime and salt are catalysts of flavours and will lift the flavour beautifully.

[3] To avoid overheating, make sure the bottom of the bowl is not in direct contact with the simmering water. At 90°–95°C cocoa solids begin to solidify and grain.

[4] Start off whisking slowly to mix the ingredients and progress to full speed. If you start on full speed you will create a cloud of icing sugar.

[5] Arrowroot is an edible starch, which helps to stabilise the mixture. It is much finer than flour and has better binding qualities.

[6] This par-baking of the fondants will give you a lovely crust on the outside. The fondants will also be easier to finish and serve – less stress on the day!

[7] Ensure you remove the metal rings as soon as they are cool enough to touch. There will be enough residual heat in the rings to overcook the fondants.

Chocolate delice

**

Serves 12

Preparation:
20 mins, plus
overnight setting

Cooking: 15 mins

Special equipment:
24 x 14cm
rectangular frame
mould (2–3cm high),
or a 20cm tart ring,
hand-held stick
blender

This is one of the most popular desserts in Brasserie Blanc. Simple, delicious and easily achievable at home, it is a wonderful chocolate experience. You can omit the base, if you like (see variations overleaf), though that would be a shame.

Planning ahead The delice needs to be made around 8 hours in advance to allow time for it to set.

For the praline and cornflake base
100g cornflakes, slightly
    crushed
200g hazelnut praline paste[1]

For the chocolate delice
2 organic/free-range
    medium eggs
325ml whipping cream
140ml whole milk
340g good-quality dark
    chocolate (70 per cent
    cocoa solids), chopped

For the caramel hazelnuts
50g skinned hazelnuts
150g caster sugar

For the coffee foam (optional)
2 sheets leaf gelatine (27x7cm)
100ml freshly made strong
    coffee
10g caster sugar

To finish (optional)
grated chocolate

To make the base In a large bowl, mix the cornflakes and hazelnut praline paste together thoroughly with a wooden spoon, to make a smooth paste that can be easily pressed into the corners of the mould. Sit the rectangular frame or tart ring on a tray lined with non-stick baking paper. Tip the praline and cornflake paste into the mould and spread evenly with the back of the spoon to an even 4mm thickness. Refrigerate for 30 minutes until firm.

To make the chocolate delice Lightly whisk the eggs together in a bowl. In a medium saucepan, bring the cream and milk just to the boil[2]. Slowly pour onto the eggs, whisking as you do so. Add the chocolate and stir until melted and smooth. Pour on top of the cornflake base. Leave to set in the fridge overnight.

To prepare the caramel hazelnuts Preheat the oven to 170°C/Gas 3. Scatter the hazelnuts on a baking tray and toast them in the oven for 8–10 minutes[3]. While the nuts are still warm, carefully push the sharp end of a cocktail stick into each one. Affix some Blue-tac pieces under a shelf near to the cooker and place a tray underneath to collect any excess caramel[4].

In a small heavy-based saucepan over a medium heat, melt the sugar and then cook to a dark golden caramel[5]. Immediately dip the base of the pan in cold water for 2 seconds to stop the cooking process[6]. Leave to cool slightly for about

a minute, until thickened to a coating consistency[7]. Now, holding the cocktail stick, dip each hazelnut into the caramel to coat. Press the other end of the stick into the Blue-tac, to suspend the caramel-coated hazelnut vertically. After a minute the caramel will have set hard with a beautiful long tail. Place on a tray lined with greaseproof paper. Repeat with the rest[8].

To make the coffee foam Soak the gelatine leaves in a shallow dish of cold water to soften for a few minutes. In a small pan, heat the coffee and stir in the sugar to dissolve. Drain the gelatine leaves and squeeze out excess water, then add to the hot coffee and stir until melted. Now whisk in a large bowl or pour into a large jug and foam using a hand blender[9].

To serve Using a sharp knife dipped in hot water, slice the delice and sprinkle with grated chocolate, if using. Arrange on serving plates with the coffee foam alongside. Garnish with the caramel nuts.

Variations To simplify the dish, omit the cornflake and praline base. Pour the hot chocolate cream into a serving dish and leave to set; serve with vanilla ice cream.

Or to make chocolate ganache, set the chocolate cream in a tray, cut into cubes and dust with cocoa powder.

To make a divine chocolate tart, pour the filling into a pre-cooked pastry case.

[1] You can buy praline paste from good confectioners or make your own: in a pan, melt 200g sugar and cook to the hard-crack caramel stage. Add 200g skinned hazelnuts, stir and pour onto a tray lined with non-stick baking paper. Cool until set, then blitz to a paste in a blender, adding a little warm water if needed.

[2] It is important that the cream and milk mixture is boiling hot when you add it to the beaten eggs, as this will partially cook them and help to set the mixture.

[3] Toasting the hazelnuts releases their natural oils, giving a more intense flavour.

[4] Sometimes as a cook you have to improvise. Using Blue-tac to suspend the hazelnuts on cocktail sticks allows them to form decorative caramel tails.

[5] Don't take the caramel off the heat too early. You need a pronounced caramel flavour; a pale caramel will be overly sweet and uninteresting.

[6] Be careful at this point, as the intense heat of the pan will make the water it is dipped into boil instantly. This step is necessary to stop the caramel cooking and keep it at the right colour.

[7] You need to catch the caramel at just the right stage; too hot and it will be too thin; too cool and it will begin to set. *Bonne chance!*

[8] Due to the humidity in a kitchen, it is best to prepare the caramel hazelnuts within a few hours of serving, to ensure they don't become limp and sticky.

[9] This magic foam will not last forever, so do this at the last moment, just before you serve. If you make it too far in advance it will collapse, but don't worry, to rescue it simply whisk again.

Café crème in a chocolate cup

Serves 4

Preparation:
3 hours, plus
making sabayon,
overnight freezing
and 4 hours
minimum setting

Special equipment:
four 13cm saucers,
sugar thermometer,
4 acetate rectangles
(17.5 x 6.5cm)[1],
four 5.5cm plastic
rings (3cm high),
small greaseproof
paper piping bag,
2mm nozzle, four
5cm dariole
moulds, 16 x 23cm
rectangular or 19cm
square frame (about
2cm deep)

Unravelling the secrets of pâtisserie is something I particularly enjoy, not least this elegant dessert, which took me 6 months to elaborate. There were so many things that could (and did) go wrong – the thickness of the chocolate, the textures, the presentation. In our quest for perfection, Monsieur Benoit and Le Manoir pâtissiers made thousands, but it was worth it - café crème has become a classic at Le Manoir. It appears to be a complex dish, but once you have mastered the various techniques, you will find it is not so difficult. A fourteen-year-old boy accomplished the recipe and sent me a photograph to prove it!

Planning ahead The chocolate cup, iced parfait and sabayon can all be prepared a day in advance. Keep the chocolate cups in a cool place, but not the fridge. The dessert needs to be assembled a few minutes before serving.

*For the chocolate coffee cups,
saucers and handles*
500g good-quality dark
    chocolate (65 per cent
    cocoa solids), chopped[2]

For the sponge layer in the cups
4 x 3cm sponge rounds, soaked
    in 50ml espresso coffee

*For the coffee parfait and
kirsch sabayon*
300ml prepared sabayon
    (see page 21)
40g ristretto coffee (double-
    strength espresso)
1 tsp kirsch

For the ganache sugar cubes
100ml whipping cream
100g good-quality dark
    chocolate (65 per cent cocoa
    solids), chopped
50g demerara sugar, for
    coating

To finish the dessert
40g caramel or coffee essence
    (available from major
    supermarkets)

To prepare the saucers Brush the base of the saucers with a little oil[3]. Place a saucer bottom-side down a piece of cling film and wrap in the cling film, pulling the edges of the film up over the top of the saucer and twisting them together tightly to ensure the underside is completely smooth. Repeat this for the other three saucers.

To temper the chocolate In a heatproof bowl over a pan of simmering water, melt two-thirds (330g) of the chopped chocolate. Take the bowl off the heat and add the remaining third (170g), stirring to cool rapidly until the temperature is 32°C as registered on a sugar thermometer[4].

To make the chocolate saucers Holding the saucer by the twisted cling film, dip the base into the chocolate up to the rim, then lifting and holding the saucer vertically, push any excess thick chocolate off the rim with your finger, so as to achieve the thinnest possible chocolate saucer. Lastly, encircle the saucer with your thumb and forefinger to push away chocolate from the rim, so it will be neat and perfectly round; this also ensures that once set the saucer will be easily released from the cling film. Lay on a tray with the chocolate surface up[5]. Repeat this for the remaining three saucers. Allow to set for a minimum of 4 hours.

To make the chocolate cups One at a time, spoon melted chocolate along the middle of each acetate rectangle. Using a small palette knife, evenly spread the chocolate to create the thinnest possible layer on the acetate. Carefully lift a corner up using a paring knife and hold the acetate by the edges. With the chocolate facing inwards, bend the rectangle around to form a circle, slightly overlap the ends and slide the cylinder into the plastic ring to hold the shape. To ensure that there is a good seal all along the join, dip your finger in the chocolate and cover the join with a thin layer. Stand on a tray lined with greaseproof paper. Repeat for the remaining three cups. Allow to set for a minimum of 4 hours.

To make the handles Put some tempered chocolate into a small piping bag fitted with a 2mm nozzle. Pipe 'S' shapes onto the greaseproof paper lined tray, about 3mm thick and 3cm tall. (Prepare extra to allow for breakages.) Allow to set for a minimum of 4 hours.

For the coffee parfait and kirsch sabayon Spoon 250ml sabayon into one bowl and fold in the coffee. Put the remaining 50g sabayon into a small bowl and fold in the kirsch; reserve in the fridge.

Fill the 4 dariole moulds up to the top with the coffee sabayon and place in the freezer for a minimum of 4 hours.

Once frozen, briefly dip the base of each dariole mould in boiling water for 3 seconds and de-mould the parfait. Reserve in the freezer until needed.

To prepare the ganache for the sugar cubes In a small saucepan over a high heat, bring the cream to the boil, then pour over the chocolate in a bowl, whisking until melted and smooth. Pour the ganache into the rectangular (or square) frame and allow to cool, then refrigerate for at least 4 hours until set.

Once set, cut the ganache into 2cm cubes and roll each cube in demerara sugar to coat. Reserve in the fridge until required.

To assemble the chocolate coffee cups Delicately unwrap the cling film from each saucer to release it, then peel the cling film away from the chocolate saucer; set aside. To de-mould the cups, gently lift the plastic ring from the acetate cylinder and then peel away the acetate from the chocolate, leaving a smooth, shiny, thin chocolate cup; set aside. Carefully release the handles from the paper.

Dipping the saucer in chocolate.

Removing excess chocolate.

Releasing the chocolate saucer.

Lifting the chocolate strip.

Inserting into the ring mould.

Peeling the acetate from the cup.

Making a small piping bag.

Piping the chocolate handles.

Setting the cup on the saucer.

Place a chocolate saucer in front of you. Quickly and lightly melt the base of the chocolate cup cylinder by briefly touching it on a warmed tray (or other hot surface) and then place in the centre of the saucer to set it in position. Repeat with the remaining cups. In a similar way, lightly melt the edge of the handle and then hold it against the surface of the coffee cup until set in position[6].

To assemble the finished dessert Carefully place a coffee-soaked sponge disc in the bottom of each chocolate coffee cup, then slide in the frozen parfait. Spoon the kirsch sabayon over the parfait, right up to the rim of the coffee cup. Place a ganache sugar cube or two on the coffee cup saucers. Thread the caramel or coffee essence in a swirl on top of the sabayon and serve to your guests.

Variations In place of the sponge disc, you can use biscotti.

For a lovely petit four to end a dinner party, dust the ganache cubes with cocoa powder, rather than coat them in demerara sugar.

---

[1] You can buy plastic acetate in most craft shops and good cake decorating shops. You may have to cut it to size. Ensure the surface is clean and free of any moisture by rubbing a piece of cotton wool over the surface. This is essential, as the finish of the cup will depend on the smoothness of the surface you spread the chocolate onto.

[2] This looks like a lot of chocolate, as you will only need to use about 200g of it, but you need to temper this amount so that you can easily form the saucers, coffee cups and handles. Any remaining chocolate can be cooled down and reused for other desserts. Choose a good chocolate, such as Valrhona.

[3] Cling film is the secret to the fine, smooth chocolate saucer. A film of oil allows the cling film to slide over the saucer, creating a smooth surface for the chocolate to mould to. It also helps you when you come to unwrap the saucer for assembly. Before discovering how to make the perfect saucer, I learned a great deal from my failed attempts; for example, painting chocolate directly onto a fine china saucer will not work as china is quite porous and makes the chocolate stick.

[4] Tempering makes chocolate easier to work with. Adding the cold chopped chocolate to the hot melted chocolate cools the latter quickly. As the chocolate cools, the cocoa butter within crystallises, making the chocolate the right consistency to work with and giving it a shiny appearance and a nice smooth texture. The optimum temperature for tempered chocolate is 32°C; beyond this, it will become dull.

[5] As the chocolate cools, it will firm up, then solidify, turning shiny and crisp with a perfect cracking texture.

[6] Setting the handle will take more than a few seconds, so be prepared to hold it in place until the chocolate cools and creates a seal. Be careful if you have warm hands – enlist the help of a cool-handed (warm-hearted) friend!

Glossary

Equipment

Having the right kitchen tools and equipment is essential for successful cooking. Alongside each of the recipes, I have listed any special items of equipment required. The Directory (on page 313) provides a list of suppliers.

Acetate Flexible plastic sheets used to mould melted chocolate into shapes for desserts. It is available from specialist cookware and cake decorating shops.

Bain-marie Essentially a container filled with hot water, which holds the container of food to be cooked. It can be a deep roasting tray filled approximately two-thirds full of water and placed in the oven (as for a chicken liver parfait or delicate custard), or a heatproof bowl suspended over a pan of gently simmering water (as for sabayons and melting chocolate). In this case, the bowl must not be in direct contact with the water otherwise the food is liable to overheat. This method of cooking in a bain-marie surrounds the food with very gentle heat, enabling it to cook gently and evenly.

Baking stone These can be made of a variety of materials, but the best are made of clay, which is sturdy and has the best heat conduction. A baking stone is used for items that need a kick-start at the beginning of cooking, such as breads and pastries – the raw product being placed directly on the preheated stone in the oven. The benefits of using a baking stone are numerous, but the main ones are: a better crust on breads, a crisp base to tarts, and more uniform cooking – as the baking stone diffuses the heat more evenly than a baking tray.

Bread basket This is normally a wooden or taught wicker bowl, lined with cloth and liberally dusted with flour that can be used to shape breads prior to baking, as well as for the second proving. The raw dough is placed in the basket and allowed to prove for a second time before being turned out and baked in the oven. The dough retains its shape when baked. Bread baskets come in a variety of shapes and sizes.

Cook's blow-torch A small blow-torch specially designed for use in the domestic kitchen. Once ignited, a small narrow jet of flame is emitted, which is directed and waved over foods, such as crème brûlée or sabayon-topped fruit, to quickly caramelise the surface. It is also suitable for charring peppers and skinning tomatoes.

Free-standing electric mixer with dough hook A valuable appliance that can be used to whip, mix and beat. It is perfect for whisking egg whites for meringues, making doughs for breads and pastries, and preparing cake batters. A variety of models are available, with the standard capacity between 4 and 6 litres. I would recommend that you opt for a larger electric mixer, as you will find it more versatile.

Mandolin A traditional Japanese tool that allows you to produce ultra-thin and even slices quickly and easily. It comprises a very sharp metal blade fixed to a metal or plastic frame which the food is passed over. The angle of the blade can be adjusted to achieve the desired thickness. It is perfect for slicing vegetables for crudités, potatoes for gratins and fruits for desserts. Do use the guard provided to hold the food as this will prevent you cutting your fingers on the very sharp blade.

Peel An essential tool which will make your baking so much easier. It is a shovel-like tool used by bakers to slide loaves of bread, pizzas, tarts and other baked goods in and out of the oven. Essentially it is a simple wooden tray with a handle that pastries and breads can be formed on, which is then slid onto a baking stone in your oven. You line the peel with a sheet of greaseproof paper or non-stick baking paper before forming your dough or lining your tart ring, to allow easy and smooth transfer of the product into the oven. A peel also comes in very handy when removing things from the oven as it can be slid under items easily, avoiding damage to the food and the risk of burning yourself.

Plancha A thick solid piece of steel that is heated from below upon which food is directly cooked. In essence, a plancha acts as a large frying pan and is perfect for sealing meat and fish. Many superior cooker models can now be specified to include a plancha. Pans may also be placed on the plancha to cook liquids, making it a very versatile piece of equipment. Solid metal plancha tops can be bought that fit over a gas burner. If you do not own a plancha, a good, solid, heavy-based frying pan can be used instead.

Sous-vide A useful item of equipment that seals raw food in a plastic pouch under a vacuum and then cooks it at a very consistent temperature, usually in a bain-marie, water bath or steamer. A sous-vide ensures that food will not overcook, as the water bath will maintain a temperature of your choice. Because the food is cooked in the pouch at a relatively low temperature, you get better flavours, tastes, colours and textures. The loss of nutrients is also minimised when cooking in a sous-vide.

Cooking techniques

Blanching To immerse food in boiling water for a short time (usually a minute or so), not necessarily to cook it, but to get it ready for the next stage of preparation or cooking. After blanching the food is generally refreshed in cold water straight away to stop the cooking process. Vegetables, for instance, are often blanched before they are frozen to reduce the activity of enzymes, which leads to deterioration.

Braising A lengthy, slow cooking process most often applied to tougher cuts of meat which require long, gentle cooking in a liquid to tenderise them. These include shin of beef, ox cheeks, hock of pork, shoulder and neck of lamb – parts of the animal that are worked hard and are therefore more muscular with lots of connective tissue.

Confit The most popular cooking technique in the southwest of France – and they live until 100 there! Food, such as game or poultry cuts, is immersed in oil or fat and cooked slowly at a low temperature. The medium is often duck fat.

Curing A traditional preserving process. In salt-curing, the meat or fish is covered with salt or immersed in a brine solution for a period of time. The salt will kill most bacteria and germs which cause spoilage, thus allowing the food to be preserved. Smoking is another method of curing, which is effective because chemicals in the smoke inhibit bacterial growth. With hot-smoking, heat is also involved and the food is partially cooked. Some foods, like bacon, may be both salt- and smoke-cured.

Deep-frying To cook food in oil or fat at a high temperature. The best oils to use for this are vegetable oil, safflower and rapeseed oil – as these have the highest burning point. The process will brown the food, giving it flavour and a crusty texture. The amount of oil must be at least three times the volume of food. Usually the food is first coated in batter or breadcrumbs to protect it. Clean oil must be used. It can be recycled, provided it is strained after use and kept for the same type of food. Foods must be dried of any moisture to prevent spitting. Care must be taken when deep-frying as the oil is very hot.

Deglazing Adding wine, stock or water to the pan after roasting or pan-frying, stirring and scraping up the sediment as you do so, to create a tasty jus.

Pickling A method of preserving in an acid, such as vinegar or lemon juice. The acid permeates the food and kills the bacteria; it also softens the foods.

Poaching To cook food by immersing it in barely simmering salted water or stock. If the food is cooked in stock, the flavours will permeate the food. The liquid must not boil.

Roasting To cook food, usually meat, in the oven by dry heat (originally used to describe cooking over an open fire). Roasting is suitable for prime cuts of meat. Small and medium joints are often first seared on the hob before roasting. When a roasted joint is removed from the oven the residual heat will continue to cook it. After roasting, a joint must be rested to allow the juices to re-distribute through the meat. A resting time of 20–30 minutes is needed.

Sautéing To cook food quickly, usually cut into small pieces, in oil or fat to brown it lightly.

Searing To brown food quickly in a little fat or oil to caramelise the surface.

Sous-vide The process of sealing raw food in a plastic pouch under a vacuum and then cooking it at a consistent, relatively low temperature, usually in a bain-marie. It is excellent for retaining flavour, colour, texture and nutrients.

Steaming To cook food in a perforated container over boiling water in a sealed pan. This food cooks gently in the trapped steam, so the method is ideal for delicate foods, such as asparagus, fish and chicken breasts. It is a good cooking technique, which retains the nutrients, although I prefer to use emulsions, particularly for cooking vegetables (see page 157).

Stir-frying A Chinese technique whereby foods are cooked very quickly in hot oil. It uses very little oil and the food is cut into even pieces and shaken and stirred throughout the cooking.

Sweating A term used to describe the gentle cooking of vegetables in oil or butter. The low heat softens the vegetables and converts the starches into sugars, enhancing the flavour.

Directory

John Lewis
(for general cooking equipment)
www.johnlewis.com
Tel: 08456 049 049

Oxford Chefshop
(for general cooking equipment)
www.oxfordchefshop.co.uk
Tel: 01993 899 155

For pots, pans and utensils
www.raymondblancbyanolon.com
Tel: 0151 482 8282

For the tarte tatin dish
www.emilehenry.co.uk
Tel: 020 8877 7180

For the sous-vide and vacuum-pack machine
www.sousvidesupreme.com
Email: customerservice@
sousvidesupreme.co.uk

Acknowledgements

I would like to thank the team who has helped me bring together this lovely little book. First to my publishing team at Bloomsbury: thanks to my editors Richard Atkinson, Natalie Hunt and Janet Illsley.

For making the book beautiful, thanks to Jean Cazals, Paul Wearing, Lawrence Morton, Cynthia Inions and Penny Edwards. Thanks also to James Steen for all his tremendous work, and to my agent Rosemary Scoular.

Of course huge thanks to my close partners, the magnificent Adam Johnson and Ankush 'Kush' Bhasin; Gary Jones and Benoit Blin from Le Manoir, Mark Peregrine from the Raymond Blanc Cookery School; George Auckland who looked at the science behind the secrets, and Sian Shepherd, Dr Carina Ventner and Natalia Traxel who were equally brilliant in this department. And of course Leanda Pearman, who is on the front line; thanks also to Anne-Marie Owens and Jo Campbell from the garden.

Et bien sûr a big thank you to the whole BBC team for their support.

For all these recipes, I have used Anolon cookware. I use only the best; my reputation depends upon it.

Index

First published in Great Britain in 2011
This trade paperback edition published in 2012

Bloomsbury Publishing Plc, 50 Bedford Square, London WC1B 3DP
Bloomsbury Publishing, London, New Delhi, New York and Sydney

A CIP catalogue record for this book is available from the British Library

ISBN 978 1 4088 2211 1

10 9 8 7 6 5 4 3 2 1

Project Editor: Janet Illsley
Art Direction and Design: Lawrence Morton
Photographer: Jean Cazals
Illustrator: Paul Wearing for PW Art/CIA
Stylist: Cynthia Inions
Indexer: Hilary Bird

Printed and bound in Italy by Graphicom

www.bloomsbury.com/raymondblanc